The English language owes a debt of
gratitude to Fritz Spiegl.
So does everyone who cares about it.
This latest book adds to the debt.

John Humphrys

Fritz Spiegl was born in Austria (a distant relation of Mahler) and
came to England as a child, first apprenticed as a graphic designer
but eventually training as a musician at the Royal Academy of Music.
His love affair with the English language and its eccentricities began
as soon as he stepped off the children's boat at Harwich, with hardly
a word of English but a dictionary in his hand.

Throughout the rest of his life he wrote many books, about both
music and English. These include *MediaWrite/MediaSpeak* and
Keep Taking the Tabloids, lampooning the abuse of English by the
popular press, radio and TV. Other works include two gravestone-
shaped books, *Dead Funny* and *A Little Book of Grave Humour*,
The Joy of Words: a bedside book for English lovers, *Sick Notes*, *MuSick
Notes*, *Music through the Looking-Glass*, *A Book of Musical Blunders* and
Lives, Wives and Loves of the Composers. As proprietor of the Scouse
Press, he produced *Scouse International* (the Liverpool dialect in five
languages, including Japanese) to accompany four earlier volumes
of *Lern Yerself Scouse*.

In addition, for more than ten years he delighted readers of the
Daily Telegraph with his 'Wordplay' and 'Usage and Abusage'
columns. His most treasured possession was a letter from Leonard
Bernstein, received when he was writing in the *Listener*: 'It's a
weekly joy to read you; I adore your courageous whimsy.'

Fritz Spiegl died in 2003 at the age of 77, just after finishing
work on this book.

Contradictionary

an A–Z of confusibles, lookalikes and soundalikes

Fritz Spiegl

Kyle Cathie Limited

This edition published in Great Britain in 2010 by
Kyle Cathie Limited
23 Howland Street
London W1T 4AY
general.enquiries@kyle-cathie.com
www.kylecathie.com

First published in 2003

ISBN 978 1 85626 954 4

© 2003 by Ingrid Spiegl

Project editor: Caroline Taggart
Text edited by Peter McAdie
Designed by Robert Updegraff
Typeset by Mick Hodson Associates
Production by Sha Huxtable

Ingrid Spiegl is hereby identified as the author of this work in accordance
with Section 77 of the Copyright, Designs and Patents Act 1988.

A Cataloguing in Publication record for this title is available from the
British Library.

Printed and bound in Great Britain by CPI Group (UK) Ltd, Croydon, CR0 4YY

Proem*

Fritz Spiegl died days after he finished work on the main part of this book but before he could write its introduction. Had he lived, he might have written something like this:

I came to England as a child in the 1930s, knowing hardly a word of English, and have been fascinated by the language ever since. As time goes by, however, I feel an increasing sympathy with the character in *My Fair Lady* who, having decided that Eliza Doolittle is a Hungarian princess, pronounces, "Her English is too good…that clearly indicates that she is foreign." To someone learning English other than as an infant, the language often seems to have been specifically designed to confuse. There are so many homonyms and homophones, so many "false friends" and near misses, that it is never possible to assume that a word means what you think it ought to mean.

On top of that, journalists have for so long been pleasuring themselves (or making each other groan) with intentional puns of the TALK/TORQUE, RIGHT/RITE/WRIGHT variety that they have forgotten that many readers automatically assume that what they see in print is correct. A reader whose command of English is not fluent may therefore emerge neither pleasured nor groaning but more confused than ever.

Nor do you have to be a foreigner to succumb to this confusion. It is twenty years since I wrote my first diatribe against the ABUSE/MISUSE of the English language, *Keep Taking the Tabloids*, but the principal target of that book was the notorious "popular" press who have never been held up to the rest of us as purveyors of good English. In the intervening years, the trend towards bad puns, clichés, bizarre archaisms and mistakes pure and simple has spread from the tabloids to encompass many writers and broadcasters who should know better – newsreaders and others on the BBC (once an infallible source of

---

* See page 192

"correct" usage) and journalists in our broadsheet newspapers (perhaps never quite infallible, but certainly less fallible than they are now). There is no better way of learning to use any language well than to read its best authors, but what chance do young readers today have when they are constantly bombarded by the errors, deliberate or accidental, of writers who do not read, or who read only enough to learn of the existence of unfamiliar words, but not enough to learn what they mean?

There is a serious message here – as the conservationists say, once a species is lost, it is lost forever. "Correct" English usage may be considered an endangered species too and, to those who maintain that it doesn't matter, that this is the stuff of pedantry and nit-picking, I can only reply as I have written elsewhere, "You *can*, in a makeshift sort of way, use a chisel as a screwdriver; but eventually you will ruin the chisel, and it may not do the screw much good either." Words are precision tools and should be treated by the writer with the same respect as a jeweller might accord his eyeglass or a striptease dancer her BASQUE.

That said, this book's purpose is only partly informative – and partly, I must confess, an excuse to vent a certain amount of spleen (see BILE) against ABUSES which never fail to INCENSE me. Some of the entries do aim simply to clarify common confusions (see, for example HOARD/HORDE and PRONE/SUPINE), but *Contradictionary* has no desire to gather dust alongside po-faced works on the reference shelves. Many of the misuses quoted here are frankly hilarious – see, for example, the image of the sinking *Titanic* conjured by the confusion quoted under FLOUNDER/FOUNDER; the illness of the late Princess Margaret under FLU/FLUE; or the residence of the sculptor Jacob Epstein under PENURY/POVERTY. Even when words are used correctly – and by a master such as Shakespeare – their meanings can change over the centuries to give us a bit of fun: see *King Lear*'s Chinese cook under HA/HO and Peter Quince's Irish friend in *A Midsummer Night's Dream* under PAT/PADDY/IRISHMAN/PATSY/STALKING-HORSE/ STOOL-PIGEON.

The attentive reader who goes through this book from start to finish (and I expect there to be very few of those) will notice the frequent appearance of some papers and apparent neglect of others. The reasons for this are simple: the vast majority of the research for this book comes from my own reading and listening, and I generally don't read the national tabloids. Also, the *Guardian*'s "Corrections and Clarifications" and the *Independent*'s "Mea Culpa" columns themselves often point out mistakes or confusions, so I would not like it to be thought that I was singling these papers out for special treatment – on the contrary, I am grateful to them for the help they have given me.

This book could not have been written without the help of the extraordinary scholarship that went into compiling the second edition of the *Oxford English Dictionary*, to whose CD-ROM version I have referred constantly for guidance on definitions, early usage and changing meanings. I am also grateful to the many readers who have written to me with contributions, and continue to do so ten years after I ceased writing a regular *Daily Telegraph* column on usage and abusage. Specifically, Frank Thornton sent me the quote from the *Daily Telegraph* that appears under BRAKE/BREAK; Naomi Hill the one from the *Stroud News and Journal* under DIE/DICE/DYE/DIED/DYED; and Robert Hopkinson the *Daily Telegraph* under PENURY/POVERTY.

— A —

aboriginal/aborigine(s) *Aboriginal* comes from the Latin *ab origine*, meaning from the beginning; so aboriginal people are the earliest known inhabitants of a country. Any country, not just Australia: the Romans were the aboriginal Italians, the ancient Greeks those of Greece. From the 17th century, the natives already in possession of America were described by the settlers as being aboriginal, but the Australians later invented a bogus noun and called their natives "the" aboriginals – resulting in the inevitable abbreviation "abos" – which some now regard as disrespectful.

abortion/aborting A writer in the *Independent*: "...following the abortion of the planned air attack upon Iraq". The verbal noun *aborting* is less ambiguous: "...the aborting of a planned air attack" – and no-one will think that a pregnancy is being terminated, with which the proper noun has become irretrievably linked.

absent/absent The adjective, like the noun *absence*, is stressed on the first syllable, but the verb on the second. A radio reporter who said "He *ab*sented himself from his unit..." may have *read* English at university but had not *heard* enough of it spoken, especially in scanning/rhyming verse. Such stress differences as are printed in this book have been tested where possible with poetry, because metre usually confirms established syllable-accentuation. But unfortunately under-trained and word-deaf radio and television reporters have a greater influence on the language than Shakespearean actors are able to do, so that wrong may eventually replace right.

> From you I have been *ab*sent in the spring,
> When proud-pied April, dress't in all his trim,
> Hath put a spirit of youth in every thing.
> > Shakespeare: *Sonnet 98.*

absent

> If thou didst ever hold me in thy heart
> Ab*sent* thee from felicity awhile...
>> Shakespeare: *Hamlet* (1602).

abstract/ab**stract** As with *ABSENT/ABSENT*, above (and several other examples below) *Abstract* is usually defined as the opposite of *concrete*, except in art, where it may mean a work that is non-figurative and does not clearly represent a recognizable subject. But *to abstract* something is to remove it, and to be *abstracted* is the same as being removed from reality, or absent-minded. When an arts critic of the *Liverpool Daily Post* wrote of "abstracted paintings" at an exhibition she thought she was being smart, and did not imply they had been stolen, or abstracted, let alone that they were feeling a little absent-minded.

abuse/misuse/self-abuse/disabuse When I was a boy I was abused by a neighbour: I was practising my recorder, when he shouted "Stop that b***** racket, you noisy little b*****!" and he went on abusing me in this manner for some time. Had the newspapers made a story out of it they might have headed it,

NEIGHBOUR ABUSES BOY, 10

and no-one would have given it another thought: rude people were abusing each other all the time. Today such a headline would be ambiguous and sinister, for *abuse* can mean anything from name-calling to criminal assault. It could be verbal, mental, physical, sexual and even ritual abuse. Blame American sociologists, who started it all with the euphemism "alcohol abuser" for an alcoholic or drunkard. Alcohol *misuse*, surely? Similarly, drug *ab*use is *mis*use of legitimate drugs, although some drugs have no legitimate use and are therefore always *mis*used. The loose euphemism *sex abuse* is common, but avoidable. If it is assault, why call it abuse? Even the once dreaded *self-abuse* is no longer taboo, having been elevated to therapeutic status – what Woody Allen described as "sex with someone you love". But *disabuse*? In the rush for new understandings of abuse its much rarer negative has almost got left behind and, if used at all, seems to be reserved for pompous utterances: "Sir–May I be permitted to disabuse your correspondent..." It means "to free from abuse, error or mistake", usually in the sense of correcting someone's misconception or mistaken belief.

abusing/abusive The same remarks apply as in the foregoing paragraph. When the *Guardian* wrote "Naseem killed her abusive lover..." the writer meant a man who physically, not verbally, abused her.

accents/diaereses/umlauts/cedillas etc. In spite of all the computer-based facilities now available to writers, many treat the troublesome little marks that sit above or dangle below foreign words as optional luxuries for which they have no time. These marks, of which English is for the most part happily free, can change singular to plural, masculine to feminine, alter pronunciation, and indeed change the very nationality of words. Taking only French-based words, imagine a *blase* woman with a *retrousse* nose looking *soigne* in a *lame* dress eating a *pate* and *creme brule* in a *cafe* with her *fiance*, a *passe old roue*, to whom she gave his *conge*.

accepted/excepted The two may be confused because of careless diction, but an interesting ambiguity was spotted in a Chinese takeaway, staffed by obviously first-generation Chinese still struggling with their English. Behind the counter was the notice: "No Dogs – Guide Dogs Accepted". See AFFECT/EFFECT.

acetic/ascetic *Acetic* means sharp and sour, from Latin *acetum*, vinegar. *Ascetic* is derived from the Greek word *asketes*, a monk, a person in training, and signals self-discipline, austerity and self-denial. The Greeks also had the useful word, *askesis*, which would have meant the strenuous physical exercise they depicted in their art – what might now be called a work-out.

acrid/arid A BBC reporter, describing the area in the Sahara where a round-the-world balloon had landed, said it was "...an acrid wilderness of sand". Did he go down and lick it? *Acrid*, from Latin *acris*, sharp, means bitter, hot or pungently stinging to the taste. What he intended was *arid*, from *aridus* – dry and parched with heat. See also POIGNANT.

acronym/abbreviation "Is IDS an acronym for 'In Dire Straits'?", asked a correspondent in the *Daily Telegraph*? No, it is an abbreviation. The Greek prefix *acro-* has various meanings, like highest, topmost, tipped, pointed, but an *acronym* is a *word* formed from the initial letters or syllables of other words.

11

activist/trouble-maker *Activist* is journalists' and politicians' code for a person they consider an agitator or trouble-maker, as in "trade-union activist" or "black activist".

actor/actress The *actresses* Vanessa Redgrave and Glenda Jackson, and a few others, have let it be known that they wish to be described as *actors*, because they consider the feminine form to be as patronizing as authoress and poetess (although both describe themselves in the 2002 edition of *Who's Who* as actresses). To call females actors sounds more politically correct than sensible, but ultimately people can call themselves what they like, however silly. And the quip "as the Bishop said to the Actor..." takes on an entirely new meaning.

ad nauseam/towards revulsion Had Violet Elizabeth, in Richmal Crompton's *Just William* stories, been a Latin pupil, she might have said "I'll sqweam and sqweam *ad nauseam*", for it means "to the point of revulsion, or sickness" (in her case, "until I'm sick"): or, as the *OED* says, "something that happens so long or so often as to excite disgust" or even vomiting; and quotes a writer of 1616: "We have heard this often enough. Ad nauseam usque." See also NAUSEOUS/NAUSEATED.

adamant/vehement/inflexible/stubborn *Adamant* comes from the Greek/Latin *adamas*, hard, but in modern journalese, e.g. "He is adamant that...", usually indicates only a strong denial or disagreement, or stubbornness and inflexibility of opinion. There is a useful noun, *adamance*, which sits neglected and forgotten in the bigger dictionaries.

adherent/adherence/adhesion All come from Latin *ad + haerere*, to stick fast, CLEAVE to, or remain firmly attached to something. See also COHERENT/COHESIVE, which too has the Latin "sticking" word *haerere* as a basis but with a different prefix.

admissible/admitted/permissible/permitted/permissive What is *admissible* can be *admitted*, e.g. evidence in court, except when it is ruled inadmissible; and similarly the *permissible* is *permitted*. But *permissive*, as in "the permissive society", is now usually interpreted as freedom to express or pursue sexual licence. It orginally had alcoholic undertones and goes back to the 1860s and 70s, when the English Parliament introduced "permissive bills" that gave each parish the right to issue or withhold licences to sell intoxicating liquor. In those days sexual licence would not have been a subject for discussion in newspapers except in the most general and moralistic terms. Occasionally one sees a conditional right-of-way signposted "PERMISSIVE FOOTPATH".

adopted/adoptive Both come from Latin *adoptivus*, meaning "due to adoption", e.g. "The holy kyng Edward made William Norman his sone adoptivus" (ca 1440), but precise modern usage should distinguish between, say, a child that is *adopted* and the parents who adopt it: the child is adopted, the parents *adoptive*. An adopted child is no more "adoptive" than an abused one is abusive. See also ALTERNATE/ALTERNATIVE and COMPULSIVE/COMPULSORY.

advance/advanced "Rommel's advanced knowledge of the 1944 plot to kill Hitler", wrote *The Times*, meaning *advance* knowledge. The same applies to "The theft of documents is thought to have given the Egyptians advanced warning", in the *Independent*. Both statements suggest that the information is "at a superior level of education", like the advanced A-Level exams, rather than "forward in space or time", "in advance", which is what the writers actually meant.

advancing/making advances *Advancing* indicates moving or going forward, e.g. troops in combat; but *making advances* has, by common usage, acquired associations of another kind of forwardness, that is, an attempted initiation, by either physical or verbal means, of sexual intimacy. So the BBC reporter who said, "Opposition forces are said to be making advances throughout the country" made an ambiguous statement.

aerobic/beneficial/healthy The adjective *aerobic* denotes the presence of, or need for, air (in modern terms, oxygen) from Greek *aer*, air + *bios*, life. That which is *anaerobic* can exist without it. *Aerobics*, meaning a form of strenuous exercise, usually to loud music, was a careless American coinage dating from the 1960s which makes no sense: all it says is that exercise makes us breathe harder and may be *beneficial*. *Anaerobics* would be impossible, except perhaps on Mars.

affect/effect "The general affect is one of chaos...", in the *Daily Telegraph*; and "Peterborough" in the same paper, "The bleak weather has had the most awful affect on Gosford House." In a *Guardian* consumer advice column: "How does this effect your rights?" These misunderstandings are possibly brought about by the modern "big-

13

mouthed" pronunciation (as seen on television) of the short *e*: "best" and "west" becoming "baast" and "waast". Thus "effect" becomes a soundalike of "affect" and spelling confusions are a consequence. In general usage, *affect* is only ever found as a verb, meaning to have an *effect* upon. *To effect* is to bring something about, as, for example, a change, or a cure for a disease.

afrikaner/afrikaans An *Afrikaner* is a white native South African whose language is *Afrikaans*.

aggravation/aggression/annoyance *Aggravation* comes from Latin *aggravare*, to make something heavier, worse, more burdensome or troublesome. It does not mean to annoy, and aggravation is not the same as *annoyance*, let alone a provocation or *aggression*, now popularly abbreviated *aggro*. But see AGRO-, below.

agnostic/atheist When the British Prime Minister Harold Wilson declared himself *agnostic* about some policy or other he was ridiculed by journalists who thought it meant the same as *atheist*; but it was a perfectly valid statement. The atheist denies the existence of God (it comes from Greek for "no God"), whereas the agnostic is not sure – Greek for "no knowledge" – of or about whatever is under discussion, whether it is God or politics.

agro-/agri-/aggro The Greek *agros*, field, has provided a host of prefixes relating to agriculture [sic!], from agrochemicals to agrotechnology. So should the prefix be *agro-* or *agri-*? There appears to be no rule and we can presumably please ourselves – so long as it is not "agroculture"; or *aggro*, which is a word coined in ca 1960 that relates to both AGGRAVATION and AGGRESSION (see above).

airbrush out/delete/censor *Airbrush* was the trade name for a spray-gun which (until computer retouching made it obsolete) was used for improving or altering photographs by spraying paint over unwanted parts to obliterate them. NATURIST magazines made extensive use of *airbrushing* to make it seem that women had no pubic hair, which it was an offence to show on a photograph. Airbrushing later became a political weapon; and expressions like "Trotsky was airbrushed out of history..." are figurative references to the way the Soviets and other despotic regimes *deleted* or *censored* parts of photographs to make it seem that former leaders and others wielded no influence; or even that they never existed. Airbrushing (more accurately "spray-gunning") has become a cliché archaism, like "hanging up" the telephone or "pulling the chain" of a lavatory. It has no connection with AIR-GUITAR/MIMING. But see also BLUE-PENCIL and, for a similar archaism, BLUEPRINTS.

air-guitar/miming Playing *air-guitar* is a pretend action in which a SINGER/CROONER/VOCALIST/ENTERTAINER goes through the motions of pretending to play pop music but remains mercifully silent.

aisle/isle The decline in church-going is evident in many ways, especially the ways of newspapers. Writers have admired rude (see ROOD) screens and gazed up in awe at a "knave"; or written that "the bride was led down the isle".

alibi/excuse *Alibi* is Latin for elsewhere, in another place. Old law reports make this clear: "The defendant was able to prove himself *alibi*."He has to prove he was in some other place. It does not mean he has an excuse or a pretext, or just pleads innocence.

aliens/foreigners *Aliens* was formerly a general term for *foreigners* or foreign visitors to Britain, now often lumped together as "asylum-seekers", especially if they mean to stay in the United Kingdom. In World War II *alien* was almost tantamount to "suspected spy", and was qualified, i.e. "enemy aliens" (also "undesirable aliens") for Germans and "friendly aliens" for Austrians. After the War, with the rise of space-travel and the science-fiction associated with it, many people now expect aliens to be little green men rather than full-size people with funny accents. See also EMIGRANTS/IMMIGRANTS and SUBJECT/CITIZEN.

allegory/analogy/parable All three are forms of comparison: *allegory* from Greek *allos*, other + *agoreuo*, speak: a way of describing, or speaking of, one subject in terms of another, as in John Bunyan's *The Pilgrim's Progress* (1678), where Despair is personified as a giant and Despond is a geographical location. *Analogy*, Greek *analogia*, from *ana*, against, compared with + *logos*, reason, ratio, means a correspondence or partial similarity e.g. the *analogies* (topical at the time of writing) between Saddam and Stalin, Baghdad and Stalingrad. *Parable* comes from Latin (and before that from Greek) *parabola*, a placing side-by-side to make a comparison. The parable is now usually associated with the Bible and is close to an *allegory*.

allegory

alliterate/illiterate To *alliterate*, or practise *alliteration*, is to begin words with the same letter or group of letters. *Illiterate*, from Latin *illiteratus*, means unlettered, and is generally characterized by a lack of learning. Mr Paul Savill, a reader of the *Daily Telegraph*, reported that a line in his son's essay, "Wild, wet and windy weather", had been annotated by the boy's teacher, "Well done, an excellent example of illiteration".

alma mater/old school *Alma mater* is Latin for "bounteous mother", a name given – at first facetiously, then seriously and sometimes pompously – by university GRADUATES to their former temple of learning, though newspapers also use the term for schools. The phrase was introduced by the Romans, who applied it not to learning but food production – to Ceres, the Goddess of Agriculture (who gave us cereals). Americans are especially PRONE to this term; and when Alma Mahler, widow of the Austrian composer Gustav Mahler, died in America in 1964, to less public notice than she deserved, an obituary referred to her throughout as "Alma Mater". See also ALUMNUS, SOPHOMORE.

alternate/alternative "The Princess should spend alternative Christmases with her own family…" wrote the *Liverpool Daily Post* in its self-appointed role of adviser to the Royal Family. The writer meant *alternate*, that is, every other Christmas by turns, whereas *alternative* indicates a *choice* between *two*: either one or the other. But a newer meaning entered the language during the 1960s, as in "alternative lifestyle", which refers to a supposedly better, simpler and more basic lifestyle – with plenty of free cannabis, coloured headbands and state support – as lived by members of the hippie movement and their followers. At about the same time a committee of Church of England scholars were beavering away at the Alternative Service Book, which put the ancient liturgy of the C. of E. into lame, modern English (see also under DELICIOUS).

aluminium/aluminum At first sight it looks like the usual "You say tomato, I say tomayto" difference, another example of Americans thinking that by omitting a letter they can save the planet and make life simpler for everyone (they don't: see PAEDOPHILE/PEDOPHILE). But this time, if only by accident, the Americans got it right and English PEDANTS were wrong. For when in about 1810 Sir Humphrey Davy discovered this white, malleable metal he indeed called it *aluminum*. But he was "only" a scientist and was almost immediately, in 1812, called to order by the classicists: the *Quarterly Review* wrote: "*Aluminium*, for so we shall take the liberty of writing the word, in preference to *aluminum*, which has a less classical sound..."

alumnus/old boy *Alumnus* is Latin for a foster-child or nurseling, later meaning a graduate or former student of, usually, a university. John Evelyn's *Diary* (1645): "We saw an Italian comedy acted by their alumni before the Cardinals." In Britain an *alumnus* of a public-school is more likely to be called an *old boy*, even though he may be 95 years old. See also under ALMA MATER and SOPHOMORE.

amanuensis/secretary/handyman/handmaiden/PA An *amanuensis* is a *secretary*, usually one who copies his master's writing or writes from his dictation, from Latin *(servus) a manu* + the *-ensis* suffix, "belonging to" – therefore a kind of *handyman* or (if female) a *handmaiden*. The *amanuensis* has been associated with creative blind persons, like the composer Frederic Delius or the poet John Milton; or with sighted but rather unpractical (or deaf) important people, like Handel and Beethoven. Persons in those categories would today have a *PA* or personal assistant.

amatory/amrous/erotic/salacious/concupiscent/libidinous etc.
All relate to love, but *amatory* is a more general and less personal description, e.g. *amatory* verse; while *amorous* tends to be stronger and express personal feelings, of a (usually though not necessarily) sexual nature. We may feel *amorous* towards someone but do not usually call these feelings *amatory*. *Erotic*, the adjective derived from Eros, the Greek god of love, usually serves as an alternative (see ALTERNATE) but in commerce often just means sexually suggestive. Eros's Roman equivalent Cupid, on the other hand, has altogether stronger, or more *cupidinous*, associations. CUPIDITY means ardent desire or plain lust, not necessarily for sex but perhaps wealth and possessions. *Concupiscence* in its *libidinous* sense could also be laid at Cupid's door – via *cupere*, to long for or desire carnal things – and is always mentioned with great gusto, e.g. Tyndale's 1526 translation of the New Testament (James 1. 14): "Euery man is tempted, drawne awaye, and entysed of his awne concupiscence", and Chaucer's "Fuyr [fire] of fleisschly concupiscence" (1386) – but is not a word that can be spat out with distaste, like plain "lust". Eventually concupiscence became a kind of obituarists' code word with which tactfully to suggest randiness. Thus a contemporary of Thomas Arne

hinted that it was "his concupiscence" that stood in the way of his becoming the greatest English composer after Purcell. More about Arne under COSTIVE/ COSTLY/ DEAR/ EXPENSIVE. See also EXPLICIT/SALACIOUS.

ambassador/envoy/diplomat The first two are generally holders of diplomatic posts, and both come from words meaning "one who is sent", or who is "charged to carry out a task", though an *envoy* may merely be a messenger sent to fulfil a specific assignment. Sir Henry Wotton's famous definition (1604), "An ambassador is an honest man sent to lie abroad for the good of his country" had a clever double meaning, for to "lie" in some place then meant to live there; and of course he also had to tell *diplomatic* lies. Another CYNICAL derivation of *ambassador* could be construed from the Latin prefix *amb-*, double, in the same way as the *diplomat* is related to Greek *diploos*, double: ambassadors and diplomats need to be skilled at not only lying but also engaging in double-talk and half-truths. Witness the letters dutifully sent to newspapers by diplomats from terrorist regimes who claim that their countries are run by philanthropes who would never dream of hurting anyone. The *BBC Style Guide* of 1993 says an ambassador is "always *to* a country, or *in* a capital..." This rule is now so often breached as to have become irreparable, for almost anyone can be an "ambassador" – *to*, *from*, *by*, *for* or *of* almost any organization to anywhere or anybody. The United Nations made a pop singer into its "Goodwill Ambassador", whatever that means; UNICEF (the United Nations International Children's Emergency Fund) plumped for an English film actress noted for her nude scenes to be its "Special Ambassador"; and for a time Liverpool's "Ambassador for Merseyside" was an elderly soap actress who has no connections with the city but is (as the local paper put it) "a household face". The New Labour government of England elevated a retired pop entertainer then aged about 20 and misdescribed as a SINGER, to be its "International Women's Ambassador". So much for the need of an ambassador to "lie abroad".

amputate/behead Latin *amputare* means to cut off a limb or any other part of the body, from *am* + *putare*, to prune or lop, originally branches and limbs of trees but now confined to limbs – although a report in the *Liverpool Echo* told of someone whose head was amputated. Although strictly correct, it is absurd in modern usage, which prefers the unequivocal if regrettable *beheading*. Nevertheless, carelessness often attends the subject, as when the noted writer Monica Dickens (a descendant of Charles Dickens) wrote in one of her hospital novels of "a patient who had an amputated leg", inviting the questions – whose was it, and where did he keep it? The *OED* dates the ugly and rather unfeeling word *amputee* with a jingle from the *Journal of St Bartholomew's Hospital* of 1910, quoted in the OED,

> Please put the patient both to bed
> And then perhaps we'll see
> Which is the amputated part
> And which the amputee.

and/plus *Plus* for *and* is an American bad habit enthusiastically adopted by commerce and advertising: "It tastes good plus it's good for you."

angst/anxiety/trauma *Angst* is the ordinary German word for fear or anxiety, or just mild apprehension. It was introduced into English in a letter by George Eliot (1859), and as it was a foreign word she put it into quotation-marks. Only when C. J. M. Hubback translated some of Freud's writings in 1922 did the word (which like all German nouns takes an initial capital) become naturalized as a pseudo-English clinical word *angst*. As soon as journalists got hold of it they worried it to death like a dog a bone – at least until they discovered that they could have just as much sport with *trauma*, the everyday Greek word for a wound.

annex/annexe The verb to *annex* comes from Latin *annexum*, that which is joined, hence also the annexation of a country. If it is a building, e.g. an extension to a main site, that is *annexed*, the resulting noun is an *annexe*. To speak of "an annex" is wrong.

announce/enunciate Latin *nuntius* means a messenger (remember the Vatican and its Papal Nuntius). What he does is *enuntiare*, to state, proclaim, utter or pronounce. He also *announces*, of course, and this word came to England via French *annoncer*. When a critic praised "Miss Agutter's perfectly annunciated contribution" he merely got the related forms muddled. *Enunciated* was what he meant.

anon./anon *Anon.* is short for *anonymous*, and as an abbreviation requires a full-stop. *Anon*, as in "It shall be done anon", is an adverb that goes back to 1200 AD or earlier, a contraction of "on one" or "in one" – meaning at once, straightaway, forthwith.

anon

anorak/nerd/enthusiast *Anorak* is ESKIMO/INUIT for a warm, weatherproof, padded working-jacket. Such a garment is now popular, but not usually with well-dressed English gentlemen; and since a warm anorak is almost obligatory wear for train-spotters, persons following this and other harmless pursuits have themselves been nicknamed "anoraks". A *nerd* is rather cruelly defined by the *OED* as "an insignificant or contemptible person ... conventional, affected or studious; a 'square', a 'swot'"; and probably has its origin in one of Dr Seuss's unlovely but successful American children's books of the 1950s (which also brought us the "preep", the "proo" and the "nerkle", all mercifully forgotten). The computer industry has bred many *enthusiasts* with intimate knowledge of both hardware and software but not a lot of other intellectual accomplishments and, it is usually implied, few if any social skills. Such "computer nerds" must not be despised: they may wear anoraks but are often the only people able to rescue intellectual non-nerds from computer-related disasters. See also FIEND/BUFF.

anorexia/bulimia Together with dyslexia, *anorexia* and *bulimia* are probably the three commonest medical conditions bandied about by the MEDIA. *Anorexia* comes from the Greek *orexis*, appetite, with the *an-* prefix denoting an absence, or lack of it: in other words, a sickness of compulsive fasting which can result in emaciation and even death. (The proper adjective is not "anorexic" but *anorectic*, as is the noun for a sufferer, just as sufferers from *dyspepsia* are *dyspeptics*, not "dyspepsics"; and the same applies to *dyslectics*, who are not "dyslexics", as is usually claimed. But these small battles appear to have been lost). *Bulimia* (*nervosa*), which is defined by the *OED* as "an emotional disorder occurring chiefly in young women in which 'binges' of extreme over-eating alternate with depression and self-induced vomiting, purging or fasting, [usually combined with] a persistent concern with body shape or weight". Both conditions are blamed on the pressures of modern life, and *bulimia* was associated with Diana, Princess of Wales. However, it has been known and named since the 14th century, when it went under the English word *bulimy*, via the Latin *bolismus*: "Bolismus is immoderate and unmeasurable, as it were an hounde's, appetite" – which is not quite accurate, as it comes from the Greek *bous*, an ox + *limos* hunger , "eating like an ox". The bulimics' frantic alternation of guzzling and fasting was described as early as 1598: "One while the boulime, then the anorexie, ... rage with monstrous ryot."

anschluss/annexation When used in English without further qualification the German word *Anschluss* means – or should mean – specifically the *annexation* of Austria by Germany in 1938, a word much used by ENGLISH-SPEAKERS before, during and after that event. In German, however, it is the ordinary word for a connection which (like BLITZ) requires qualification, e.g. *Netzanschluss*, which is a connection to the mains electricity. It does not mean annexation: the Austro-German *Anschluss* was a political joining-up or, as Germans and Austrian Nazis maintained, a unification on the part of the Nazis which in 1938 was welcomed by the majority of Austrians, who did not feel in the least annexed. See also ANNEX/ANNEXE, above.

ante/anti *Ante* in Latin means "before", *anti* "against". The sign "To the Anti-Natal Clinic" seen outside a hospital would have been more appropriate for the family planning department.

antediluvian/antiquated Latin *ante*, before + *diluvium*, deluge, but what is specifically meant is Noah's flood as recounted in the Bible. But people often call things *antediluvian* when they mean outdated, obsolete, unfashionable or just "very old".

antic/antique An *antique* figure is an old one – by traditional definition 100 years or more – whereas an *antic* figure is a bizarre or grotesque one, such as a gargoyle, caryatid or other "human figure represented in an impossible position", as the *OED* cryptically puts it.

anticipate/expect *Anticipate*, from Latin *ante-* + *cipare*, to take before, is to look forward to something. Gradually, however, another meaning came to the fore, namely to *expect* something to happen, to have (or claim to have) foreknowledge. As a celebrity said to a gossip columnist, "Paul and I are just good friends but we are anticipating marriage" – and for once was doubly accurate.

antimony/antinomy *Antimony* is a metallic substance, chemical symbol Sb. It is not to be confused with *antinomy*, which is a contradiction in law, Latin *antinomia*, from Greek *anti*, against + *nomos*, law.

anxious/keen/eager An *anxious* person is troubled or uneasy in his mind, perhaps even suffering from clinical ANGST. The cliché "anxious to please" means *keen* or *eager* to please.

any more/any more (than...)/anymore A London politician's
statement, "I don't like Tony Blair any more than Ken Livingstone"
could mean either "I don't like Tony Blair any more than I like Ken
Livingstone" or "I don't like Tony Blair any more than Ken Livingstone
does". A third way would be "I don't like Tony Blair anymore", meaning
that the speaker's initial liking for him was not "for ever" – or FOREVER,
which please see.

apiary/aviary Latin *apis* is a bee, so that an *apiarium* is a bee-house or,
in English, an *apiary*. Latin *avis* is a bird, so an *aviarium* is a birdcage or
bird-house. The *Guardian* improbably had "...an aviary where two
hooded beekeepers were extracting honey..."

apogee/nadir/zenith When the sun reaches its highest point it is said
to be at its *apogee*, from the Greek words for "away from"and "earth",
also *zenith*, meaning the point directly overhead. Both are used
figuratively to describe a highpoint, climax or culmination; or, loosely
and perhaps poetically, the zenith is the general expanse of sky above.
The lowest point, both astronomically and figuratively, is the *nadir*, the
Arabic word for "opposite" – e.g. a time of greatest depression or
degradation.

apology/apologia *Apologies* are in vogue – no longer merely saying
"sorry" or otherwise expressing regret but as a way of trying to
absolve or distance oneself, one's company or country, from possible
blame. Thus young Germans have apologized for the HOLOCAUST on
behalf of their guilty grandparents, and Englishmen for the slave trade
of 300 years earlier, for which they, too, can take no conceivable
blame. Such apologies are often pointless, designed merely to make
the apologizer feel better – and will probably have by now been
offered to the iceberg with which the *Titanic* COLLIDED. But issuing an
apologia is something far grander. Although simply Latin for apology, it
is now applied only to a formal, written justification or defence of
something of a usually theological nature. Cardinal Newman's famous
Apologia pro Vita Sua (1864) and its lasting appeal to converts to
Catholicism set the ball rolling and was largely responsible for the
introduction of the word into English – and often into journalists'
prose because they look upon it as merely an elegant variation. See
also PROTEST/PROTEST AGAINST.

apostate/convert An *apostate* is one who renounces his religion, from the Greek *apostates*, a deserter. Apostates are almost always assumed to be Roman Catholics who leave the church or the priesthood without legal permission or dispensation from the Pope. The difference between an apostate and a *convert* is that the apostate's leaving the church is not necessarily followed by his joining another.

apposite/opposite *Apposite*, from Latin *appositus*, something that is in the right place, or appropriately positioned or placed. *Opposite* is from Latin *oppositus*, that which lies or is placed on the other side of something, such as a line or space, or the opposite side of the road, etc.

appraise/praise/apprise To *appraise* means to estimate something, e.g. an amount, value or price; to *apprise* is to inform or instruct, hence to be *apprised*, to be informed or have knowledge of something, usually taking the form *apprised of*. Neither has anything to do with praise: "He was warmly appraised by the panel of judges..." is a trying-to-be-clever howler; and when a man is said to be "appraising the woman's looks" he might have hated the way she looked. See also HALLMARKS/SIGNS.

arcane/archaic *Arcane* means hidden, concealed or secret, from Latin *arca*, a chest, hence *arcare*, to shut away and possibly hide, as in a trunk or chest, adjective *arcanus*. Hence *arcana*, often applied to works known only to a few and therefore considered rare and probably collectable. *Archaic*, from Greek *archaikos*, old-fashioned, means just that; though probably not as old as ANTEDILUVIAN, above.

ariel/aerial *Ariel*, the character in Shakespeare's *The Tempest* (1610), was "an airy spirit" but originally came from the Old Testament, where it is both a person's name (Ezra 8.16) and a place (Isaiah 29.1). It is also a Hebrew CHRISTIAN NAME/FORENAME and, to astronomers, one of the satellites of the planet Uranus. The up-in-the-air *aerial* meaning was reinforced with the coming of wireless telegraphy at the start of the 20th century, when the wire that gathered the transmission through the ether was named aerial – short for "aerial wire", as it had to be placed as high as possible. In the early days of domestic wireless it became a household-word but for some years onwards the spelling remained uncertain: a Revivalist Hymn of 1928 written in praise of the then new BBC begins

I have a wonderful wireless set,

ariel

Sublime is the music and message I get.
No loudspeaker, crystal nor valve is there,
For the name of my set is Believing in Prayer.
My Aeriel's [sic] fixed to the Cross
Away on the brow of the hill at Calváry,
And often I'm thankful when tempted to sin,
That my Earphones are on and I'm listening-in.

arse/ass The Americans did themselves a disservice by settling on the near-homophone euphemism *ass* for respectability's sake, instead of retaining the old and respectable English *arse*. Such tampering always spells trouble, and where in 1 Samuel 25.23 of the *Authorized Version* of the Bible Abigail gets off her *ass*, the American *Good News Bible* plays safe with "When Abigail saw David she quickly dismounted", without revealing what Abigail had mounted in the first place. Another word disapproved of by Webster's *American Bible*, which will be found under COCK-UP.

artful/artistic Both are to do with art; *artful* is concerned more with deceit, cunning and artifice than with artistry, for which sense the *OED* gives numerous positive, *artistic* examples from earlier centuries. The change is probably to do with Charles Dickens's Artful Dodger in *Oliver Twist*.

aryan/arian Before around 1930 the word *Aryan* had precise ethnographic meanings that related to certain ancient peoples or linguistics, but then Hitler's Nazi regime twisted its meaning to denote people of non-Jewish extraction. Thus the German Nuremberg Laws of 1935 attempted ludicrously to classify who was or was not an Aryan. An *Arian* is an adherent of the doctrines of Arius, more about whom will be found in a good book on Christian theology. Also, for believers in star-diving twaddle, a person born under the zodiacal sign of Aries. More about astrologers under ASTRONOMY.

assiduous/acidulous To be *assiduous* means to be diligent and unwearyingly persevering, with the implication of sitting down to do or learn something. It comes from Latin *assidere*, to sit by. *Acidulous* means sour; or, figuratively, sour-tempered. The common misspelling "aciduous" confuses the two concepts: there is no such word.

assure/insure/ensure *Assure*, to render safe or give confidence, but also sometimes an alternative for *insure*, which is the usual meaning of the process of assuring someone that, for example, he will be recompensed if certain events occur. This should *ensure* that he is not out of pocket. All three words share the same root, but each acquired specialized meanings. See also ENSUE, which is sometimes accidentally printed or erroneously "corrected" as "ensure". What is now almost always called (life) *insurance* was in the 19th and early 20th centuries more often called (life) *assurance*.

asterisk/asterix An *asterisk* is a little star, from the Greek word *asteriskos* (Latin *asteriscus*), diminutive of "star". It is also a typographical device which can serve as a pointer to an explanation or addendum that is similarly marked, usually at the bottom of the same page. Asterisks also indicate omitted letters, especially in the interest of decency, e.g. "f****ing h*ll!" for, possibly, "flipping hell". Three asterisks printed in triangular formation are called an *asterism* – a device used for different attention-drawing purposes on the printed page. *Asterix* is a cartoon character created by the French team of Goscinny and Uderzo. For many young people *Asterix the Gaul* is more familiar than asterisk the typographical character.

astronauts/cosmonauts The distinction has arisen since the beginnings of space travel. Americans send up *astronauts*, from Greek *astron*, Latin *astra* + Greek *nautes*, a sailor, whereas Russians send *cosmonauts*, coined from *cosmos*, the universe, from a Greek word meaning "perfect order and arrangement". This is what Pythagoraeans believed of the universe – possibly overlooking a few hundred tons of space debris. When men began to take to the air, first by balloon and then heavier-than-air craft, the press called them *aeronauts*, "air-sailors", but *airmen* became the more popular word.

astronomy/astrology Those who confuse *astronomy* with *astrology* are in good company, as for centuries the two were interchangeable, with a common etymological ancestry. But from the 17th century the Latin *astronomia*, the arrangement of stars, parted company from *astrologia*, which then became star divination. Today *astronomy* is the science of the heavenly bodies and their relative positions, while *astrology* propagates the foolish (or worse, fraudulent) belief that the stars' mutual relationships and relative positions influence human actions and destiny.

astronomy

Even newspapers and magazines which purport to CATER FOR intelligent people print astrology columns, largely for their female readers. A comparison between the wildly disparate predictions made by different astrologers for the same birth-signs proves the only absolute and incontrovertible truth of astrology: there is a fool born every minute. Now that it is possible artificially to control the date and time of a child's conception as well as his or her birth, these follies and falsehoods have become even plainer.

Shakespeare, who knew everything about everything, dismisses astrology in *King Lear* (1608) as part of "...the excellent foppery of the world, that, when we are sick in fortune – often the surfeit of our own behaviour – we make guilty of our disasters the sun, the moon and the stars: as if we were villains by necessity; fools by heavenly compulsion; knaves, thieves and treachers [sic – meaning those disposed to treachery] by spherical predominance; drunkards, liars and adulterers by an enforced obedience of planetary influence... My father compounded with my mother under the dragon's tail; and my nativity was under Ursa major; so that it follows I am rough and lecherous."

Shakespeare may have been familiar with a diatribe against astrology by John Chamber, Prebendary of the Chapel at Windsor and a Fellow of Eton College. Chamber, contrasting astrology with witchcraft, condemned it as "...a damnable superstition, which dishonoureth God, polluteth Heaven, deceiveth and seduceth men, goeth without touch or check; the astrologer 'scaping while the witch is punished". An early rogue astrologer, Shakespeare's contemporary Simon Foreman, had a lucrative practice in London in which he advised rich ladies wishing to conceive a child of the most propitious time for its conception. If he liked them he would tell them that the very best moment to "compound" with them for an act of procreation was there and then, while they were alone with him in his consulting-room.

attorney/solicitor Now chiefly an American-versus-English distinction: The Americans have *attorneys*, the British *solicitors*, which in the USA means persons who solicit. A New York hotel whose lobby is a meeting-point for prospecting prostitutes displays a notice "SOLICITORS ARE NOT WELCOME".

auger/augur An *auger* is a carpenter's tool for making holes, usually in wood, the name derived from an old Teutonic source adopted into English by early mediaeval craftsmen. But in ancient Rome an *augur* (written *avgvr*, as the Romans used a 'consonantal *u'* to represent a *v*) *au-* being the bird prefix and *gar-* that of *garrire*, to talk) was an official whose duty was to predict future events. He did this by interpreting omens derived from various phenomena, including the habits of birds (talking birds?), which were thought to augur well or badly, according to his findings. His other name was *avispex*.

aural/oral Confusion is caused by the fact that in modern informal speech the two words sound almost the same, but they refer to different senses: *aural* from Latin *auris*, ear, for hearing; *oral* from *os*, *oris*, mouth, for speaking. Things can get even more confusing because, for example, *oral* examinations are *aural*, too. See also PERFORM/CARRY OUT.

avoidance/evasion A pair of words whose near-synonymity is a tribute to the British system of assessing Income Tax, which is expensively adversarial and requires the deployment of opposing armies of experts – those who collect taxes and those who try legally to avoid having to pay them. Hence the often fine difference: the *avoider* knows and exploits the rules and loopholes, the *evader* simply ignores and FLOUTS them.

award-winning/allegedly good Like the ubiquitous …OF THE YEAR sobriquet, the almost meaningless and usually bogus description *award-winning* can be attached to anyone – from a Nobel Prize laureate to a jobbing journalist, much-loved tea-lady or veteran road-sweeper – or indeed to anything or anyone that has ever won anyone's approbation, as in "Award-winning cookery writer Delia Plinge…" The *Independent* for years displayed a banner on its front page reading

AWARD-WINNING NEWSPAPER

without stating what the award was, when it was given, by whom and for how long. Most "of the year" awards are incestuously awarded by members of interested groups, to each other, for CYNICAL publicity purposes. Much the same goes for "BEST-SELLING".

award-winning

— B —

bachelor/batchelor/singleton *Bachelor* goes back to the Middle Ages, when it meant a young knight, a novice in arms – presumably a novice also in the lists of love and therefore unmarried: whether he was CELIBATE or not was immaterial. The precise origin is unclear, but Latin *baccalaris* has been suggested; also the Welsh *bach*, little; and the French *bas chevalier*, a low-ranking knight. Various spellings occur: Chaucer (ca 1386), had a "Bacheler of lawe"; and Samuel Johnson (1750) wrote about "the unsettled condition … of a batchelor". The latter form was the preferred spelling until the 19th century, but has survived only as a family name (as did Gardiner, Smyth and Taylor, and other nominal misspellings) although English writers are often confused or misled by Batchelor's Peas. However, an advertisement by the University of Teesside still offers a "Batchelor's Degree", which suggests that they read more can-labels than books. In recent years *singleton* has been revived in newspaper "lonelyhearts" and advice columns (Letter to a newspaper: "I'm a 33-year-old singleton…") – a useful and admirable 19th-century word with several uses relating to singularity, perhaps formed by analogy with *simpleton*. See also LONE/SOLO AND CELIBATE.

bacterium/bacteria *Bacterium* is a Latin adaptation from the Greek *bakterion*, a little rod or staff (the shapes *bacteria* take when seen under a microscope). *Bacterium* is the correct singular noun: to speak of "a bacteria", as so many people do now, is wrong on all counts, especially as the little devils come in such large numbers that single ones must be impossible to isolate. So if your doctor tells you he thinks you've "got a bacteria" you might be wise to get a second opinion. But alas, the singular "bacteria" seems to be going down the same road of no return as "the media"- for which see MEDIUM/MEDIA. Another Latin (and less common) word for the *bacterium* is *bacillus* – whose plural *bacilli* is not in danger of being singularized (viruses are different things altogether). See also INFECTIOUS/CONTAGIOUS and SALMONELLA; and other plural confusions cross-referenced under MEDIA.

ballpark figures/estimates *Ballpark figures* are figures or sums that are *estimated*, being calculated or guessed at within a broad area of possibilities. It is an American term and comes from places where baseball is played – places that are known as ballparks. Its non-sporting, international use seems to have started in 1960, with reference to the place, designated a "ballpark area", where the Discoverer XIV space capsule was expected to land.

banana republic/poor country *Banana republic*: "a small country that is economically dependent on a single crop, such as bananas, or a single product, such as tin [and] often governed by a dictator or an officer of the armed forces – countries where savings are hoarded rather than invested in productive enterprises" —*The American Heritage Dictionary of the English Language*, which might have added that such savings usually find their way into the dictator's personal Swiss bank account. The American poet Ralph Waldo Emerson (1802–1882) must have had banana republics in mind when he wrote:

> "The highest civility has never loved the hot zones.
> Where snow falls there is usually civil freedom;
> Where the banana grows, man is sensual and cruel."

Perhaps it is the hot climate required for the successful cultivation of the banana which tends to create hot-headed people and produced the expression "going bananas", first heard in the USA from the early 1930s, and defined by the *OED* as "crazy, mad, wild with excitement, anger, frustration, etc." Banana is an African word, and also an African family name. The first President of Zimbabwe, the Rev. Dr Canaan Banana, will be remembered chiefly for his disagreements with the President who succeeded him, the dictator Robert Mugabe, as well as the famous headline denying that a quarrel had taken place between the two men:

NO SPLIT, SAYS BANANA

When things were still amicable between the two politicians, Mr Mugabe, risking a BANANA SKIN, passed the world's first and only law banning jokes about a fruit (eat your hearts out, lettuces and cucumbers). But when the banana was first introduced into Europe and people "went bananas" for it, its name was thought poetic enough for Douglas Grant Duff Ainslie to write a "Serenade" beginning

> Lady of the lovely thighs
> Curving like banana fruit.

After that it was downhill all the way. Partridge's *Dictionary of Slang* says "Have a banana!" was "an early catchphrase expressive of contempt"; and that the phrase "Having a banana with…" meant (ca. 1905–1930) "to coit with a woman, after a line in an earlier song, 'Burlington Bertie from Bow': I had a banana with Lady Diana." (quoted verbatim from the second edition of the *OED*).

banana skin/embarrassment For some reason humorists have pretended to enjoy the spectacle of someone slipping on a *banana skin*. P.G.Wodehouse is probably to blame for popularizing the expression, in *Right Ho, Jeeves!* (1934): "Treading upon Life's banana skins". A few years later, living in wartime France, he himself slipped on one by allowing himself – perhaps innocently – to be recruited as a propagandist for Hitler. Most banana skins are now political and are likely to cause what the press calls "red faces". Before the British New Labour government brought in its SPIN DOCTORS in 1997 a previous administration briefly had an unofficial "Minister for Banana Skins".

barbecue/barbeque/barbeq etc. Only the first of these – three of many spellings – is right: *barbecue*, for outdoor cooking, an American adoption from the Spanish *barbacoa*, a raised gridiron placed over a fire to support food to be dried, smoked or cooked. Mis-spellings like those given above, or "Bar-B-Q" and the abbreviation BBQ, are commercial affectations or journalistic distortions. The barbecue has nothing to do with either a CUE or a "queue" meaning a tail. See also BOIL/BROIL and GRILL/GRILLE.

basically/well/er/um/if you like "Basically I got on the plane with a bomb. Basically I tried to ignite it. Basically yeah I intended to damage the plane", a terrorist admitted in court. There is nothing *basic* about *basically* in the way it is now used in EVERYDAY conversation, especially by the less articulate – for it is just a throat-clearing noise, often an attempt to, *er*, gain a little, *um*, thinking-time before the subsequent remark or statement. It has become the 20th/21st-century companion to *well*, which has been the almost self-parodic "I-am-about-to-speak" signal of the Englishman for more than a thousand years. Shakespeare in *The*

Tempest (1610) has: "This is a very scurvy tune to sing at a man's Funerall. Well, here's my comfort. – *Drinkes*". Earlier examples date from ca 888 AD; and, from 1382, in the Wyclif Bible, where Isaiah 44.16 has "He...seide, Vah, or weel, I am hat" (in the 1611 Bible, "Aha, I am warm"). *Well* is now often pronounced like "wah", and is rapidly being combined with basically, resulting in the ubiquitous "Wah bicycally..." So basically we can expect a long innings for basically. On the other hand, the fashion for filling internal sentence-hesitations by slipping in *if-you-like* or *if-you-will* seems to be waning. See also INITIALLY/FIRSTLY/AT FIRST/IN THE BEGINNING.

basque/bask The adjective *Basque* (written with a capital B) refers to something from the *Basque* region, a northern part of the Hispanic Peninsula (where coincidentally one *may* bask in sunshine); but to those interested in women's fashions a *basque* is a tight-fitting, low-cut bodice which is supposedly SEXY and worn to please men – almost a cliché garment when old-fashioned prostitutes are portrayed on film. The spelling "bask" for the garment is described as wrong, but there seems to be no good reason against anglicisation. According to an 18th-century cookery-book, Mrs Raffald's *English Housekeeper*, a source for the *OED*, a basque can also be a dish of minced mutton mixed with breadcrumbs, eggs, anchovies, wine, lemon-peel, etc., baked "in the caul of a leg of veal" (mutton dressed as veal?).

bate/bait *Bated* means diminished, reduced, which is an abbreviated form of *abated*, and would therefore originally have carried an apostrophe before it. It is usually found coupled with "breath" – part of a cliché that has survived only because Shakespeare used it in *The Merchant of Venice* (1596): "With bated breath and whispering humbleness, say this..." Its virtual disuse in other applications has caused confusion with the homophone *bait(ed)*, as if one could use breath as a bait. (Perhaps a "HARE'S BREATH"?). A *bait*, as every fisherman knows, is food, from an insect or animal, that is used on a hook or in a trap to entice a prey. This comes from an Old Norse word *beita*, food, also German *beissen*, to bite. The reverse confusion is more rare, although *Private Eye* added its own dimension by claiming that "[the schools minister] would bate teachers..." A related trap for the verbally unwary is sometimes sprung by STRAINED/(CON)STRAINED. And see also HARE'S BREATH/HAIR'S BREADTH as mentioned above.

bath/bathe The customary difference between *bath* and *bathe* (as verbs) seems to be between indoors and outdoors: you *bath* a baby or have a *bath* yourself, but *bathe* in a river or the sea. Americans, incidentally, do not *have* a bath but *take* one.

baton/batten Conductors and police use *batons*, but whereas the former uses his stick to beat time, not his players, the police have been *batoning* people since at least 1520, when they were still watchmen: "They battouned her quhill thay saw her bliud". ("Quhill" is an old spelling of "while" – which in north British usage means the same as "until" – see WHILE). The *Guardian* chose the wrong one of the two homophones when it reported that "the RUC battened marchers in full view of television cameras", instead of *batoned*. "Battening down the hatches" is a familiar phrase, meaning to make oneself secure, originally by closing a ship's hatch with battens (lengths of wood, or *scantling*) and wedges. To *batten* an animal is to feed it so that it grows fat.

beatify/beautify In the Roman Catholic faith *beatification* is a sort of half-way house on the way to full canonization – a happy kind of LIMBO which a person marked out for sainthood can enter only after his death. Latin *beatificare* means to make someone supremely happy (albeit posthumously) – hence the cliché "beatific smile", a rare survival of the word in EVERYDAY English. I suggest *beatification* might be secularized for, say, a self-made MOGUL who donates large sums to a ruling party and is supremely happily waiting for his expected knighthood or peerage. *Beatify* is a difficult word to get past some sub-editors, who suspect a mistyping for cosmetic treatment and put *beautify*. Thus a news-reader on BBC Radio Merseyside: "The Pope has beautified Father Colbert, a priest who in World War II saved the lives of concentration-camp inmates..." See also TITIVATE/TITILLATE.

before/in front of "The case was heard in front of the chancellor of the diocese..." claimed the *Independent on Sunday*. Cases are heard *before* the judiciary, not *in front* of them: they would hardly be heard *behind* them.

beleaguered/troubled In wartime cities are *beleaguered*, as were Mafeking in the Boer War and Stalingrad in World War II. Today it is a cliché description of politicians or other public persons who figure often in the news in some derogatory way – and are probably under pressure to resign. But to call them *beleaguered* (as in "beleaguered SPIN DOCTOR Jo Moore") is to use a term that is STILTED and better suited to war. For to *beleaguer* means to surround, or lay siege to, a town, or an encampment of enemy forces. It was also used in the sense of laying a figurative and amorous siege to a person, as in Samuel Richardson's *Pamela* (1740/1): "The girl is beleaguering, as you significantly express it, a worthy gentleman."

bended/bent *Bended* was the original past participle of bend, now almost universally expressed as *bent*. In modern – and usually facetious – usage only knees and swords, sometimes also spears, are *bended*.

benefactor/beneficiary "He was the chief benefactor of her £150,000 will", said the young *Guardian* writer. A *benefactor* (a Latin word meaning literally a "do-gooder") gives, but the *beneficiary* takes, i.e. benefits from whatever it is that is being given.

benefited/benefitted The accepted way of modifying *benefit*, is to *write benefited*, not *benefitted*, and the confusion probably arises because *fit* changes to *fitted*. A rule about whether or not to double letters (usually *s* or *t*) was devised by Charles Harris, a 19th-century Yorkshire printer – and it seems to have few exceptions: "If the *last* syllable is stressed (forget, commit, abet or beset), or there is only one syllable (sit, fit, rot, bed, bet) the last letter is doubled":

> bed/bedded/bedding
> beget/begetter/begetting
> beset/besetting
> bus/bussed/bussing
> commit/committal, committed, committing
> fit/fitted, fitting
> forget/forgetting, forgotten
> regret/regretted
> rot/rotted/rotting
> sit/sitter/sitting
> wed/wedding/wedded
> wet/wetting.

"If a syllable *other* than the last is stressed, then the final letter is *not* doubled":

> ballot/balloted/balloting
> bayonet/bayoneted/bayoneting

benefited

benefit/benefited/benefiting
bias/biased
budget/budgeted/budgeting
carpet/carpeted/carpeting
eyelet/eyeleted/eyeleting (not "eyeletting", like
bloodletting)
facet/faceted/faceting
focus/focused/focusing (not "focussing")
gusset/gusseted/gusseting
leaflet/leafleted/leafleting (not "leafletting")
target/targeted/targeting (not "targetting")

And yet, computer language *has* changed format into formatting, but that is a recent change rooted in the often haphazard language of information technology. Twentieth-century English airmen, including those in World War II, used the word "formating" to describe the action of forming up for formation-flying. Other occasional exceptions include dial/dialling, signal/signalling (both of which the Americans spell better, with one *l*), but tranquil/tranquility (which is to be preferred to "tranquillity").

-berg/-burg The German pioneer of book-printing was Gutenberg, not "Gutenburg", as it is often written by his less fussy successors; and Hindenburg was not "Hindenberg", as *The Times* claimed as long ago as Armistice Day, 1918 and has occasionally been claiming ever since. The trouble is that *burg* and *berg* are pronounced differently in German but sound the same in English. The Germans cannot confuse them, because a *Berg* is a mountain and a *Burg* a (fortified) castle. The Battenbergs' name originated from a mountain, not a castle, so when they changed their name at the start of World War I they literally translated it to Mountbatten (which, it was said, caused a Mr Ginzberg to change his to the more aristocratic-sounding Mountginz). The Battenberg cake that was named in honour of the family was a favourite of Queen Victoria but was not so called until 1902 – and in 1914 did *not* change to a Mountbatten cake.

(the) best part/greater part I can truthfully say that I have lived "the best part of my life" in Liverpool, in both senses of the expression, i.e. the *greater* as well as the *better* part; but statements like "The best part of the article was omitted" are ambiguous. It is an ancient quirk of the language: "Twenty nobles [a coin worth one-third of a pound sterling], of which I think he doth owe the best part for his rent", wrote an author of 1538 – and was confusing his readers even then. See also ENJOY/EXPERIENCE.

bevy/bevvy A *bevy*, says the *OED*, is "the proper term for a company of maidens or ladies; also of roes, quails, or of larks". A *bevvy* is an alcoholic drink, probably abbreviated from *beverage* but some say it was current among 19th-century English soldiers serving in India, who jocularly corrupted the word *bevali*, cheap or common beer. Perhaps they were scousers, for in the Liverpool dialect *bevvy* is an EVERYDAY word, which is why the local papers persist in writing about "a bevvy of bathing-beauties".

biannual/biennial *Biannual* means half-yearly or twice a year; *biennial*, once every two years.

bigamy/trigamy/quadrigamy *Bigamy* comes from the Latin *bigamus*, twice married, and this has been the preferred word in English, although there is the NICE home-grown mediaeval *twie-wifing*, used in the earliest translation of Genesis and Exodus: "Bigamie is unkinde thing, on engleis tale, twie-wifing." The word has also been used in ecclesiastical writings as a second marriage after the decease of the first spouse, or the lawful annulment of the first marriage (either way it is a happily prophetic form of the modern slang term "two-timing"). In modern use *bigamy* strictly means marrying a *second* wife or husband while legally still married to the first. Therefore three wives must be *trigamy*, which the *OED* quotes from a writer of 1615: "For [priests] it is lawfull to marry: but bigamy is forbidden them, and trigamy detested in the Laity." The *OED* also admits *quadrigamy*, albeit half-heartedly, but after that *polygamy*, literally "many marriages", sets in. However, the press goes straight from "two" to "many", and absurdly uses terms like "serial bigamists" (absurd, unless of course the offence is committed and recommitted in recurring groups of two). The semantic side of the problem has occupied many – even an anonymous limerick-writer.

> There was a young fellow from Lyme
> Who married three wives at a time.
> When asked "Why the third?"
> He replied "One's absurd
> And bigamy, sir, is a crime".

big brother/authority In 1949 George Orwell (real name Eric Blair) wrote a futuristic novel, *Nineteen Eighty-Four*, in which he postulated a Soviet-style Communist-ruled Britain. In the novel, images of "the Leader" are displayed everywhere (as is still the custom in dictatorships), with the warning: "Big Brother is watching You". Happily, by the time the year 1984 dawned, Communism – far from having spread to Britain – was in its death throes everywhere, strangled by its own bureaucracy, corruption, NEPOTISM/CRONYISM and the kind of incompetence only centralized control can produce. *Big Brother* entered popular consciousness, not with reference to state *authority* and authoritarian officialdom but with the introduction of hundreds of thousands of surveillance cameras, most of them trained on criminals and anti-social ELEMENTS.

In the early years of the 21st century *Big Brother* was appropriated by showbusiness as a title for a much-copied television "format" of unimaginable stupidity, with a large dash of cupidity (see AMATORY) and immense popular appeal, with the result that most of its viewers are unlikely now even to recall the novel *1984*. Orwell called his *Nineteen Eighty-Four* hero Winston, imagining that by then this would be the most common CHRISTIAN NAME, in homage to Winston Churchill. In fact the English continue to christen their sons James and John, Charles and Andrew, as they have always done, while the few Winstons one encounters seem to come mostly from Afro-Caribbean stock.

bile/gall/choler/spleen *Bile* is a fluid the liver secretes to aid the digestive process. It was believed to be one of the "four humours" which, in pre-scientific medicine, were thought to govern man's behaviour. It has a bitter taste, was also known as *choler*, and became a synonym for anger, ill temper or peevishness (adjective *choleric*). Another name for *bile/choler* is *gall* ("bitter as gall"), which, too, has connotations of irascibility but with suggestions of impertinence ("He has a gall!") – all of them archaic ideas that are gradually losing currency. Even *bilious attacks* are no longer spoken of as they used to be: the complaint is now more likely to be diagnosed as *reflux*. The *spleen* is a different organ again, with a different function, which in ancient medicine included the seat of various emotions, from merriment and capriciously changeable feelings to sudden impulses and a hot ("splenetic") temper. See also DANDER/GANDER.

black/negro/afro- *Black* is "a word of difficult history...", wrote the
19th-century editors of the *OED*, making one of the great
understatements of the 20th, for they could not have guessed what a
MINEFIELD it would become – in the media, in politics and in EVERYDAY
use. They defined the word as "dark, sombre, dusky, gloomy, deeply
stained with dirt; soiled, dirty, foul, having dark or deadly purposes;
malignant, pertaining to or involving death; deadly, baneful, disastrous,
sinister, iniquitous, atrocious, horribly wicked; clouded with sorrow or
melancholy, dismal, gloomy, sad, threatening, boding ill..." and so on for
page after page, some 130 inches of small type; with associations ranging
from funerals and mourning to deadly snakes and spiders, the *Black
Death*, *black Fridays*, the *black sheep* of the family, the *Black Hole* of
Calcutta; *blackguards* giving each other *black looks*, getting into each others'
black books or selling on the *black market* to boost the *black economy*;
motorists skidding on *black ice*; judges donning their *black cap* before
condemning criminals to death; people squeezing *blackheads* or bringing
up *black bile*, naming union *blacklegs* or SCABS in *black books* or on *blacklists*
– and numerous similes, like *black as the devil*, *black as sin*, *black dog*
depression, and hundreds more "black" expressions used by people who
would never dream of saying an unkind word about a person of different
skin-colour. For such a person euphemisms abounded, the most common
of which was *Negro* (simply the Spanish work for black) and others which
were (or now sound) patronizingly offensive, such as lady of colour, a
touch of the tarbrush, of darker hue, etc.

All that changed in the 1960s, with the rise of movements like Black
Power, Black Consciousness and Black is Beautiful – and suddenly those
who were formerly called *negroes* were proud to carry the black label. The
position of the two words was reversed: *black* was declared good and
Negro bad. It was as if Jews had decided they wished henceforth to be
called "yids" and disabled people preferred "cripples". So we were back
where we started – and with equal inaccuracy: "black" people come in a
variety of attractive shades of brown, but seldom in a real black;
similarly, if I were to see a genuinely "white" person I should be much
alarmed. The only section of the population that has benefited from the
change is the well-meaning "equality" industry, which keeps trying to
banish from the English language ancient and innocent terms like those
above, even when they have no conceivable RACIST/RACIALIST meaning.
Most style books rule that when referring to people of African or Afro-
Caribbean origin, the word Black should take a capital initial, as do

Catholics, Jews, Methodists, Muslims, etc. – but not, curiously, whites. For further confusions see ETHNIC; also ESKIMO/INUIT, SCAB/BLACKLEG/FINK.

blanch/blench Sue Arnold, in the *Independent*, recounting how she had come face to face with a flood of overflowing raw sewage in her flat: "I came, I saw, I blanched". *Blanching* and *blenching* are not the same, although a person who has just had a fright might do both. She could have *blanched* if her face was drained of colour (old French *blanchir*, to whiten), or blanched some almonds by covering them with boiling water. Or she might have *blenched*, which means she flinched, quailed or gave a sudden start out of fear or shock (from Old English *blencan*, which also gave us blinking) – as one would when confronted with a flat-ful of raw sewage. (Or even cooked sewage? But no; raw here means untreated).

blaze/fire/inferno Ordinary people talking to each other would say things like "There was a *fire* in our street last night", whereas journalists invariably reach for the word *blaze* or, if only slightly bigger, an *inferno*.

blond/blonde Men are *blond*, plural *blonds*, women *blonde*, plural *blondes*. A woman may be called "*a blonde*" but to call a blond-haired man "a blond" neither looks nor sounds right. In archaic sources quoted by the *OED blonde* is made to serve for both sexes. See also FIANCÉ/FIANCÉE.

bloody/blooming It now seems strange but until about 1970 few if any newspapers would have printed the EXPLETIVE *bloody* except by disguising it with asterisks, or euphemizing it in some facetious way – "blooming", "blessed", "blithering", "blankety-blank", etc – or give it in some facetious circumlocution, like "the sanguinary expletive". George Bernard Shaw in 1912 outraged the English-speaking world by using the word in his play *Pygmalion*. The resulting public outcry became a long-running *cause célèbre*, and produced the euphemism "Not *Pygmalion* likely!" (now all but forgotten). It took another half-century for bloody to be accepted in polite society, at least until it was used by Royalty. In 1999 the Food Editor of Australian *Vogue* at the age of about 85 was able to publish a best-selling COOKERY-BOOK/ COOKBOOK which she called *Bloody Delicious!* and indeed Australia (unlike England) has accepted bloody as a parliamentary expression, along with "shit" and "Bullshit!" The formerly taboo expression "pissed off" has also been gentrified, and like bloody has become an accepted parliamentary expression, if only in Australia. And see BLUE-PENCIL below.

blue-pencil/censor/cut Another archaism. From World War I and again in World War II to *blue-pencil* referred to the military censors' use of heavy blue crayon to obliterate and make unreadable written information (in letters and newspaper articles, etc.) that might have been of help to the enemy. It became the term for any act of censoring or cutting material, usually for moral reasons. It also became a euphemism for BLOODY, as in "not blue-pencilled likely", and BLOODY would have been one of the words censored (except in its legitimately sanguinary application). See also CENSOR/CENSER/SENSOR/CENSURE.

blueprints/plans/schemes The *blueprint* method of photographically reproducing plans in an image composed of white lines on a dark-blue ground, dates from the 1880s and was superseded some 90 years later by more effective ways of plan-printing. Its figurative use, by which any *plan* or *scheme* is called a *blueprint*, dates from the 1920s and is now a journalistic archaism, like "dialling" a number on the telephone. See also AIRBRUSH OUT.

blue-rinse/female-conservative The idea that Tory women dye their hair in lurid shades of blue is probably based on some one-off comment by a political journalist which caught his mates' imagination and became a stock cliché. Even the most cursory comparison between women attending a Conservative political conference and, say, people staging an anti-Tory protest outside, will show that blue-dyed hair (as well as purple and green) is more popular with punks and students than among GENTEEL ladies with aspirations to good taste and class. The cliché is usually incomplete unless expressed in pseudo-military terms as the "blue-rinse BRIGADE". Another stereotypical cliché with social or political undertones is the "chinless wonder", a man of presumed aristocratic origin who lacks firmness of character, and who naturally votes Conservative. However, the post-1997 Labour government headed by Tony Blair in fact had a minister of impeccably LUMPEN origin to whom nature had forgotten to give a chin – a total deficiency EXACERBATED by his attempt to hide its absence with a beard.

boar/boor/bore Kamal Ahmed of the *Guardian* described two of Newcastle United's directors as "...loud-mouthed and chauvinistic boars". *Bores*, probably, *boors* possibly, but male pigs, no. *Boors* were originally associated with Dutch or South African peasants (from *boer*) but have figured in English from at least 1598, when Florio's *A Worlde of Wordes* gives "a lubber, a clowne, a boore, a rude fellow". For *chauvinistic* see under JINGOISM.

boche/bosch/hun/kraut *Boche* was the World War I French nickname for the Germans, whom the English called "the hun" (a term first used for German soldiers in 1900 by Kaiser Wilhelm II himself). *Bosch* is a German firm making domestic appliances. Not so in the *Daily Telegraph*: "The Bosch has spotted us!" cries the leader of the Maquis. "Run, *mes braves!*" The American nickname for Germans during World War II was *Krauts* – and *Kraut* is cabbage (so is *Kohl*, like a former German Chancellor), which Americans use as an abbreviation of *Sauerkraut*.

boffin/scientist A *boffin* was originally a wartime scientist, usually one who worked anonymously, probably on secret assignments. In peacetime it means any scientist working on any project a journalist may not understand. No earlier examples than World War II have yet been found, but some say boffin had previously been naval slang for a British officer nearing or past retiring-age.

bogie/bogey When a newspaper described rescue workers as "…hoisting a bogey from one of the crashed trains", the reporter meant a *bogie*, the wheeled section of a railway carriage, plural *bogies*. A *bogey* is what children – and some adults – call a piece of solidified mucus picked from the nose: the larger the more satisfying, but not so large as to require a crane (note also the SNOOTY/SNOTTY difference). A bogey is also something bad in golf, and in football a *bogey team* is one that is dauntingly difficult to beat – like a team of *bogeymen*. In this sense *bogey* is thought to be related to *bug* or *bugge*, a terror, bugbear or scarecrow, and these kinds of bogey take the plural *bogeys*. See also BUGBEAR/BUG BEAR.

bog standard/box standard When said of manufactured items, one assumes that the term (at any rate in British English) is derogatory and that "bog" refers to a latrine or other primitive toilet arrangement. But recent *OED* researches suggest that it is motorcyclists' jargon and is a corruption of *box standard*, that is, basic, unused and unmodified – just as it came out of its packing (*were* new motorcycles ever delivered in cardboard boxes?). The first recorded dating in the *OED* is 1983 but an antedating to the 1950s is possible.

boil/broil "There is no such English word [as *broil*]", claimed a writer in the *Independent*. American housewives would disagree, as would English cooks and cookery-writers down the ages, from Mrs Raffald (1769) to Dr William Kitchiner (1821) and Mrs Beeton (1861). Broil, "to burn, char with fire...or on a gridiron..." – in other words, to GRILL or BARBECUE. Broil is now regarded as American, but like so many words it emigrated to the USA and was forgotten by the people back home, especially sub-editing folk who suspect a misprint for *boil*. Even the Bible refers to this method of cooking. William Tyndale's version of 1526, has, in St Luke 24.42, where Jesus reappears to the doubting disciples and asks for MEAT: "And they gave hym a pece of a brouled fisshe, and of an honycombe". The translators of the King James Bible of 1611 made it "broyled fish", and later versions had broiled, but they must all have considered the mixture of fish and honey non-KOSHER (or gastronomically improbable), for they omitted the honeycomb.

bolshy/unco-operative/obstructive/truculent *Bolshy* as an abbreviation for *Bolshevik* dates from 1920, when a new political system in Russia sent waves of fear across the Western world. It is Russian for "the bigger ones". Both D. H. and T. E. Lawrence were early users of *bolshy* (D. H. in 1918) and *bolshie* (T. E. in 1922), while H. G. Wells used both spellings from 1930 onwards. In its political sense the word had gone into decline even before the fall of Communism and become general slang for "obstructive or recalcitrant behaviour or temperamental disinclination to obey authority". Paradoxically such behaviour is possible only in a free society, and in countries whose citizens are allowed to show their opposition. Under Bolshevik rule no-one could legally be *bolshy*. It is one of the minor accidents of history that had their counter-revolutionary opponents the *Mensheviks*, the "smaller ones", triumphed, we might now be telling people, "Don't be so menshy!" See also BIG BROTHER.

bonanza/wealth/riches/windfall etc. *Bonanza* is Spanish for fair weather, especially that experienced when a ship is becalmed at sea. In its anglicized form it means a source of wealth, riches or good trade, but it was originally adopted into American English as a mining-term relating to the discovery of rich veins of silver in Mexico. The Irishman's *bonanza* is GALORE.

bonanza

41

bottleneck/hold-up When a traffic *hold-up* is under discussion the word *bottleneck* is not only overworked but can also become a self-cancelling cliché. "A big bottleneck on the M25" would suggest an *increased* flow of traffic, not an obstruction. *Hold-up* has been compromised by its criminal meaning, which is an originally American term for a robbery in which villains surprise their victims, who are stopped from what they are doing and "held up" for money or valuables.

boy/buoy The subject for endless confusion, both by punsters ("A mermaid sitting on a buoy") and bad spellers ("The ship was tied to a boy anchored in the Formby Channel"). Only sticklers for pronunciation distinguish between them by giving the floating object two syllables, something like "bw-oy" and one to the young male.

brake/break One would think no-one could possibly confuse them but the *Liverpool Daily Post* had a music critic saying (probably over the telephone) that the movements of a piano concerto had been "played without brakes" (a runaway success?); while the *Daily Telegraph* claimed, conversely, that the car in which Diana Princess of Wales died "had an automatic breaking system".

brand/brandish "Winnie Mandela is today brandished a liar and a charlatan..." wrote the *Independent*. *Brandish*, to flourish, to wave something about, by way of threat or display, or to prepare for action, comes from the Teutonic word *brand*, a sword. *Brand*, also from Germanic languages, meaning fire, is to mark or stamp with infamy, to burn with a hot iron, to mark indelibly. Mrs Mandela's preferred form of punishment for political opponents was, IRONICALLY, to "necklace" them by setting fire to a rubber tyre placed round their neck.

breach/breech A *breach*, meaning a break or fracture, comes from the Teutonic and German *Bruch*, *brechen*. A *breech*, now used more often in the plural, *breeches*, since they come in pairs, is a garment covering the loins, thighs and knees (pronounced "britches"): confusing the two gives extra meaning to the cliché "More in the breech than the observance". One of the earliest examples of possible confusion (especially for schoolboys) is found in the Old Testament, Judges, 5.17, where Deborah says, "Asher continued on the sea-shore and abode in his breaches." That does not mean he kept his trousers on – those kinds of *breaches* were breaks in the coast or in small harbours, not *breeks*, which is sailors' slang for wide trousers. And what is one to make of Thomas Shadwell (1642?–1692) writing of William III after the King was wounded at the Battle of the Boyne: "But Heav'n of you took such Peculiar Care/That soon the Royal Breech it did repair"?

bridal/bridle A *bridle* is (part of) the headgear of (usually) a horse, by which the animal is controlled or guided. It also denotes other forms of restraint, like the mediaeval "scold's bridle", with which allegedly erring or scolding wives were punished. *Bridal* relates only to brides – making an advertisement for "Bridle Wear" a POIGNANTLY alarming error. The declining ROLE of the horse has also produced the REIGN/REIN confusion.

brigade/movement/crew etc. A *brigade* is a recognized subdivision of the British Army, consisting of a certain number of battalions under the command of a Brigadier. Also, less specifically, a civilian group of people united by a common purpose or profession, like the Fire Brigade, Boys' Brigade, etc. As a deprecatory collective noun for adherents of a certain *movement* with shared opinions, like the BLUE-RINSE brigade of Tory women, it is older than its current clichéd over-use suggests. William Drummond's *History of the five James's* (ca 1640) anticipates the non-military *brigade* by more than three centuries – also another recent vogue-word, *crew*: "Ye are such a brigade of papists, and antichristian crew". *Brigades* and *brigadiers* have their origin in *brigands*, who from mediaeval times lived by pillage and robbery, which only heightened Drummond's invective.

brisk/brusque These two words were once closer than they are now, but their meanings gradually diverged. To be *brusque* means to have an offhand manner, to be blunt, sourish and perhaps act rather hastily, from the Italian *brusco* (think of *Lambrusco*, the Italian wine industry's answer to *Coca-Cola*). Being *brisk* is to be active, sparkling, lively. Perhaps Shakespeare means both, in *Henry IV Part I* (1597): "A cup of Wine that's briske and fine".

brit/briton/british/britisher/english Because *Brit* is now often used derisively ("Brits misbehaving on the Costa") it is taken for a modernism. In fact it was the proper word for certain non-Scots, especially in Scotland, until about AD 1300, and later specifically meant the Welsh: "All Albione wes in gude rest and peice [peace], both Scot and Brit, and Inglismen also"

43

(1535) – note the distinction made between Brits and Englishmen. *Britons* did not really come into their own until what the *OED* calls "the Rule Britannia period", from the middle of the 18th century. In the 19th and early 20th centuries people were more likely to speak of *Britishers* (E. M. Forster, in *A Room with a View* (1908): "I do detest conventional intercourse. Nasty! they are going into the church, too. Oh, the Britisher abroad!"), but this gradually disappeared after World War II, supplanted by the now lazily over-used Brit, often attached to other words, e.g. Brit Art, Brit Pack, Brit Pop, etc. Abroad the word *British* has always taken second place to *English*. When the Germans cried "Gott strafe England!" during World War I they lumped together the English, Scots, Irish and Welsh as *die Engländer*, and the same misapprehension persisted during and beyond World War II. In the same way the French still prefer *les anglais*, much to the chagrin of non-English Britons.

britain/brittany/britannia/breton *Britannia* is the Latin word for *Britain* and has one *t* and two *n*s, whereas the Greek-based form has two *t*s and one *n*, giving rise to *Brittany* – whose natives are *Bretons*, with one of each.

broncho-/bronco "The cause of death on a certificate signed by Dr Shipman was given as broncopneumonia" (*Guardian*). This alarming condition would have been caused either by an untamed horse (Spanish *bronco*, rough, rude) or the old, "hard" toilet-paper with that trade name. *Broncho-*, on the other hand, is the medical prefix relating to the windpipe or the breathing process, from Greek *bronchos*.

bucolic/alcoholic *Bucolic* means rustic, countrified or peasant-like, from the Greek *boukolikos*, a herdsman. It has nothing to do with drink or drunkenness, although the *-(c)olic* syllable may mislead one to assume connotations of alcoholic, rollicking jollity.

budget/cheap As an adjective *budget* is a newcomer largely linked to sales-talk meaning *cheap*, as in "budget fares","budget airlines", etc.; but the verb *to budget*, meaning, broadly, to make prudent financial plans and look after one's pennies, goes back to the 17th century. The original noun is older still, from the late Middle Ages, French *bougette*, a leather bag or big purse. It was such a bag that earlier Chancellors of the Exchequer actually opened when presenting their periodic account of the national finances. Before long it gave its name to what we now know as the Budget and at some point the budget bag was replaced by a red dispatch-box.

bugbear/bug bear A *bugbear* is "a kind of hobgoblin supposed to devour naughty children", says the *OED*: "Hobgoblines and Buggebeares, with whom we were never acquaynted" (1581). But more recently it has come to mean an object of dread, an annoyance or bane: see also BOGIE/BOGEY. It is is neither a bug nor a bear and should therefore be written as one word, or else two joined by a hyphen, though newspaper writers spell the creature "bug bear" when it suits them to space out a headline.

bullets/pellets/shot/rounds Firearms such as rifles, pistols and machine-guns fire *bullets*; air-guns discharge *pellets*; and shotgun ammunition is called (lead) *shot*, singly also sometimes pellets. "The victim was hit by a bullet from a shotgun" is nonsense. Machine-guns fire *rounds* – which sounds cheerfully harmless.

burger/burgher *Burger*, as used in the USA since the 1930s, is short for that ubiquitous fast-food, the hamburger – also beefburger, cheeseburger, eggburger or whatever combination of filling is served between two halves of a cottonwool-textured bread-roll. The common assumption that a hamburger originally contained ham is false: it meant a "Hamburger steak", which German immigrants popularized in the USA at the end of the 19th century. *Burghers* are the inhabitants or citizens of a borough, burgh, town or city. Although related, the two are separated by different spelling. When a *Guardian* writer referred to the "Burgers of Calais" he meant the famous sculpture-group by Auguste Rodin but in fact evoked McDonalds.

buxom/bosom/well built As a description of a woman attractively or comfortingly plump, especially her breasts, *buxom* now sounds dated and coy, but this is a relatively modern meaning, as the word comes from the old Dutch/German *buigzaam/biegsam*, pliable to the touch (T. S. Eliot's "pneumatic bliss"?) or submissive. The English spelling was from the 12th century *buhsum* but the likeness of this word to *bosom* and suggested AMATORY availability (as it was from the 18th century) seems to be happy chance. Today's boring press euphemism is *well built*.

byline/byeline A *byline* is printed line giving the name or names of the author(s) of a newspaper article or report. A *byeline* is the painted white line that extends the alignment of the goalposts on a soccer pitch.

byline

cache/store/arsenal/dump *Cacher* is French, meaning to hide. Its noun, *cache*, has been in English use for a hiding-place since the middle of the 19th century, though pronounced in the French way, to rhyme with "rash". It looks and sounds good in an English sentence only when used as an elegant alternative, (or a coy one, like the *cache-sexe*, French for a woman's g-string or the "posing-pouch" of a male artist's model). When speaking of terrorists' and criminals' hoards of weapons or explosives, journalists tend to prefer the elegant French word to the more homely *store*, or *dump* or, when bigger, *arsenal*. See also HOARD/HORDE.

callous/callus Both come from Latin *callosus*, hardened, but a *callus* is hardened skin, *callous*(ness) a hardened state of mind. The famous soprano was neither of those, but Maria *Callas*.

camp/township/reservation/ghetto/quarter A *camp* is a place where people lodge in tents or other temporary means of shelter, such as canvas sheets slung between trees. This description clearly does not apply to *townships* in which the shelter consists of permanent buildings constructed of concrete blocks, yet when displaced Palestinians live there they are always called refugee *camps*. Far from temporary, they have deplorably been in existence for nearly half a century, their construction indistinguishable from that of other urban quarters. *Reservations*, however, are bad news all round: tracts of land set apart by a government for the exclusive use of native people. They were first set up by 18th century Americans so as to keep their NATIVE AMERICANS/RED INDIANS under control, and the word never became respectable.

The first *ghetto* for Jews was established in 1516 in Venice on the site of an iron-foundry, for which the Italian word is *getto*: "The place where the whole fraternity of the Jews dwelleth together, which is called the Ghetto" according to the *Crudities* (1611) of Thomas Coryate, who left a fascinating account of his travels, mostly on foot, throughout Europe and the near East. (He also wrote a book called *Thomas Coriate Traveller for the English Wits* – which saved the "wits" the bother of embarking on their own Grand Tour, as the Travel Sections do still in our SUNDAY PAPERS). Early ghettos (and again under the Nazi oppression of 1933–1945) were places where Jews were confined behind walls and not allowed out without special permits, but what today's press calls a (Western) ghetto may merely be an area, like a Jewish or Muslim quarter, where people of a common race, religion or nationality have chosen to live in close proximity to their relations, for notional ghettos can be occupied by ETHNIC folk of all kinds.

canard/canaille The late prolific columnist and calumnist Auberon Waugh (favourite word "hideous") had the enviable ability to write articles faster than the time it took to read them. In his haste, one day, he wrote in the *Daily Telegraph* about "a *canaille* pushed around ... that Edward VIII had a bastard child by an Australian aboriginal". Waugh here confused a duck with a dog (strange for a man who once tried to become an MP for the Dog Lovers' Party). *Canaille*: riff-raff, rabble, from pre-17th-century Italian *canaglia* and ultimately from Latin *canis*, a dog. *Canard*: literally a duck, but also "an extravagant or absurd story circulated to impose on people's credulity, a false report". This also has canine associations, though only indirectly: from *un bailleur de canards*, or duck salesman, "a cousener, guller, cogger, foister, lyer" (1611), in other words, one who "sells a pup". Waugh's law: if you must use foreign terms, check that you've got them right. Perhaps we must blame cheap foreign holidays for foreign half-knowledge. As a 16th-century English sage complained "Some far journayed gentlemen at their retourne home, like as thei loue to go in forraine apparell ... will pouder their talke with ouersea language. He that cometh out of Fraunce will talke Frenche Englishe and never blush at the matter. An other choppes in with Englishe Italianated, and applieth the Italian phrase to our Englishe speakyng."

canvas/canvass *Canvas*, the strong coarse fabric used for making sails etc., was originally *canevas*, a 12th-century word for hemp, as is *cannabis*. The verb to *canvass* is remotely related to the sail-cloth, and at first meant "to toss in a canvas sheet, as a sport or punishment", in which sense Shakespeare has it in *Henry IV Part 1* (1597): "Ile canuas thee in thy broad Cardinalls Hat, if thou proceed in this thy insolence". The modern meaning of soliciting votes, opinions etc. dates from as recently as the early 19th century.

47

carbon copy/copycat/copy *Carbon copy*, as in "carbon copy murder", is a journalistic cliché description of a crime that closely follows the pattern of a previous one. It is an archaism that will soon puzzle younger readers, as few writers now make copies of their work by laboriously interleaving and then winding into a typewriter sheets of carbon-coated paper (which journalists used to call "blacks", but now don't, albeit for different reasons). Electronic keyboards, copying-machines and desk-top printers have made them all obsolete. *Copycat*, "a derogatory term for one who copies another" is also senseless, for although it goes back to the middle of the 19th century, whoever coined it forgot that cats are independent creatures who do not demean themselves with slavish copying.

carbuncle/eyesore In a memorable speech to the Royal Society of British Architects in 1984, Charles, Prince of Wales, described a proposed extension to the National Gallery, London, as "a kind of monstrous carbuncle on the face of a much-loved and elegant friend". It probably had greater influence than any other utterance in protecting London from some extravagant excesses of modern architects. The real *carbuncle* is a precious stone of a red and fiery colour, from Latin *carbunculus*, small coal. The word was also used for an inflammatory skin eruption or, as the first editor of the *OED* warned, "a red spot on the nose or face caused by habits of intemperance".

careen/career *Careening* is a nautical term for turning a ship or boat on her side, usually to scrape barnacles off her bottom, though it sometimes refers to a vessel that keels over of its own accord. Either way the *Independent's* report of two American presidential candidates "careening round the South" EVOKED/INVOKED an unlikely spectacle. Normally the confusion is in the other direction, for many attempts to use "careen" in a newspaper FLOUNDER/FOUNDER on the MURPHY'S LAW/SOD'S LAW principle of well-meaning but erroneous "correction". Thus a sub-editor may suspect a mistyping and change *careening* to *careering*. Careering is an equestrian term for a horse's gallop at full speed while "turning this way and that in running", but the 20th-century rise of motor transport annexed the word, usually for vehicles running out of control.

carousal/carousel A *carousel* is a merry-go-round or roundabout as seen at fairgrounds, though the word originally came from a mediaeval jousting tournament (the ancestor, perhaps, of the wooden fairground horse). A *carousal* is what the *OED* engagingly defines as a "drinking-feast" and few print-journalists now hesitate to call a piss-up.

(a) **carpeting/reprimand** For its definition of *carpeting* the *OED* evokes a bygone social system, explaining the expression as "To call (a servant) into the parlour, etc., to be reprimanded... to 'call [sic] over the coals'..." – for servants would have had no carpets in their quarters, though they would have had coal. The *OED* also gives a surprisingly early example, dating from 1840: "They had done nothing? Why were they carpeted?" Newspapers are fond of carpet clichés, like "Blood on the carpet". Notice "call" over the coals, where now "haul" is normal. See also FACING THE MUSIC.

cartoons/caricatures The *OED*'s priorities are sound, for its first definition of a *cartoon* is "a drawing on stout paper, made as a design for a painting of the same size...." etc. Only then comes "a humorous or topical drawing in a newspaper, etc." This second meaning was invented, appropriately, by the humorous magazine *Punch* in its second year (1843), when it warned politicians of the impending "...publication of several exquisite designs, to be called Punch's Cartoons!" When *Punch* published cartoons they were recognizable representations of the public figures of its day but made no attempt at exaggeration, as do *caricatures*. Even Queen Victoria occasionally figured in *Punch* cartoons, but in a good – if not always flattering – likeness. It was not until the 1970s that newspapers tentatively began to draw caricatures of royalty, which were sometimes cruel and impertinent. In truth few modern cartoonists, political or general, can draw by professional art-school standards – and those who can stand out far above the rest. Most do not even attempt to create likenesses – unlike the great cartoon artists of the second half of the 20th century, like Sir David Low and "Vicky" (Viktor Weisz) who have few successors that measure up to them. Certain conventions act as a kind of shorthand: burglars wear jerseys with horizontal stripes, prisoners have arrows on their clothes, and many a joke is "explained" by the inclusion of a news placard, or a name written on trouser-turnup or lapel. The chief strength of modern cartoonists lies in their comic ideas and situations, which they then illustrate – some with no more than a crude, schoolboy line. The *OED* defines caricatures as "grotesque or ludicrous representations of persons or things by exaggerating their most characteristic and striking features". In spite of the fact that caricatures attempt to delineate a person's character the occasional misspelling "characature" is without etymological basis.

cassock/hassock/tussock/hillock/hummock/pillock If writers come away from church confused by the SURPLICE/SURPLUS difference, what hope is there of their distinguishing between the garment that clerics wear and the cushion they kneel upon? The *cassock* was at first a riding-cloak – presumably related to the *cossack* – and originally a Turkish word that took on its English ecclesiastical meaning during the 17th century. A *hassock* was originally found outdoors (where it is also known as a *tussock*), a tuft or clump of matted vegetation, like grass, with which the kneeling-cushions would be stuffed, hence the thick, firm kneel-upon cushions used in church. Also related are the *hummock* and *hillock*, a small hill. This leaves only the *pillock* – current from the 1500s for "a fool, a stupid person" (*OED*) maybe one who would confuse a surplice with a surplus. It is a contraction of a humorous mediaeval term of abuse for a man or boy, *pillicock*, the penis ("Mi pilcok pisseth on mi schone [shoes]" – quoted by the *OED* from *Reliquiae antiquae*, 1300–1325) though it is also found as a form of intimate endearment.

cast/caste A *cast*, in the sense of the possible confusion that concerns us here, is the group of actors in a play or other production, particularly with reference to the role assigned to each player. *Caste* is a RACIALIST term chiefly associated with the religious and cultural divisions that obtain in India, from Latin *castus*, pure, unpolluted. "The caste of an Asian soap…" in the *Guardian* was no more than a happy coincidence.

catamite/sodomite The *OED* says a *catamite* is "a boy kept for unnatural purposes", without specifying what these were (and besides, what is considered unnatural by one generation may be placed on the schools curriculum by the next). The word comes from Latin *catamitus*, a corruption of the Greek *Ganymedes*, Jupiter's cup-bearer and catamite: child-abuse was part of "normal" life for all-powerful ancients (and no doubt many not-so-ancients who had young servants in their charge). But the catamite never became part of the popular language and today he would be called a rent-boy, among other names. The *Sodomite* was at first simply an inhabitant of the biblical city of Sodom and this word, too, did not come into popular use, at least until it figured LARGE in the trial of Oscar Wilde. The citizens of Sodom and Gomorrah were said, in Genesis 18 and 19 to have been generally debauched, and finally added incest to homosexual injury. But the word occurs in so many quotations about them (e.g. William Caxton, in 1474, in *The game and playe of the chesse*: "the vnnaturell synne of lecherye of the sodamites"), that the idea arose that *sodomy* was specifically the act of buggery. Sodom was always twinned with Gomorrah, and because of all the evil-doing the Lord destroyed both cities (clearly something of a tradition in the Middle East). Apart from that Gomorrah got off relatively lightly, at least in that it never had a vice named after it. See also the difference between SOD/SOT.

cater for/cater to/pander to Shakespeare makes it plain with his near-proverb in *As You Like It* (1600): "He that doth the Rauens feede, Yea prouidently caters for the Sparrow." The word comes from the French *acheter*, to buy (provisions). Catering has become almost synonymous with cooking – which one does *for* people, not *to* them (in spite of the fact that W. M. Thackeray in 1840 got it wrong with "Catering to the national taste and variety"). The clumsy catering *to* did not catch on until the 1980s, when columnists took a fancy to it, perhaps confusing it with *pandering*, which does take *to* – as in their "pandering to the vulgar taste". Pandering means to minister to others' gratification – which in its original dictionary-recorded form was exclusively sexual – from Pandarus, the character who figures in Chaucer, Bocaccio and Shakespeare and procures the love of Cressida for Troilus. Hence the generic *pandar*, *pander* or *pandor* for a procurer or pimp. Could Troilus, incidentally, have been responsible for giving us *troilism*, which the *OED* prissily defines as "Sexual activity in which three persons take part simultaneously" and the tabloids call "Three-in-a-Bed Romps"? The *OED* rather lamely postulates, "Perhaps from French *trois*, three". Troilus, Cressida and Pandarus all in one great mediaeval fourposter?

cavalry/calvary The music critic (or his typesetter) who reported a performance of "Suppé's Overture *Light Calvary*" probably got his fingers in a twist, because normally the confusion works in the other direction – *Calvary* being changed to *cavalry*, since television and schools tell us more about mounted warfare than the Crucifixion at *Calvary* – Latin *calvaria*, Greek *golgotha*, originally "the place of the skull".*

*A jeweller, asked if he had any PENDANT crosses, replied, "Do you want a plain cross or one with a little man on?"

celebration/commemoration/jubilee A caption-writing sub-editor of the *Guardian* wrote a paragraph about "the [anniversary] celebrations" of *Kristallnacht* – a day of particularly vicious Nazi atrocities in 1938 – and BBC Radio 3 presenters sometimes say things like, "Today we celebrate the death, seven years ago of..." Both are theoretically correct, for to celebrate comes from Latin *celebrare*, to perform solemn rites, but they are wrong in the spirit of usage. *Celebrations* are for joyful events, *commemorations*, from *memor*, mindful, for deaths, disasters and other deplorable occasions. But *jubilees* are by definition joyful. For complete authenticity they should include music for trumpets (a tradition well observed by Western CLASSICAL composers in their oratorios and cantatas), for the word comes from Hebrew *yobel*, trumpet and, via later Latin *jubilum*, a wild cry. Strictly jubilees occur every fifty years (like golden weddings) and are a time for forgiveness and restitution. As Leviticus 25.10–12 says, "And ye shall hallow the fiftieth year, and proclaim liberty throughout the land unto all the inhabitants thereof... for it is a jubile [sic]; it shall be holy unto you". See also MEMENTO.

celebate/chaste It is commonly believed that *celibate* and *celibacy* refer to the abstention from sexual intercourse, or the following of a chaste life. *Celibacy* in fact means living in an unmarried state, which in Latin is *celibatus*, as in "St Paul's advice for cœlebacy, or single life", as told by one Laurence Womock in 1663. Although St Paul might not have approved, most of the merry monks among his followers were fornicating their socks off while technically remaining fully *celibate*. See also BACHELOR/SINGLETON.

cellophane/celluloid/plastic *Cellophane* is the proprietary name of a transparent cellulose material made from about 1912 and, like many trade-marked products, remained a generic name after newer plastics (with their own proprietary names) had superseded it. The statement in the *Liverpool Daily Post*, "The drugs were hidden in small cellophane wraps..." is outdated to the point of absurdity: the writer meant either "clingfilm" or "polythene". *Celluloid*, which was originally also a proprietary trade-name, goes back to a British patent of 1871 and was formerly used in the manufacture of photographic film, hence its transferred use for the cinema, e.g. "a celluloid hero" (1922) to mean a film star. Celluloid was highly combustible and caused many fires in cinemas, before it was replaced by less FLAMMABLE plastic film; it is now merely a MEDIA archaism.

censor/censer/sensor/censure In ancient Rome the *censor* was a magistrate whose duties included the supervision of public morals. The nearest to such a post in England was held by the Lord Chamberlain who until the middle of the 20th century acted as theatrical censor and was able to BLUE-PENCIL certain passages in stage plays. A *censer* is a vessel for burning incense, from Latin *incensarium*. The spelling goes back to the Middle Ages: Wyclif's Bible has an "aungel hauing a golden censer" (Revelation, 8.3). A *sensor* is a device capable of sensing or giving a signal, now usually electrical, and is often fitted to burglar-alarms. *Censure*, meaning an adverse judgement, hostile criticism or expression of disapproval, comes from the same source as the *censor* but via French *censure*: "No might nor greatnesse in mortality can censure scape" – Shakespeare's *Measure for Measure* (1603). The *Guardian* inadvertently harked back to the unlamented Lord Chamberlain and his blue pencil when one of its theatre critics wrote: "The audience was encouraged to wander over the stage and activate hidden censors."

centurion/centurian/centenarian A *centurion* was a Roman officer in command of a hundred men (some of whom were doubtless DECIMATED) – Latin *centurio*. In England a cricketer who scores 100 runs, i.e. makes a century, has also been facetiously called a *centurion*, though more fastidious sports-writers spell the word *centurian*. A person who has reached the age of 100 is neither a centurion nor a centurian but a *centenarian*, from Latin *centenarius*.

chairman/chair/chairwoman/chairperson The *chairman* was one of the first victims of political correctness (surely *social* correctness might be a more fitting term?) and is a regular target of the non-discriminatory-language BRIGADE. People with two arms, two legs and two of everything else that matters, suddenly find themselves reduced to *chairs*, although they had got along perfectly well with a single-sex *Chairman* or *Madam Chairman*, or the ugly *chairperson*. Yet the problem of what to call female holders of posts previously occupied only by men is not a new one. In 1884 *Punch* printed a neat verse about it, having reported that "At the half-yearly meeting of the Convocation of the University of London, Lady Graduates for the first time took part in the proceedings..." The writer postulated the then remote possibility that some day (see EVERY DAY) one of them might become President, and wondered how she would then be addressed:

> If *place aux dames* should make the fair
> Preside, a curious question this is -
> How should a man address the Chair,
> If Mr Chairman is a "Missis"?

Those who insist on the all-embracing *chair* can point out that it has long been used as a gender-free *symbol* of authority, as in "a reproach from the chair", just as one speaks of a pronouncement "from the throne". But for a BBC reporter to say of a brave thalidomide victim, "Although she had no arms or legs she was the chair of the Thalidomide Society" was even more insensitive than my quoting him here. However, it does show how supposedly politically correct usage blunts the meaning of words. See also HEAD/HEADMASTER/HEADMISTRESS/HEAD-TEACHER.

charisma/charm/attractiveness *Charisma* is today considered an essential attribute for persons who occupy positions of power and influence, although many politicians lack it and achieve office nevertheless, while others who do have it don't. The over-use of the word in this context might have raised a Churchillian eyebrow: Sir Winston would have understood the word but not in the sense in which it is used today. *Charisma* is Greek for the gift of grace; and while he would not have doubted that he possessed this, he would not have boasted of it, nor expected others to attribute it to him; for charisma was in Churchill's day used chiefly in a religious context (anglicized in the 17th century as *charism*). It was the German sociologist Max Weber (1864–1920) who secularized it, in his *Wirtschaft und Gesellschaft* ("Economics and Society") into a briefly useful term that eventually became a crashing cliché: "A gift or power of leadership or authority … hence the capacity to inspire devotion or enthusiasm". Weber, incidentally, was the man responsible for much of the ludicrous sociological gibberish which the Americans translated into what they thought was English and English sociologists blindly adopted because they thought that as it sounded unintelligible it must be good. Politicians in truth need more than this new-fangled kind of charisma, but English lacks an appropriate word. *Charm* is inadequate for the purpose. It means a magic quality, sometimes a spell, that influences, beguiles or enchants. Charm is discerned only by the beholder: as soon as the possessor knows (or thinks) he has it he has lost it. The Italians, French and Germans all have adjectives like *simpatico*, etc. but the English "sympathetic" acquired different meanings. There are also self-described "charismatic" Christians, who use the word in a religious sense but do not fall within the scope of this book.

charted/chartered The difference is simple and clear: territory and seaways are *charted*, that is, they appear on charts; ships may be *chartered*, or hired in accordance with a legal contract or *charter*. "We are all in completely unchartered territory…" is nonsense.

cheesy/tacky/inferior Described as "a vague term of depreciation", *cheesy* was spotted in Gore's *Student Slang* as long ago as 1896. From the last couple of decades of the 20th century, cheesy has acquired wider meanings, all of them derogatory or associated with bad smells or decay. And that in the country that produces Cheddar, Stilton, and other fine cheeses. Significantly there is no pejorative French equivalent. *Tacky*, originally English for something slightly sticky, like insufficiently dry paint or varnish, in the mid-19th-century became American for something thought to be in bad or questionable taste.

chemist/pharmacist Unlike qualified ENGINEERS, who look with disdain on repairmen who usurp their job-title, qualified, degree-bearing *chemists* – analytical, industrial and other – seem to co-exist happily with *pharmacists* who are also informally called chemists, but (although they, too, are fully qualified in their own field) do not PRACTISE chemistry but dispense chemical materials, in other words medicines – accurately, one hopes. As a notice in a chemist's shop proclaimed, "We Dispense with Accuracy".

cherub/cherubs/cherubim/angels/putti *Cherubs* go back to biblical times; in fact they *are* biblical, up there with the *angels*, where they have various alleged functions, including the ability to fly. But whereas angels usually took adult forms, especially the fierce avenging ones, cherubs are traditionally depicted as well-nourished babies – either male or sexless but "cherubic". They also inspired a boys' CHRISTIAN-NAME, the rascally young cross-dresser Cherubino in Mozart's *The Marriage of Figaro*. The plural is either *cherubs* or *cherubim*, the *-im* suffix indicating a Hebrew plural; but the "double plural" *cherubims* has been mistakenly used by so many great poets that it became an accepted alternative. Secular cherubs, often represented in art, are called *putti* (singular *putto*, Italian for a boy).

choir/coir/chorus "They entered the threshold and walked over a simple choir mat…", wrote the *Liverpool Echo*. Unlikely, unless they were singing in massed harmony. *Coir*, from Malayan *kayar*, cord, is a much-used material for doormats made from fibres of the coconut. A *choir* (archaic and poetic spelling quire) is a body of singers found usually in a church or cathedral. Just to trap the unwary, in the theatre or opera-house such a body is always known as the *chorus*.

christian name/forename *Christian name* has long been an anomalous term – ever since Christians started to give to their offspring Jewish or Hebrew names from the Old Testament. "Christening-name", that is the personal name given at a Christian christening, would be one solution, but in a supposedly multicultural society it is probably safer to say *forename*, especially if the child is called Hussain Chaim Krishna Goldberg. Forename is undenominational and acceptable to Christians, Hindus and Muslims, as well as those who give family names to their offspring.

chronic/acute *Chronic* does not mean the same as very bad, annoying, intense or severe (pain or illness): a *chronic* disease is one that lasts for some time (from the Greek *chronos*, time) as opposed to an *acute* illness (Latin *acutus*, sharp), e.g. pain of short duration. A chronic invalid is therefore by definition a long-term sufferer.

chunnel/channel tunnel A tunnel under the English Channel was proposed as long ago as the 18th century, and in the 19th one was actually started. The portmanteau word *chunnel* was coined early in the 20th (also *chunnelling*, *chunnellers*, etc), but after the tunnel became a reality at the end of that century, nobody seemed to bother with the silly word, reverting to – *channel tunnel*. A rare case of common sense triumphant? No, more likely because most speakers now fail to disinguish between "channel" and "chunnel".

chutzpah/cheek *Chutzpah* is probably the Yiddish word that is most commonly borrowed by Gentiles. It represents one of several spellings of the Hebrew word for insolence or audacity, brazen effrontery, impertinence or downright cheek, though its operation may generate some admiration or approval. The most often quoted example is the story of the man who, accused of having murdered his parents, pleads for leniency on the grounds that he is an orphan. But chutzpah also takes the form of argumentatively answering a question with another question ("How should I know?", or "Do you think I'm made of money?"). This Jewish habit can be traced back to the Old Testament, which laid the foundations of Jewish thought and culture. So already (!) in Genesis 4.9, where "The Lord said unto Cain, where is Abel thy brother?" (as if He didn't know, for surely God knew everything), Cain answers God back by asking Him what must the original, the supreme, the ur-chutzpah counter-question, "Am I my brother's keeper?"

clapboard/clapperboard The journalist who wrote in the *Independent*: "The Kennedy estate, set in a picturesque town of clapperboard homes…" had perhaps seen too many films in the making, with clapper-boys using *clapperboards*. He meant *clapboard* homes, an American method of house-building used by the Pilgrim Fathers, as their fathers had done before them in Eastern counties of England: "No man shall sell claboards [sic] of five foot in length for more than three shillings per hundred…" – *Salisbury, Massachusetts Records* (1641). A clapper-board (one word, or two hyphenated) consists of two pieces of wood hinged at one end and brought sharply together to provide information, both AURAL and visual, to film-makers before each take. The person operating it is a junior employee called *clapper-boy*, even if he is a girl.

cleave(together)/cleave(apart) *Cleave* is a two-faced word, which can mean either to hold or stick fast to something or somebody, as in Wyclif's Bible of 1382, "He shal clyue to his wyf"; or else to split something asunder, as with a cleaver. The word has been used in both ways from at least AD 890, the dawn of modern English, and even gave us the cleavage, the separation-line that may be seen between a woman's breasts, especially if they are constrained or compressed in a certain manner: see CORSET/CORSAGE.

climactic/climatic/climacteric/menopause The first three words all derive ultimately from the same Greek word, but their meanings have diverged considerably. *Climactic* is the adjective derived from *climax*, climatic from *climate*. The *climacteric* is any critical period in human life, most commonly a woman's "change of life", or *menopause*. This, too, is sometimes confusing, as it means the *cessation* of monthly periods, not a *pause* in them. The clue lies in the misleading derivation: *meno-* is the Latin "monthly" prefix, but *pausis* means a cessation, not a pause. There are also potential musical confusions, for the Italian tempo-marking *meno* means less (*meno forte* = less strong), whereas a pause symbol (shaped like a raised eyebrow) instructs the performer to make a note longer.

57

clinical/precise Latin *clinicus*, from Greek *klinikos*, means "of or pertaining to a bed", later with the implication of a sick-bed. From this came the medical *clinic*. One hopes that *clinicians* are *precise* and coolly detached in their dealings with patients – but *clinical* is not an apt word for sports-writers, who call the scoring of a goal a "clinical finish" and speak of a "clinical knockout" when a boxer is rendered unconscious – though these may well find themselves in a PRONE/SUPINE position and in need of clinical attention. See also CRITICAL/SERIOUS and SURGICAL/ORTHOPAEDIC.

clod/clot The first meaning of *clod* is a lump of soil or clay, hence also in (religious) descriptions of the human condition: Edmund Spenser's "...us wretched earthly clods" (*Epithalamion*, 1595); and Cardinal Newman's "low-born clods of brute earth" (*Gerontius*, 1866). A *clot* is also a lump, as perhaps one formed from coagulated liquid like blood or milk, but in the most common and informal usage means a dull, clumsy or stupid fellow, like Ben Jonson's "clots and clowns" in *The Magnetic Lady* (1632). Compare the unrelated SOD/SOT.

closet/cupboard/secret A *closet*, from Latin *clausum* or *claustrum* (compare *claustrophobia*, the fear of being shut in one) is a chamber used for private purposes – and these, from the 1660s, referred also to the emptying of the bowels or bladder. It was often called a "closet of ease", later a water closet. The implied privacy has also given us the *privy*. It has become the most common meaning in English, while Americans say *closet* where the English mean a *cupboard*. Hence *closet communist*, *closet homosexual*, etc.: a secret practitioner of whatever it is that is being hidden; one who has not admitted his allegiance or proclivities, and has not "come out [of the closet]".

clover/shamrock The *shamrock* plant, from the Gaelic *seamrog*, is held in great affection by the Irish, especially nationalists. According to Campion's *History of Ireland* (1571) it was one of the staple vegetables in Ireland before the potato was introduced: "Shamrotes, water-cresses, rootes and other hearbes they feede upon"; and St Patrick supposedly used it to illustrate the doctrine of the Holy Trinity (presumably having some explaining to do when encountering a rare four-leaved example). Apart from its religious and patriotic significance it is identical with the English *clover* – so shamrock is perhaps nothing but the clover's political wing. For another Irish-nationalist division see DERRY/ LONDONDERRY.

coca/cocoa The *coca* plant, *Erythroxylon coca*, produces the medicinal drug cocaine, which is highly addictive when made available for ABUSE/MISUSE. *Cocoa* is derived from the same Hispanic word as coca but from a different seed – *Theorbroma cacao*, the cocoa bean, which produces, among other things, the pleasant, chocolatey drink that shares its name.

cocktail/small A *cocktail* is by definition a drink mixed from several ingredients (hence "a cocktail of drugs"), but has become also a commercial euphemism for things that are *smaller* than normal: *cocktail sausages*, *cocktail gherkins*, *onions*, etc. Scraps of, say, smoked salmon left over from carving big, neat slices are sold as *cocktail pieces*, suggesting to gullible consumers that such morsels may be conveyed to the mouth with small *cocktail sticks* and served as an accompaniment to the cocktails they may drink. A *cocktail dress* denotes a short one – perhaps "a little black number", as the current cliché has it – indeed the *cocktail party* itself is a social gathering short enough not to encroach into dinner-time. Guests may be entertained by a *cocktail pianist*, who however can be full-grown: he merely plays a mixture of small, short and light musical numbers.

cock-up/blunder *Blunders*, mistakes or general confusion caused daily by those in government (both national and local) or in public life generally, now attract the almost automatic description of *cock-ups*. Although the word is linked with the newly acceptable "balls-ups" (or the still unacceptable "f***-ups"), its origin lies not in sexual imagery but in printers' jargon. In letterpress printing, a cocked-up letter was one that accidentally protruded higher than others and caused an uneven image. Cocks have troubled Americans since the 18th century. Noah Webster (1758–1843), the compiler of *Webster's Dictionary* (1828), who laid the foundation of the simplified American spelling that most English people hate, also bowdlerized the Bible: his version of St Luke says that "The rooster crew thrice". His successors who dealt with the *American Bible* changed the famous passage in Acts 9, 5, which Wyclif's Bible (1382) translated as "It is hard to thee, to kyke agens the prickes", to "goads". This revealed that they had dirty minds: *pricks* were proper and legitimate words for spurs (and to this day Americans find mere "roaches" in their kitchens). See also under ARSE/ASS. The expression "pissed off", which not long ago would have been unacceptably obscene, is now used unthinkingly by many speakers who would not utter the f- or c-words. See also CAROUSEL/CAROUSAL.

coherent/cohesive That which is *coherent* is in modern usage usually abstract, relating to ideas that "hold together" and therefore make sense, whereas the *cohesive*, although it, too, has *cohesion* as a basis, now nearly always sticks together materially, as for example two or more substances. Think of the impassioned appeal to Cloacina, Goddess of the Sewers, thought to have been composed by Lord Byron:

> Soft yet cohesive let my offerings flow
> Not rudely swift, nor obstinately slow.

See also ADHERENT/ADHESION and
INCHOATE/INCOHERENT/INARTICULATE.

collide with/hit/strike Latin *collidere* means to clash *together*, so "A car collided with a lamp-post", seen daily in the papers, suggests that the lamp-post came out to hit the moving car. "The two planes collided together…" is a tautology, for *col-* already means "together".

colombia/columbia/colombo/colon The name of Christopher Columbus (1451–1506) figures in names of many places in America, both North and South, but in different ways. Only the English-speaking world uses the above anglicized form of his CHRISTIAN name: his mother would have addressed her letters to Cristobal Colón ("Is there really an opera house named after the great intestine?", a reader asked after seeing a reference to the *Teatro Colón* in Buenos Aires). And another confusion: in the 18th century the Americas were given the poetic name *Columbia* – but in homage not to Columbus but to the dove (Latin *columba*), hence the difference between *British Columbia* in Canada and the United States *District of Columbia* on the one hand, and the South American country *Colombia* on the other, named after the Spanish-Italian discoverer. The difference in pronunciation between British Columbia and South American Colombia is that the one contains a *bum* sound, the other a *bomb*. Then again, the capital of Sri Lanka (*quondam* Ceylon) is *Colombo* – related to the dove, not the explorer, nor indeed to the intestine.

combat/combat The noun *com*bat is stressed on the first syllable, the verb *to* com*bat* on the second.

> The *com*bat deepens. On, ye brave,
> Who rush to glory, or the grave!
> > Thomas Campbell (1777–1844): *Hohenlinden*.

> To com*bat* a poor famish'd man
> > Shakespeare: *Henry VI* (1592)

combine/combine The verb is *to* com*bine* and (as Shakespeare showed us with COMBAT) is stressed on the second syllable.

> God, the best maker of all marriages,
> Com*bine* your hearts in one.
> > Shakespeare: *King Henry V* (1599)

This accent on the second syllable of the verb com*bine* is confirmed in countless poems, but farmers speaking of their *com*bine harvester have chosen to stress the noun on the first. This has absurdly been copied by news reporters: "Christian militia forces have *com*bined with Israeli troops" – suggesting that they brought in the harvest together.

common-law (husband/wife)/mistress/lover/concubine As a euphemism the *common-law husband/wife* for a live-in *lover/mistress* is on the wane, for now that the sin has been removed from "living in sin" and cohabitation is made fashionable by irregular unions of celebrities, euphemisms are no longer needed. "Partners" rule the marriage-bed. Some papers carried the common-law absurdity so far as to treat their readers to a (hyphen-starved) "common law brother in law" and "common law grandfather". Although used even by lawyers there is nothing lawful about "common-law" partners, in common or any other law. Common Law certainly exists, but is a term permitting various interpretations (ask a lawyer, if you can afford it) and the original Common-Law Marriage goes back to 1563, when weddings in England had to be solemnized with the rites of the Church of England, and civil marriages were not legal. Thus it came about that an emergency marriage, e.g. one conducted in a Muslim country where there were no Christian priests, or on board ship with only a Captain to officiate, was called a Common-Law Marriage. Scottish law recognizes "unions of habit and repute", whatever *that* means: a habitual "partner" for a year, a month, or a week? Or just a "meaningful overnight relationship"? At one time Scotland had Gretna Green "marriages", arrangements which

common-law

61

satisfied the eloping partners and perhaps their relatives but not the law. In truth, "common-law" is a meaningless term. One might equally call a vegetarian nut-cutlet a "common-law steak". At one end of the social spectrum there are gipsies who "live over the brush" (in reference to a traditional "wedding" ceremony in which the partners step over a broom), while at the other, Lord Bath, the master of Longleat, has mistresses he calls *wifelets*. Mistress ("something between a mister and a mattress" – schoolboy definition) is thought by some to have too stark, and possibly sexist, overtones, and is inaccurate to boot, as a man's mistress is not usually in a position to boss him about in the way the mistress of a house may rule her servants. There is an old English word *fere*, "my fere" being my companion, comrade, mate, partner (of either sex) and even the vulgar "my bird" has a charming "beloved pet" LINEAGE: from *birdsnie* or *birdsnye*; also *pyggesnie*: "She was a prymerole, a pyggesnye ffor any lord to leggen in hys bedde." – Chaucer: *The Miller's Tale* (ca 1386). See also MRS/MISS/MS.

community/group/people etc. With the rise of sociology in the second half of the 20th century the English language received large and painful injections of socio-academic jargon. This came mostly from German academics who had found refuge in post- World War II America, and much of it reads and sounds like flawed or badly translated American-English (see also under CHARISMA). For example, one of the commonest and over-used socio-jargon terms is the all-purpose *community*. Sticking this word in front of an existing term, like Arts Centre, Sports Ground, Recreation Hall or Birth Control Clinic, "Community" was thought to make these places sound more socially beneficial (in some instances "Neighbourhood" did the same trick). Used as a suffix word it would help (or so sociologists believed) to bring *people* together, as a shared religion, churches and other places of worship had done for centuries – like the "Quaker community" or the "Jewish community". But when the *Daily Telegraph* described the nation's gun-licence holders as the "shooting community", the crowds at Epsom Racecourse as the "racing community", and homosexuals as the "gay community", the mind began to boggle. (Although there is a gay community there is curiously no PAEDOPHILE community: if paedophiles congregate at all they come in RINGS). What next? The "redhaired community"? The "white-socks-wearing community"? Or the "hermit community"? Community is merely one of many "feelgood" words pressed into service by sociologists.

compass/compasses A *compass* is a navigation-aid whose needle points towards North. The word is from old French *compas*, meaning measure. The compass, or *mariner's compass*, is always singular. *Compasses* are a single, albeit two-legged, instrument used for navigational or geometrical purposes, and traditionally come in pairs, i.e. a *pair of compasses*, like pairs of scissors, stockings or trousers.

complacent/complaisant/compliant Both *complacent* and *complaisant* are derived from Latin *complacere*, to please, but went their separate ways, distinguished by different spelling. Complaisant has come to mean complying politely with another's wishes – especially, it seems, amorous ones, hence a complaisant husband is one who chooses to ignore or condone his wife's activities with another person. If he cannot be bothered to do anything about it he may also be complacent – that is, satisfied with existing circumstances. That was perhaps why John Bayley in a book review in the London *Evening Standard* called Sir William Hamilton (husband of Horatio Nelson's mistress Emma) "complacent"; and Lord David Cecil's celebrated biography of Max Beerbohm also refers to a "complacent husband". Perhaps both these fine writers dictated their work to a young and inexperienced (or old but hearing-impaired) AMANUENSIS. The complaisant husband's wife was probably *compliant*, that is "ready to yield to the wishes or desires of others" (*OED*).

compliment/complement/complimentary "These wall lights will compliment the decor in your sitting-room...", said a puff for some electrical fittings. If they could speak, they might pay *compliments* to the decorator who wrote that in the women's pages of *The Times*. What she meant was that they might *complement* the effect, from Latin *complere*, to fill up, or complete (see also under EXPLETIVE). *Compliment* – "to flatter with polite and delicate praise" (*OED*) – comes from the French *complimenter*, and while both words have the same root, over the centuries useful separate meanings became established. Samuel Pepys got it "wrong" in 1668, in the opposite direction, when he proudly reported "being complemented by everybody with admiration", but then his spelling was as free as his amours. However, in the late 1990s there was no excuse for Debenhams to offer bath towels with printed labels claiming that they have "absorbuncy [sic] and have been designed to compliment our range of bath sets". *Complimentary* means free of charge, at no cost, "with the giver's

compliment

compliments", so when the *Daily Telegraph* wrote that twin brothers "held complimentary office as Church of England bishops" it suggested they received no stipends. There is also *complementary* medicine, which complements the REGULAR kind.

compound/com**pound** Cattle are kept in *com*pounds, but actions are com*pound*ed.

> Com*pound* for sins they are inclin'd to
> By damning those they have a mind to.
>   Samuel Butler (1612–1680): *Hudibras.*

comprise/compromise *Comprise*, to bring together. *Compromise* has many shades of meaning, the commonest being that of damaged reputations, so a confusion can result in howlers like "The party will compromise several girls" (*Liverpool Daily Post*).

compulsive/compulsory Things that are *compulsive* we usually do ourselves (like the journalist's clichéd "compulsive womaniser") whereas that which is *compulsory* is forced upon us by others.

concert pianist/pianist People who know a little about how classical music is spoken or written about find the qualifying word "concert" superfluous – almost a solecism. Musicians just say "pianist", without needing to specify that they are not speaking of a COCKTAIL, jazz or bar pianist. The same applies to other instruments and their players, yet the *Guardian* announced the death of Jacqueline du Pré's famous teacher under the headline

CONCERT CELLIST DIES

What else might he have been? A circus cellist? A pub cellist? SEA CAPTAIN is a similar howler.

concordat/agreement *Concordat* means exactly the same as *agreement* (from Latin *concordare*, to agree). Although it can have certain religious connotations, such as a concordat between church and state, its use by would-be-clever politicians and journalists is nothing but showing off.

conform/confirm *Conform* means to have, or to share, the same shape or character; *confirm*, to strengthen or add strength; but the two are often used as if they were interchangeable. Even the venerable Travellers' Club in London, in a printed notice stating its dress code, asks that "Ladies should confirm to this standard".

conjugal rights/marital rights The first appears to concern sex, the second property. Although both were formerly lawful rights they are now largely obsolete, or have been replaced by a thicket of family law. See also RIGHTS/RITES, and other punning opportunities which British print journalists find perennially hilarious.

conjure/conjure *Conjure* has different meanings according to how it is pronounced. This is best seen (or heard) in Shakespeare's plays, where the metre of the verse governs placing of the stress. In *A Midsummer Night's Dream* (?1595/6) "To *con*jure years up in a poor maid's eyes" refers to *con*juring, as in magic tricks, and rhymes with "sponger"; whereas, in *The Two Gentlemen of Verona* (?1594/5) Julia says, "And even in kind love I do con*jure* thee", which is con*jur*ing, meaning "to entreat or solemnly charge, as by a common oath". However, in *A Comedy of Errors* (?1594) Shakespeare himself makes play on the difference by using both meanings in one speech (albeit in just the first-syllable stressing): "Thou art, as you are all, a sorceress: I *con*jure you to leave me and be gone." His audiences would have appreciated the joke.

console/console/consul In spoken English there is sometimes confusion between the noun "*con*sole" (such as a combined television, radio and video apparatus, or the keyboard and pedals of an organ) and the verb "con*sole*", meaning to alleviate someone's sorrow or distress (which anyway has been all but ousted by "counselling"). The average English-speaker has no difficulty with a sentence like "He would console himself at the console of an organ". In Roman – later also in French – republics, the *consul* was the chief magistrate, the top official who wielded supreme powers (e.g. Napoleon Bonaparte), often forgetting that the consul's job was to *consult*, Latin *consultare*. Today's consuls are usually agents appointed by a government to represent certain interests in a foreign country, but in Britain the Consul was for a time best known as a popular kind of Ford car. Just to confuse its foreign visitors a well-known hotel promised its guests "a television consul in each room".

consultant/specialist Senior medical practitioners, both physicians and surgeons, working either in hospitals or privately in their own consulting-rooms, have long held the honorary title of *consultant*. They were originally called *consulting* surgeons or physicians – a curious misnomer as they are consulted rather than themselves consulting others. This kind of consultant is little more than a hundred years old in name, and is in fact an abbreviation: consultant surgeon, consultant physician, etc. In English medicine these titles are carefully allocated and jealously guarded – *specialist* being the popular and more or less general appellation by patients. Since the end of the 20th century numerous other walks of life have seen a proliferation of (usually self-awarded) consultancies. With many professional people made REDUNDANT/UNEMPLOYED, some enterprisingly continue to practise privately, on a freelance basis, borrowing the grand title from medical people in the hope of gaining extra status and recognition. A cautionary parable is told of a group of tomcats who used to meet on the rooftops every night, doing what tomcats like to do on rooftops. One of their number disappeared from the scene – only to return a week or two later, looking very pleased with himself but with his hinder parts bandaged. "Sorry, boys," he explained, "but I won't be coming out to play at nights any more. I've set up a consultancy."

contiguous/continuous/continual *Contiguous*, from Latin *contiguus*, touching together, is sometimes well meaningly but erroneously "corrected" to the more familiar *continuous*, which means going on, incessant, non-stop, without pause or interruption. *Continual*, as in "I can't stand his continual snoring", suggests that there are intermissions, however brief. Both are derived from Latin *continuus*, hanging together, unbroken.

contract/contract As a noun, *con*tract is stressed on the first syllable, as the adjective con*tract*ual on the second, and as the verb to con*tract* – whether by law or physically by shrinkage – on the last.

> Come, temperate nymphs, and help to celebrate
> A *con*tract of true love: be not too late.
> Shakespeare: *The Tempest* (?1611)
> To whom the Angel with con*tract*ed brow
>
> Accuse not Nature, she hath done her part;
> Do thou but thine, and be not diffident

Of wisdom, she deserts thee not if thou
Dismiss not her.
                    John Milton: *Paradise Lost* (1667)

Similar noun/verb stress differences are found in *con*duct/con*duct*,
*con*flict/con*flict*, *con*test/con*test*, CONTRAST/CONTRAST and other words
beginning with *con-* listed below.

contrast/contrast/convert/convert convict/convict Much the same
applies as above and below.

Let the loud drum in *con*trast beat
While trumpets blare in battle's heat.
                    Anon.
I know not how long the gay dance might have lasted
With the semibreve's gravity strangely con*trast*ed.
                    Anon.

*Con*verts are persons who have been con*verted,* and *con*victs persons who
have been con*victed.*

Charming women can true *con*verts make,
We love the precepts for the teacher's sake.
        George Farquhar: *The Constant Couple* (1700)

And be you blithe and bonny
Con*vert*ing all your sounds of woe
Into Hey nonny, nonny.
        Shakespeare: *Much Ado about Nothing* (1599)

Banished he was for ever more
To the distant *con*vict shore.
                    Anon.

Lose no time to contradict her
Nor endeavour to con*vict* her
        Jonathan Swift (1667–1745): *Daphne*

cookery book/cookbook The English have *cookery books*, or more properly *cookery-books*, while Americans prefer *cookbooks*, *cook books* or (very rarely) *cook-books*. It may be modish but is not English – more a literal translation of the German *Kochbuch*. It did not go unnoticed when first seen in English: Tyler's *A Yankey in London* (1809) uses disbelieving quotation-marks: "An assortment of culinary reviews, vulgarly called 'cook-books'." Good old Tyler.

cord/chord The two spellings were formerly interchangeable, but in modern usage a *cord* is a small rope, string or sinew – or almost anything that can be tied – whereas a *chord* is an arrangement of two or more musical notes sounded simultaneously. Writers tend to err on the side of the *ch* form, so that "umbilical chords" frequently twang their way into print (apt only for very young musical prodigies?). Such chords accidentally figure so often in the *Guardian* that when the paper quoted an amusing cutting from a local paper, "Bring your newspapers (and your neighbours). Put them in paper bags or tie them up with chords" its splendid *Corrections and Clarifications* column remarked only on the ambiguity of the tied-up neighbours, not the fact that they were supposedly tied with "chords".

core/corps/corpse A tasteless headline in the London *Evening Standard* reading

ROTTEN TO THE CORPS

brought a story about dead bodies, so one might have assumed that the sub-editor responsible could not spell "corpse". I have also seen the puzzling

TANK CORP SURVIVOR

– did the writer mean *corpse* or *corp*, the British Army abbreviation of "corporal"? Neither. It was just that *corps* was one letter too long to fit the line.

corner shops/high street shops This old cliché distinction between little shops and big ones is based on the absurd assumption that all *small* shops are sited on street-corners and all *big* ones (as well as banks) on the High Street. Neither is true. But more accurate observation will confirm that in every big English town or city (and some villages) such "corner" shops are owned and run by hard-working and naturally entrepreneurial Asians. Question: "Why are there so few Asian soccer stars?" Answer: "Because every time they get a corner they open a shop on it."

corset/corsage Both *corsets* and *corsages* are worn by – usually – women, but whereas a corset is an under-garment they get into, their corsage is attached to the outside of an outer and upper garment. This is pronounced like the French word it is and consists of a small bouquet of flowers worn in the middle and front of the bosom – full name *bouquet de corsage*. The device dates from the early years of the 20th century, when women's corsets were tight-laced and dresses low-cut, so as to create the illusion of a solid, almost sculpted, one-piece bosom. To show the cleavage where the breasts were squashed together would not only have spoilt the "single-breasted" look but would have been considered indecent. "On her rounded breast a splendid corsage of orchid and lily of-the-valley..." (1911). In mediaeval English a corsage was the body itself (from old French *cors*): "Another beste [beast] of moche fayr corsage or shappe of body..." – William Caxton (1481). Later it came to mean the same as corset – until women's fashions separated their meanings again.

coruscate/excoriate/execrate When the *Guardian* said it expected the Pope (or "the pope", as it prefers to style him) to have "a coruscating moral voice" it meant to say a harshly critical one. *Coruscate* is often misused thus, and usually misspelt "corruscating", the extra *r* suggesting rough "corrugations". That word comes from Latin *corrugare* meaning to wrinkle, whereas *coruscare* means to twinkle – "to give forth intermittent or vibratory flashes of light". Confusion may also arise between coruscate and *excoriate*, to flay, to pull off the skin (of a man or beast) which now nearly always refers figuratively to savage criticism and comes from Latin *ex-*, out (of/from) + *corium*, hide, skin. To *execrate* someone is to pronounce a curse or imprecate evil upon him: Latin *ex* + *sacrare*, to "unholy" someone – the opposite of *consecrate*.

costive/costly/dear/expensive Dr Thomas Arne, the composer of "Rule Britannia" (but famous also for his concupiscence – see AMATORY) wrote a song – "You're the Dearest Girl in Town!" – addressed to a London prostitute, who would have understood why she was *dear* to him (worth "half a guinea", though she "would jump at half a crown"). In other words, she was *expensive, costly* – pricey in modern English – but

costive

not, one hopes, *costive*. That comes from the French *costive*, or constipated, from the Latin *constipare*, to press or crowd closely together. The city councillor who declared that a proposed new tunnel would prove "too costive" was wrong – though accidentally right. Compare RESTIVE/RESTFUL.

COUP/COUPe/COOP The political or revolutionary *coup*, from the Old French for a blow or stroke, is short for *coup d'état*, a sudden, violent and illegal change of government; *coupe* is French for a goblet and is used by cookery writers and menu scribes to Frenchify a fruit-and-icecream cup into, for example, a "Coupe Jacques"; and a *coupé* with an *é* at the end (though the acute accent is often carelessly omitted) is a kind of motor-car body. But a *coop* – a mediaeval English word – is an enclosure for poultry. However, the *Radio Times* plugged one of its featured broadcasters with the words, "This week he...constructs a chicken coup" – perhaps an uprising of battery-hens.

courtesy/curtsy Both are forms of *courtesy*, one meaning general politeness, the other a specific – and now rather old-fashioned – gesture, like a deep bow or servile bending of the knee. Shakespeare's "I am the very pinck of curtesie", in *Romeo and Juliet* (1592), meant the first form; but a contemporary of 1575 clearly had the (now usually feminine) gesture of obeisance in mind: "At this, the minstrell made a pauz & a curtezy..." Modern spelling is – or should be – more of a precision-tool than it was for the free-spelling Elizabethans, so we may as well observe the distinction.

coventrate/sending to coventry/ostracize *Coventrate* is a translation from the German word *coventriert*, from *coventrieren*, coined by them during World War II and meaning, as the Americans now say, "to bomb the [hell] out of a place". The Germans did just that to the civilian city of Coventry in the English midlands, but it did not coin *coventriert* until after the allies had retaliated by carpet-bombing German cities. Only then did the Germans start to complain that Dresden had been *coventriert*, thereby admitting that they started it all. Coventrate is a word English can do without, but if it *were* used it could mean "to send a person or persons to Coventry", that is, to ostracize or ignore them. *Sendings to Coventry* have for many years been undertaken by British trades unionists against colleagues who have transgressed against union rules, usually as alleged "blacklegs" (see

SCAB/BLACKLEG/FINK), but is not as modern a punishment as it sounds. As early as 1647 it was mentioned in *The History of the Rebellion and Civil Wars in England*, by Edward Hyde, Earl of Clarendon: "At Bromingham, a town so generally wicked that it had risen upon small parties of the King's, and killed and taken them prisoners and sent them to Coventry..." The expression occurs often in this disapproving tone throughout the 18th and 19th centuries, down to modern times, but – for obvious reasons – never in Coventry itself. Has anyone ever suggested where the people of Coventry should send people *they* disapprove of? Perhaps the quotation from the Earl of Clarendon, above, makes a case for Birmingham.

credulous/credible/incredulous/incredible Latin *credo*, I believe, but to be *credulous*, from Latin *credulus*, is to be ready – perhaps too ready – to believe anything, whether it is *credible* or not. Credible, from Latin *credibilis*, is that which is *worthy* of being believed. The addition of the Latin negative prefix *in-* gives rise to a similar confusion. *Incredulous*, not willing to believe, was orginally used of religious unbelievers but is now applied to doubters of any persuasion and in any context. *Incredible*, from *incredibilis*, means unbelievable. So the Romans made exactly the same distinctions as we do between these near-soundalikes. Yet a public figure, speaking on TV, said, "What an incredulous waste of time."

crescendo/climax An assertion like "the dispute has reached a crashing crescendo" is an absurd cliché with which writers or speakers try to convey the idea of a *climax*. In music, however, a *crescendo* is the *process* of *getting* louder, from Latin *crescere*, to increase (compare the crescent moon). So in the place where a score is marked *crescendo* the music will still be soft – sometimes even *pianissimo* – and merely *about* to become louder. See also PARAMETER, LOW KEY and ORCHESTRATE.

criteria/criterion A *criterion* is a means for judging a test or standard for comparison, a Greek singular word of which the plural is *criteria*. Unfortunately plural-confusions disseminated by the MEDIA "itself" have ditched the singular *criterion*, except as the name of a London theatre and restaurant. This, as the media might say themselves, is a regrettable phenomena. The *Press Gazette* (of all papers), announcing a writing competition, stipulates "The main criteria is that entrants should have..."

criteria

critical/serious/seriously ill/stable Instead of saying "He is in a critical/serious condition" the MEDIA say "He is critical/serious", etc. The *critical* word is "condition", for in such a state the victim would hardly be joking, though he really might be critical. The same mistreatment is given to *stable*: one report, however, declared that the then ailing cowboy star Roy Rogers was "in a stable condition".

crochet/crotchet To *crochet*, from French *crocher*, to hook or catch with hooks, is to knit with a hooked knitting-needle or crochet-hook and is pronounced as if it were French, "cro-shay". The musical *crotchet* (quarter-note to Americans), has the same origin, but is pronounced "crotch-et", having been longer anglicized, and is written with a *t* in the middle. *Crotchety*, meaning bad-tempered, is pronounced in the English way.

cross-section/cross section The presence or absence of a hyphen can play HAVOC with meaning, as in the advertisement claiming "Our strings are used by a cross section of the Hallé Orchestra". An advertisement in the *Guardian* showed a man holding a shepherd's crook, describing him as the "Lakeland crook and walking stick maker…" (crook- and walking-stick-maker?) Other ambiguities spotted in newspapers included "a meeting of hot air balloonists" – "a long postponed article" – "a well known criminal lawyer – "a blue bottle flying round the room" – "a group of light house keepers" – "a second half chance" – "a short fall" – "a long standing friend" – "a fast food chain" – "a stable lad" – "a stained glass artist" – and others that invite questions. "Extra mural courses": does that mean *additional* courses? "Extra marital intercourse": more sex or sex outside marriage?

crunch/decision etc. "When it comes to the crunch" is a justly ridiculed cliché – yet its invention is attributed to that master of elegant English, Winston Churchill, who wrote in the *Daily Telegraph* of 23 February 1939: "Whether Spain will be allowed to find its way back to sanity and health…depends upon the general adjustment or outcome of the European crunch." He must have brooded on it throughout World War II, for in 1948 he used it again, in his book about that war; and in 1957 *The Economist* sarcastically laid the word at his door: "What Sir Winston Churchill would have called the 'crunch' of the economic battle has arrived." Then the floodgates opened – and things have been "coming to the crunch" ever since. The African dictator Robert Mugabe coined an interesting variation: "When it comes to the crutch" – see CRUTCH/CROTCH.

crusade/campaign From the 11th to the 13th centuries European Christians sent military expeditions to recover the Holy Land from the Muslims, who had ANNEXED it. They were called *crusaders* because the symbol they carried was the cross, Latin *crux*, referring to Christ's crucifixion – with plunder not far from their minds. In popular usage it is now virtually synonymous with *campaign*, which can be any organized action for a particular purpose. According to POLITICALLY CORRECT thinking *crusade* should be used only in its historical context, although those who disapprove of changing the language in deference to such views may disagree.

crutch/crotch/crux A *crutch* is not only a device to help the lame walk but is also used figuratively: some describe the drinking of alcohol as their crutch, meaning comfort, prop or support. This appeared as early as 1581, when one J. Bell wrote, "Osorius underproppeth his Freewill here, with this crooch". The *crotch* is the point where the legs of humans join the body, the groin area. Old-fashioned doctors used to refer to it as the "intercrural region", on the assumption that crotch was related to the cross, which it probably is not: crotch is an old English word for a fork, hence the "fork of the legs". The *crux of the matter* is the chief problem, the decisive point, and does spring from the Latin *crux*, a cross. See also CRUNCH, above.

cum/come/and/with/next *Cum* is Latin for "with", and is seen in ancient English place-names, where it indicates the joining of two parishes or hamlets, as in Chorlton-*cum*-Hardy; but unfortunately its meaning is lost on Latinless writers. For example, a film critic on the *Sunday Times* described an actor's diction as "a sort of founding father come speak-your-weight machine" – twice: once in the body of the text, and again in the picture caption, so it was more than a momentary aberration. Meanwhile the *Daily Telegraph* pictured "a rosewood card cum work table", which would have been better as "a rosewood card-cum-work-table". The rustic *come*, meaning "next", as in "I'm seventy-five come Sunday" has survived chiefly as a quaint archaism. Other colloquial meanings do not concern this book.

cupidity/covetousness/greed *Cupid*, the Roman god of love, is usually portrayed as a beautiful little boy, often making eyes at – or love to – Venus, grown-up man's ideal of female beauty. However, modern usage, having plenty of words for things AMATORY, EROTIC, SALACIOUS, rude or dirty (the

cupidity

list is almost endless), gradually corrupted *cupidity* to mean an "inordinate desire to appropriate wealth or possessions; greed for gain" – when all little Cupid wanted was Venus and everything VENEREAL she could offer. See also AMATORY/AMOROUS/EROTIC/SALACIOUS/CONCUPISCENT.

curb/kerb A *curb* is a chain or strap fixed to the bit of a horse, used to control it if it is unruly, hence various expressions like "curbing or REINING IN" one's desires. The edging of a road or pavement is the *kerb*. See also RAIN/REIGN.

cygnet/signet A *cygnet* is a small swan, diminutive of the Latin *cygnus*. A *signet* is a small seal, diminutive of *signum*. So the spelling difference goes back all the way to the Romans. In the Middle Ages some writer or clerk had the idea of setting his embossed seal (which he would often use to authenticate his signature) in a ring, to be worn on the hand for immediate recognition; which is how we got our *signet* rings. *Seals* and *signets* and *signatures*, as well as aquatic seals and cygnets, provide much scope for confusion (accidental or purposely punning) – from "The cygneture tune from Tchaikovsky's *Swan Lake*" (for once not a *Guardian* pun but a happily apt spelling-mistake) to "Mink preying on fish, ducklings and signets", in the *Independent*. The fact that swans and cygnets may be *ringed* for identification is another useful bell in the media jokester's cap. See also PRAY/PREY.

cynics/stoics Both belonged to ancient schools of philosophy, the *cynics* having a reputation for being dog-like (Greek *cunos*, Latin *canis*), disbelieving, questioning and probably snarling – cynical in the modern sense; whereas the *stoics* were patient and repressed their emotions. Their name came from *stoa*, Greek for a porch under which their lectures were given.

cyrillic/acrylic A BBC correspondent in Russia reporting a demonstration by students "waving banners and shouting slogans" (as the cliché always has it) was asked by the presenter in the studio, "What did the placards say?" The reporter replied, "I'm afraid I couldn't read them because they were all in acrylic." The alphabet used by Eastern Slavs such as Russians is *Cyrillic*, a script supposedly invented by St Cyril so as to enable illiterate (!) Slavonic people to read the Gospels. *Acrylic* is a synthetic compound used in plastics and paint.

— D —

darby/derby The standard spelling for the Derbyshire county town, for the hat, the boots, porcelain, cheese and the sporting-event, has long been fixed as *Derby*, but the CHRISTIAN-NAME is *Darby*. They are pronounced the same (except by Americans, who say "Durby"). As a given name Darby was common from the 15th to the 18th century: there was a physician called Darby Ulster in Liverpool in the mid-1500s. It is now chiefly remembered as the husband's name in "Darby and Joan", the old, long-married and mutually devoted couple, first noted in 1735, when the *Gentleman's Magazine* had:"Old Darby, with Joan by his side/You're often regarded with wonder/He's dropsical, she is sore-eyed/Yet they never are happy asunder."

datum/data Latin *datum* means that which is given, such as fact or number, plural *data*. So it was until computers, statistics and the MEDIA flooded us *with data* (which seldom come singly). So the singular *datum* is all but forgotten, and data has taken its place as the new singular. "The data *is*…" still jars on some sensibilities, and there are no fines on those who continue to say "The data *are*…" But data is, alas, winning. Like the singular MEDIA. See also CRITERIA and PROPAGANDA.

deadline/lifeline When kidnappers set a supposed time-limit for carrying out their foul deeds they call it a *deadline* – but it usually means a *lifeline*. The original life-or-death deadline is thought to have been first used in the American Civil War, and was mentioned by Congress in 1864. Four years later it was given a precise and deadly definition: "Seventeen feet from the inner stockade was the 'dead-line', over which no man could pass and live" (which makes one wonder whether Tom Sawyer knew of this – see under LICK/DEFEAT). This kind of deadline was therefore a precursor of the electric fence, in prison compounds and concentration-camps. The publishing deadline did not come into use until about 1920.

deadline

decimate/devastate/reduce *Decimation* was the exaction of a tax or tithe at the rate of one-tenth of a person's wealth, though it also had a more sinister connotation: a writer named Dymok wrote, as early as 1600, in a history of Ireland: "All were by a martiall courte condemned to dye, which sentence was yet mittigated by the Lord Lieutenants mercy, by which they were only decimated by lott." The common interpretation is that decimation was a death-sentence by a kind of Russian roulette, whereas the source quoted suggests it was a one-in-ten chance of being allowed to *live*. Today the word is so often used in the sense of *devastated*, or drastically *reduced* in number, that PEDANTS have given up complaining. A BBC reporter said of a drunken killer-driver: "He was given four years for decimating three families".

defct/defecate To *defect* comes from the Latin *deficere*, to leave or desert something, e.g. a place, one's wife or husband, but is always used intransitively – ballet-dancers always defected *from* the former Soviet Union. To *defecate* from *defaecare*, means to cleanse oneself of, or to void, faeces, in other words to empty one's bowels. The *Liverpool Daily Post* reporter who had "Berliners defecating over the wall" probably felt he was introducing a spot of elegant variation. Since the fall of Communism, defectors have all but disappeared from MEDIA language, and turned into "asylum-seekers". See EMIGRANTS/IMMIGRANTS.

defensible/defendable Both are connected with defence but, in general usage and by current convention, ideas are *defensible* (or otherwise), fortresses *defendable* (or not). The same goes for their negations *indefensible* and *undefendable*.

defuse/diffuse "The statement will diffuse the tension", claimed the London *Evening Standard*; and the *Guardian*, "…diffusing confrontational situations". What the writers meant was *defuse*: to remove – figuratively – the fuse from a potentially explosive situation. Perhaps if speakers minded their diction and distinguished between "deef" and "diff" there would be less confusion. *Diffusing* the tension would be to spread it about more widely.

delicious/enjoyable *Delicious* is now associated chiefly with the enjoyment of food or other pleasures of the senses but, like LUXURIOUS, it originally had more to do with sex than with chocolates and champagne. It comes from the Latin *delicium, delicia*, 'delight', hence *deliciosus*, "sensual; addicted to sensuous indulgence, voluptuous…" etc.

Only later was its meaning widened and softened to include food and drink, comfortable surroundings and other pleasures of life. William Caxton's *Golden Legend* (1483) complains that "Thyse monckes [have] ben over delycious", and for centuries this meaning prevailed. Here is how the various versions of the Bible approached the sin of deliciousness: King James's *Authorized Version* (1611) has, in Revelation 18.9: "The Kings of the earth, who committed fornication and lived deliciously with her [the Whore of Babylon]", while the *Revised Version* (which was prepared in High Victorian times) unsurprisingly changed it to "lived wantonly with her". The *Revised English Bible* (1990) has "wallowed in her luxury", reverting to the obscure early meaning of luxury without actually giving offence, yet making it sound more like a steamy night at the Jerusalem Hilton; and the 1976 *Good News Bible* says merely that "they took part in her immorality". The *Living Bible* of 1962 (which should be called the *Leaden Bible* for its editors' unerring ear for a clumsy phrase – see also under ALTERNATE/ALTERNATIVE), seems to uncover expense accounts: "The rulers of the earth have enjoyed themselves with her, and businessmen [!] throughout the world have grown rich from all her luxurious living." Out of curiosity I looked up Luther's *German Bible*, which thunders "went whoring with her".

delirious/happy *Delirium* is Latin for madness and is a medical term for a disturbance of the brain-functions. To say "He was delirious" is therefore a clinical statement, not a report of great joy, but the cliché has been around for a long time. The "mafficking" that took place in England after the relief of Mafeking produced the headline

LONDON DELIRIOUS

deliverance/delivery A *deliverance* is a setting-free, in the sense of something or someone being delivered from evil or other major inconveniences. "We offer Nationwide Deliverance", painted on the side of a delivery van, is a promise only God can make, and even here opinions differ as to whether He can deliver it. Whether for a parcel or a baby, *delivery* is the appropriate word.

denigrate/denigrate *Denigrate* comes from the French *dénigrer* and means to blacken, sully or stain, now usually referring to a person's reputation. A quack of 1657 offered a dye for grey hair in the form of a "lotion [which] will denigrate the hairs of hoary heads". It does not mean *un*blacken, as is sometimes supposed: for the French *dé-* prefix intensifies (as happens also in many English words, like depression) – whereas the Latin-based *de* negates or reverses (as in words like DEPILATE). Denigrate changes its meaning according to the way it is pronounced: "denn-ee-grate" in the above sense of blackening, "*dee-nigh-grate*" for *un*blackening. See also DERACINATE.

dependant/dependent A man might have *dependants* who are *dependent* on him – but might prefer to be *independent* of him. The noun ends in *-ant* and the adjective in *-ent*. It is just another of those things that make the language so tricky for the learner. See also PENDENT/PENDANT.

depilate/exfoliate The two were painfully confused by a *Guardian* writer, who asserted that a woman had "exfoliated genitalia". He meant *depilated*, that is, shaved, or stripped of hair (*de* + *pilus*, hair). *Exfoliate* literally means to shed or strip of leaves (*ex* + *folium* = leaf) but as a medical term means to strip off the top layer, usually but not always of skin; sometimes to scrape away the top layer of bone.

deprecate/depreciate *Deprecate*, to express earnest disapproval of something, or to plead against it, comes from the Latin *deprecare,* to pray against. It means almost the same as to *deplore* it (though this is a degree stronger, derived from *deplorare*, to weep bitterly). Deprecate has almost disappeared from plain speech, being used mostly in formal writing: perhaps in, say, a threatening letter from a lawyer. Those who have never encountered the word suspect a misprint and "correct" it to *depreciate*, which is more familiar – chiefly because that is what their cars do as soon as they have bought them: Latin *de* + *pretium*, price.

deracinate/assimilate "By the fourth generation they had been completely deracinated and were looked upon as whites…" This statement, in a cutting from an unidentified newspaper, is based on the reasonable but wrong assumption that words mean what they sound as if they *ought* to mean. *Deracinate* is to pluck up or tear up by the roots, to eradicate or exterminate. It has nothing to do with race but with the French *racine*, root. See also DENIGRATE.

derry/londonderry Both are valid names for a city in Northern Ireland, but nationalists use the shorter form, not to save time but because they thus avoid having to say the hated word "London" as well as the ancient English title of the Marquesses of Londonderry. Their reluctance is understandable, as the place *was* called Derry until the troubles of 1613, when mercenaries recruited by City of London livery companies ANNEXED it for the English. Protestant loyalists, on the other hand, like to overstress the "London-" element, for Irish memories are long and unforgiving. The song sometimes called the "Londonderry Air" was originally a wordless folk-tune, first published in 1855 as an "Air from County Derry", where it had been noted down from a peasant by Miss Jane Ross of Limavady. The soppy "Danny Boy" words by the English barrister F. E. Weatherley are a superimposition, as are others that have at various times been attached to the tune – which the composer Sir Hubert Parry described as "the most beautiful in the world". See also CLOVER/SHAMROCK.

desert/desert/dessert A *dessert* is a course of fruit, pudding, etc., served at the end of a meal. Like many words concerning food and eating it comes from the French, in this instance from *desservir*, to clear the table, "to *un*serve". *Desert*, as in "just deserts" (with the stress on the second syllable to distinguish it from sandy *deserts*), also comes from a related French word *deservir*, this one meaning to deserve.

> What ailed us, O gods, to de*sert* you
> For creeds that refuse and restrain?
> Come down and redeem us from virtue,
> Our Lady of Pain.
> > Charles Algernon Swinburne: *Dolores* (1866)

> Fret not to roam the *des*ert now,
> with all thy winged speed:
> I may not mount on thee again –
> thou'rt sold, my Arab steed!
> > Caroline Norton (1808–1877):
> > *The Arab's Farewell to his Steed*

die/dice/dye/died/dyed A whole bank of confusibles lurks. A *die* is what the *OED* cleverly defines as "A small cube of ivory, bone or other material, having its faces marked with spots numbering from one to six used in games of chance by being thrown from a box or the hand, the chance being decided by the number of the face of the die that turns uppermost..." The plural of die is *dice*, on the near-analogy of mouse/mice. Julius Caesar is said to have said, "The die is cast"- in other words, the decision has been made. Not in the *Stroud News and Journal*, which in a story about Forest Green Rovers says, in a delightful mishmash of functions, "The dye has been indelibly cast". What has been steeped in *dye* is *dyed*; and when wool is dyed before being made into a garment it holds the dye better, hence the saying about someone "dyed in the wool"; that is to say, someone totally steeped in his convictions. Again, not in the papers, which often write "died in the wool Tories".

dike/dyke "I felt like the little Dutch boy in the fairytale who stuck his finger in a dyke and saved his town from drowning," wrote Auberon Waugh in the *Daily Telegraph*. It is generally agreed that what the little Dutch boy stuck his finger in would have been a *dike* – an earth defence against flooding – and that *dykes* are masculine lesbian women. CDs by the famous English brass-band the Black Dykes (founded early in the 19th century as the Black Dyke Mills Band) have enjoyed a surprising popularity among Afro-American women unaware that its membership consists largely of heterosexual white Yorkshiremen.

diktat/dictate/order British politicians and political commentators – usually trades unionists or those of the left – appear to be fond of the German word *Diktat*, which always sits uneasily in even the most leaden English prose, especially when English-speakers pronounce it "*dick*-tatt" (Germans say "dick-*tart*"). Its English use dates from 1933 and the rise of Hitler's National Socialist dictatorship: a decree or command, a direction given by authority. The English noun fitting this definition has been available since at least 1618, when John Donne in one of his Sermons wrote of "a faithful executing of his commission and speaking according to his Dictate". So why not dump *diktat* and revive *dictate*? Or just say an *order*?

dilemma/quandary *Dilemma* is Greek for a double proposition, or a choice between two actions – by implication a difficult one. One who is in a *quandary* is uncertain or perplexed. The presence of horns, which – except on the unicorn and rhinoceros – always come in pairs (Latin *argumentum cornatum*), suggests a choice between two possible solutions, with the additional implication that if they are on a bull, whichever you grasp you are sure to be tossed.

dinghy/dingy/dinged The sailing-*dinghy* came from India: a small rowing-boat with a single mast. *Dingy* comes from dung, making "dingy sailing" as proposed in the Guardian, something dirty and excremental. A mid-18th-century *Shepherd's Guide* specifically recommends that the "dingy" wool from the hinder parts be cut away before shearing, as it probably contains dried dung. A dingy or *dinged* metal object is (in the north of England) one with dents or irregular impressions.

direct/directly To go *direct* to some place means to do so by the shortest route; to go *directly* means to do so at once, or as soon as possible. "Directly, sir," says the archetypal butler (see also ANON). Going "directly from A to B" is not the same as "direct". It is like describing something as "nicely" instead of nice: the *-ly* ending merely makes it into a would-be posh affectation. See also FIRST/"FIRSTLY" and IMPORTANT/"IMPORTANTLY".

discomfit/discomfort The two are often used as if they meant the same thing. To be *discomfited* is like being FAZED, that is, discountenanced or embarrassed, whereas *discomfort* is a lack of comfort.

discount/discount/discourse/discourse Two more useful noun/verb stress distinctions – see CONDUCT/CONDUCT and other *con-* words, above.

> Walter works in the *dis*count trade -
> A surefire thing and he's got it made.
> Lichtenstein: *The Discount Trade*
> Dis*count* the rumours, whisper it not
> Some like it tepid, some like it hot.
> Arden: Penny

> Not by your individual whiskers
> But by your dialect and *dis*course
> Samuel Butler: *Hudibras* (1660–1680):

> Bid me dis*course*, I will enchant thine ear,
> Or like a fairy trip upon the green,
> Or, like a nymph with long dishevell'd hair,
> Dance on the sands, and yet no footing seen...
> Shakespeare: *Venus and Adonis* (1593)

discount

discrete/discreet *Discrete*, from Latin *discretus*, means separate or distinct. In medicine, discrete spots are scattered about, not coalescent or running together into patches. A person who is *discreet* shows discretion, one who (as the *OED* neatly and discreetly puts it) is "silent when speech would be inconvenient". The two have a common ancestor in *discretus* but eventually diverged in spelling. Attempts to use discrete for both meanings are to be deplored.

dishabille/scantily dressed *Dishabille* has been an English word since the beginning of the 17th century, from the French *(en) déshabillé(e)*, a state of partial undress – usually of a woman. It follows the old tradition that French things are by definition naughty, or that naughty things sound even naughtier if they have French names that have a FRISSON for Englishmen. Dishabille has various facetious pronunciations, like "dish-a-billy"; and although now usually said in a four-syllable, more-or-less French manner, Jonathan Swift (1713) wrote "Come early, out of pure good-will/To see the Girl in Deshabille", and Charles Churchill (1763): "Nor would I have the Sisters of the hill/Behold their Bard in such a Dishabill" – both imply three syllables and a rhyme with "pill".

disinterested/uninterested A *disinterested* person is one who is altruistic, unselfish and unmoved by personal considerations. One who is *uninterested* is simply not interested. Say disinterested for both and some PEDANT is sure to complain. Get it right and no-one will notice. Disinterested is misused so often that many dictionaries have accommodated the "wrong" meaning, without so much as putting a warning-sign against it.

disp**ute/dis**p**ute** In the "best" speech, known as Received Pronunciation, there is no stress difference between noun and verb, both having the stress on the second syllable – dis*pute*. *Dis*pute is thought by some vulgar and certainly has a way of impairing the rhythm of any utterance (as does ROMANCE):

> Waste not your Hour, nor in vain pursuit
> Of this and That endeavour and dis*pute*...
> Edward FitzGerald:*Omar Khayyám* (1859)

> He his fabric of the Heavens
> Hath left to their dis*putes*, perhaps to move
> His laughter at their quaint opinions wide...
> > John Milton: *Paradise Lost* (1667)

> He religion so well with her learning did suit
> That in practice sincere, and in controverse mute,
> She shewed she knew better to live than dis*pute*.
> > Matthew Prior (1664–1721):
> > *The Lady who offers her Looking-Glass to Venus*

Unfortunately the popular preference is for *dis*pute, suggesting a kind of absurd negation of "pute" – a word which in archaic English means a strumpet or whore.

distemper/emulsion More about the *distemper* that is a kind of paint (now more likely to be called emulsion) will be found under TEMPERA/TEMPORA/TEMPURA. It is also an old word for a disorder or sickness of the mind or body: "Good my Lord, what is your cause of distemper?" — Shakespeare's *Hamlet* (1602). Modern usage seems to reserve that kind of distemper chiefly for animal sickness.

diva/prima donna/fat lady A *diva* is Italian (taken straight from Latin) for a goddess or fine lady, but is now used chiefly for a distinguished female opera singer – never a *Lieder* singer or a contralto specializing in character roles. As every reasonably educated person knows it is pronounced "deeva", not like "fiver", which did not deter *Telegraph* headline-writers from making headline "jokes" like

DON'T FORGET THE DIVA   and   **HIGH DIVA**

The diva, though always famous and female, is not necessarily usually portrayed as temperamental. This assumption is reserved for the *prima donna* (Italian for "first lady") who is nearly always a high soprano (her male counterpart is *primo uomo*): only *some* are temperamental. If there is rivalry she may be called *prima donna assoluta*, the absolute first lady. Non-singing prima donnas are found in all walks of life – persons who behave in a temperamental and self-important manner. The cliché "The

diva

show isn't over until the fat lady sings", which is of unknown or disputed origin (but was probably the work of an American politician's speech-writer), is silly on all counts. Fat opera singers are no longer a stereotype – an outsize soprano is the exception, not the rule – and there is no opera in which such an expensive asset as the principal soprano appears only briefly and just before the end.

dog collar/clerical collar *Dog collar* is a jocular term for what is properly the *clerical collar*. It was first spotted in that sense by the *OED* in 1861, and has survived as a tabloid vulgarism. Dog collars are best left to dogs – or to priests themselves, who do use the term self-deprecatingly, in the same way as a SEA CAPTAIN or Admiral would call himself a SAILOR.

dog/follow The verb to *dog* means to pursue, to *follow* persistently or to beset: a word with dramatic possibilities, as Shakespeare found in *Twelfth Night* (1601): "I have dogged him like his murderer." But because the verb is rarer than the pet, ambiguities abound, especially in headlines like

AFRICA ARMS DOG PREMIER

and (about a rugby team)

INJURIES DOG LIONS

dogs of war/mercenaries *Dogs of war* is a euphemistic circumlocution and tedious press cliché for military-style *mercenaries* hired by foreign dictators and tribal chiefs. The most sought-after of these are European ex-soldiers, who are hired to teach inhabitants of Third World countries how to kill each other. These "dogs" come from a famous line in Shakespeare's *Julius Caesar* (1599): "Cry havocke, and let slip the Dogges of Warre" – see also under HAVOC. It was popularized by the title of Frederick Forsyth's novel (1974).

dominate/domineer Both come from Latin *dominus*, lord or master; to *dominate*, meaning to rule, govern or have a commanding influence, is more benevolent than to *domineer*, which is to do so in an arbitrary or overbearing manner. Husbands can be domineering, and so can schoolmasters, as Shakespeare tells us in *Love's Labour's Lost* (1588): "I that have been a domineering pedant o'er the boy". See also PEDANT.

84

don/doff Archaic contractions of *do on*, meaning to put on, usually a garment, and *do off*, to remove it. Shakespeare's *Hamlet* (1602) has "Then up he rose and don'd his clothes". Neither is much used in ordinary speech ("I donned odd socks this morning" would sound silly) though in northern-English dialect both *don* and *doff* survived into the 19th century. Now chiefly journalists use them for their brevity, even if they don't always know which is which. Martin Ivens in the *Sunday Telegraph* claimed that "many journalists have never doffed a mortarboard" (no, not unless they donned one in the first place). Harvey Cole, a correspondent from Winchester, asked, "What, not even in bed?" However, doffed is still sometimes heard in relation to hats: "He doffed his hat to her."

donor/donator/doner *Donor* comes from Latin *donare*, to give something of one's free will, so it would accurately describe a blood donor, but is not such a good word for someone whose organs are transplanted or grafted posthumously into or on to another person, though he may have given permission while still alive. It is now so closely associated with this mid-20th-century surgical advance that its other meanings, e.g. for a monetary donation, are beginning to look strange. The *Guardian* has cleverly got round this by occasionally reviving the mediaeval word *donator*. A *doner* (Turkish for turning) is a Turkish or Greek meat dish roasted on a vertical revolving spit, doner kebab in full. On the principle that an eating-house menu without at least one misprint is now a rare thing, the alarming "Donor Kebab" has become a frequent misspelling.

doppelgänger/double Whenever the German word *Doppelgänger* is used, the English noun *double* is meant, and would be just as apt. However, the German *Doppelgänger* is perhaps a little more spooky (see PSYCHOLOGICAL) than a plain English double or lookalike. In German the word can also mean an apparition of an apparently living person. The best-known and most chilling appearance of such a wraith (a "dead ringer"?) occurs in Schubert's song-cycle *Die Winterreise* (1827), which has been solely responsible for keeping this otherwise obscure foreign word in English circulation. The *OED* gives 1851 as the date of its first known English appearance – whether by someone who knew the Schubert song is not clear – but by 1830 Sir Walter Scott had already used the English soundalike translation "double-ganger", which (in spite of its hint of trades union or railway slang) seems perfectly adequate;

closer also to the Dutch *dubbelganger* and certainly preferable to the pretentious use of a German word (often erroneously as "doppelganger") when an unpretentious English one would suffice. See also TRIBUTE/IMITATION.

dormouse/"doormouse" The *dormouse*, noted for its hibernation, has nothing to do with doors but is named from Latin *dormire* or French *dormir*, to sleep. In Lewis Carroll's *Alice in Wonderland* (1865) the Mad Hatter's Tea Party has a dormouse sitting – and sleeping – between the Mad Hatter and the March Hare, who were "using it as a cushion". The little rodent has always been associated with sleepiness, e.g. John Skelton's *Dormiat in pace*, "like a dormouse" (1523); and Shakespeare's *Twelfth Night* (1601): "To awake your dormouse valour".

downsized/unemployed/redundant *Downsizing* is an American euphemism for the termination of employment or a sacking, with the implication that the employer's company has shrunk and needs fewer employees. In the UK the preferred softening term is "to be made redundant", which strictly means to be surplus to requirements or of no further use. A broadcaster said on BBC *Woman's Hour*: "Last year my husband became redundant." See also CONSULTANT/SPECIALIST.

down to/up to/because of Where previously people said "It's up to you" they now often vary it as "It's down to you" – a modish but needless confusion. *Down to* is also often used like *because of*, e.g. "It's all down to his stupidity."

doyen/doyenne The French word *doyen* is derived from Latin *decanus*, a leader or commander of men (which in the Church has produced the *deacon* and *dean*). The anglicized *doyen* (albeit retaining a semblance of French pronunciation) always means a male, senior – and by implication respected – member of a body or profession. A female doyen is a *doyenne*, but because few non-French people get the hang of unsounded consonants in French words (*"Bong jour, monsewer"*) they tend to call both a male and a female doyen "doyenne". The *Guardian* for some reason called Prince Charles a "doyonne".

draconian/severe Nigel de Gruchy, a teachers' union leader, said in a radio interview: "To call the government's education policy draconian is an insult to Dracula." For once Bram Stoker's blood-sucking Count is innocent. The culprit Mr de Gruchy was looking for was *Draco*, the Archon (or chief magistrate) of Athens in 621 BC, who was nicknamed "the dragon" because of his zero-tolerance sentencing policy. See also FRANKENSTEIN.

dual/duel *Dual*, something consisting of two parts, means two-fold or double, from Latin *dualis*, two. A *duel*, is a – usually private but now unlawful and rare – fight or combat between two persons, perhaps with the object of deciding a personal quarrel or settling a point of honour, the choice of weapons most commonly being between either swords or pistols. Common terms like *dual control*, *dual purpose* and the quaintly named *dual carriageway*, should have fixed the difference in even the most free-thinking speller's mind, but this confusion figures often in the Corrections column of The *Guardian*, which has lovingly described "a duel-function candlestick" – an interesting variation on swords or pistols.

dub/call/name To *dub* is to confer the rank of knighthood by striking ("dubbing") the recipient with the flat side of a sword – and when the Queen or other officiating member of the Royal family does so they *never* (contrary to newspaper legend) say "Arise, Sir Paul" (or whoever). Dubbing is kept alive by facetious or sarcastic use: "Since that our Brother dub'd them Gentlewomen…" in Shakespeare's *Richard III* (1594), but otherwise is chiefly a news-word, e.g. "The minister is dubbed the 'Cabinet ENFORCER…'" No-one would say, "I thumped 'im cos 'e dubbed me a wimp."

— E —

ecstasy/exstasy/extasy/"extacy" Latin *extasis*, from the Greek, literally means the state of being beside oneself, perhaps what is now called an "out-of-body experience", or being "thrown into a frenzy or a stupor, with anxiety, astonishment, fear or passion" (*OED*), though the earliest uses of the word seem to have been confined to religious *ecstasy*. Wyclif's Bible (1382) has, for Acts 3.10 "Thei weren fulfillid with wondryng, and exstasie, that is, leesyng of mynde of resoun and lettyng of tunge". Those who instinctively write the obsolete form *extasy* are in good company, for so did Shakespeare in *Macbeth* (1605): "To lye in restless extasie" (though there is no respectable precedent for the other common misspelling, *extacy*).

edible/eatable The food that has been put in front of us may be perfectly wholesome and *edible*, but may taste so bad as not to be *eatable*.

effete/effeminate Contrary to a common assumption *effete* does not mean weak or *effeminate* and, when applied to men, certainly not homosexual. It comes from Latin *ex* + *fetus*, past breeding, in other words, done with producing young, or worn out with child-bearing: in hens, too old to lay any more eggs. Oliver Goldsmith's *Natural History* (1774): "Hens after three years become effete and barren." See also EMERITUS/RETIRED, FETUS/FOETUS and FEMINIST/FEMININE.

eject/ejaculate *Eject* comes from Latin *e* = out + *jacere* = to throw. *Ejaculate* does the same, only more violently, suddenly and swiftly, for *jaculum* is a javelin. From this came both meanings – of *ejaculation: either* a sudden verbal exclamation, as when Thomas Carlyle, in *Frederick the Great* (1865), has "But where can the Prince be? he kept ejaculating" – or a male orgasm "To ejaculate seede into the matrice (i.e. the womb, though the vagina is initially meant)" (1578). For as long as the aircraft ejector-seat has been in existence, the *Liverpool Daily Post* has occasionally confused the two kinds of "throwing out", as in "The pilot ejaculated over the Irish Sea".

elderly/old The two words have come to mean the same, thanks to a combination of tact and political correctness. News items such as "An elderly widow was attacked and robbed of her life savings" may go on to reveal her age as 97. The descriptions "old woman" or "old man" are now thought to be ageist as well as pejorative. A lady of 97 may describe *herself* as an old woman but may not wish to hear others doing so. See also SPINSTER/UNMARRIED WOMAN.

elements/people/males/females In police-speak – hence also news language – *people* are often described as *elements*, especially if RESTIVE, when they become "unruly elements", meaning potential or actual wrong-doers. You never hear of elements that go about their lawful business, or elements attending a symphony concert or funeral. If Handel's *Messiah* were to be arranged for a Police Band the first tenor recitative might be "Comfort ye, my elements" (which would also fit the music better than the original "pee-hee-pull"). Police officers are trained never to refer to "men" or "women" but *males* or *females*. It absolves them from having to make judgements concerning people's age (see above) or maturity, especially from deciding when a girl becomes a woman or a boy turns into a man. It may make sense, but helps to characterize PC Plod police-speak. In 2002, Merseyside Police presented illuminated awards to four security men at Liverpool University. Each illuminated, framed certificate read: "Without fear or reservation you, together with three colleagues, detained a violent male for serious offences. Having detained the male, you were professional in your conduct, restraining him until the arrival of the Police in a manner which took account of the male's discomfort. You also dealt with the male's possession of a knife in a similarly professional manner." As Robert Burns nearly said, "A male's a male for a'that." See also HALLMARKS/SIGNS and TARGET.

elicit/illicit *Elicit*, from Latin *elicere*, to draw forth, to evoke something, perhaps a response. *Illicit*, from Latin *illicitus*, not allowed, improper, illegal. "The news *illicits* a prim 'no comment' from the palace," wrote the *Guardian* – and should furthermore have written "the Palace", meaning Buckingham Palace, where the Queen lives, not any old queen in any old palace (even Crystal Palace Football Club is known as "the Palace"). As a general rule people, places and things of whom or which there is only *one* take capital letters.

elision/eleison An *elision* is a contraction, from Latin *elidere*, to crush or squeeze out – e.g. by omitting letters or syllable: as in *"Can't* pay, *won't* pay". *Eleison* belongs to the Catholic Mass, as in *Kyrie eleison*, Greek for "Lord, have mercy".

emaciated/emancipated "The woman was suffering from the slimmers' disease anorexia and was extremely emancipated..." – well, perhaps she was that, too; but what the *Liverpool Daily Post* writer meant was that she was *emaciated*. Latin *emaciare*, to make lean, from *macies*, leanness; but *emancipate*, from Latin *emancipare*, to set free from control, servitude or restraint. See also ANOREXIA/BULIMIA.

emeritus/retired It is customary for distinguished academics or others in public life to be awarded the honorary title "Professor Emeritus", which sounds grand, with implied suggestions of "merit". But in truth it is a wholly pejorative term, from Latin *e*, out of + *meritus*, merit. It is a way of telling distinguished and formerly active figures that they have served their purpose and the time has come for them to be put out to grass: or, as the old song has it, "We don't want to lose you but it's time you ought to go". This double-edged, apparently euphemistic, malapropism seems to have originated in the USA, where the *OED* discovered an "Emeritus Professor of Divinity" who was pensioned off in Philadelphia as long ago as 1794. Orchestras have also adopted the practice and title many a sacked maestro "Conductor Emeritus", and even crown him "Conductor Laureate". See also EFFETE/EFFEMINATE.

emigrants/immigrants/emigrés/refugees/asylum-seekers People who leave their home country are *emigrants*, but become *immigrants* on arrival in the new one, just as the British are foreigners in all countries but one. The Americans, whose usage of language was cobbled together by immigrants with scant English, make no distinction between *e-* and *im-* (*out* and *in*) and call *both* kinds "immigrants", paradoxically saying things like "they immigrated from Europe". During the French Revolution, and again with the Russian pogroms (perpetrated first by the Tsars and then the Communists) the French term *émigré* was widely adopted. In British English they are neutrally called "migrants" (going in either direction, like birds), refugees or, latterly, *asylum-seekers*. English writers often forget about the acute accent and put "emigre", just as they are mean about providing asylum-seekers with the hyphens they demand.

enervated/nervous *Enervated*, from Latin *enervatus*, means deprived of nerve and strength, weak, EFFETE. When a *Guardian* writer described an event as "…enervating the multi-ETHNIC community" she intended to convey exactly the opposite, something like "energizing". See also EMERITUS.

engineer/repairman Real engineers with degrees in engineering are right to complain when repairmen (or -women) who mend washing-machines and other domestic appliances by removing some faulty component and replacing it with one that works also call themselves, or are described as, "engineers". But see CHEMIST/PHARMACIST for a more relaxed attitude to a similarly shared job-description.

english-speakers/english speakers *English-speakers* are speakers who speak English, whereas *English speakers* are speakers who are English.

enjoy/experience To *enjoy* means not only to take pleasure in something or somebody, but also, in a looser sense, to *experience* something, like a period of peace or happiness. But when *The Times* tells us that "Ten years after his death, Samuel Beckett enjoys a week on Radio Three" it stretches meaning too far. See also (THE) BEST PART/GREATER PART.

enormity/enormousness An *enormity* is a serious breach of moral conduct or of the law, something grossly improper, a wicked or outrageous aberration, coming from the Latin *e*, out of + *norma*, square, true. It has nothing to do with size, though it did provide the basis for *enormous* – which simply means abnormally large. The two forms have existed side-by-side for centuries, so it would be an enormity to start amalgamating them now, with detriment to the language. However, Tony Blair, when Prime Minister, did his best to confuse the issue by commenting in a BBC interview on "the enormity of the Labour majority".

ensue/happen In ordinary conversations reporting recent events things *happen*. Yet papers (and police officers, who often share a quaint language) keep telling us that they *ensued*; possibly in tandem with some other archaism, like "A FRACAS then ensued".

entrance/en**trance** Stressed on the first syllable, *en*trance, this is the action of coming in or going in; but with the stress on the second and a long *a*, entr*ance*, it means putting someone into a state of trance – usually figuratively – and is much the same as *enchanting* them. In verse, the metre indicates which of the two senses is meant. Shakespeare has the first stressing in *Twelfth Night* (1601): "I will answer you with gate and *en*trance, but we are preuented"; and the second in *Pericles* (1608): "She hath not been entr*anced* above five hours." But it can be confusing for unsteady users of English, like the monks of Meteora in Greece, who displayed this notice:

IT IS FORBIDDEN TO
ENTRANCE THE MONASTERY IN
SHORTS OR INDECENT CLOTHING

epicentre/centre When we write or say *epicentre* we may feel it sounds a bit grander than the plain, ordinary *centre*. Epicentre is familar from reports about earthquakes, in which context it strictly means the point on the earth or water *above* the spot where things are quaking, boiling and rumbling below; from Greek *epi*, over, above. PEDANTS, classicists and seismologists may quake with anger and boil with rage, but the MEDIA will continue misusing *epicentre* until dictionaries capitulate.

equable/equitable *Equable* means uniform, free from fluctuation or unchanging, which was what the weather forecaster *should* have said, instead of predicting "*equitable* temperatures". *Equitable* means fair, impartial or candid.

equation/position/condition/conundrum, etc. An *equation* is "the action of making equal", says the *OED*, a task familiar to those who had to struggle with algebraic equations in school. Now equation serves as a catch-all vogue synonym for *position*, *condition*, situation, question, problem and even jigsaw. Its MEDIA over-use by radio and television interviewees has brought a new pronunciation, rhyming with "asian" and not, as of old, with "station". *Conundrum* has joined this stable as a loosely used fashion word. Its dictionary definitions include a whim, crotchet, puzzle, conceit or a puzzling question. It is thought to be a facetious coinage by 17th-century academics which in spite of its Latin sound is English, with the plural conundrums, not conundra.

-er/-or A generation ago it would have been rare to see the words "protestor", "advisor" or "supervisor" in print, rather than "protester", "adviser" and "superviser"; nor, conversely, would anyone have written "imposter" for *impostor*. But *-er/-or* endings are now widely confused, with many writers putting their trust in a fifty-fifty, hit-and-miss chance of getting it right. Yet there *is* no right or wrong, no formal rule, only custom. In general, a *person* is *-er* (protest*er*, advis*er*, supervis*er*, play*er* and snapp*er*-up of unconsidered trifles), whereas *inanimates* tend to take *-or* : (mot*or*, rot*or*, carburett*or*, etc.). Inevitably there are exceptions and differences: *impostor* (above) not *imposter*; *dictator* (for a despot) and *dictater* (more appropriate for one who dictates a letter, etc.); *assessor*, *professor*; and *propeller, jailer* ; but *sailor*... etc. It is worth remembering that the Latin suffix was *-or*, not *-er*, but even Latin-based words also have their inconsistencies. One just has to get used to the *look* of words as they are written by competent authors. But in an age of television the young get less reading-practice, so if they only rarely see a certain word they can hardly be expected to remember what it looks like – just as they might not recognize their first cousin if they had never, or only seldom, seen him. See also -ABLE/-IBLE.

ersatz/imitation *Ersatz* is one of the spoils of war taken from Germany in World War II and (like FLAK and STRAFE from World War I) became a naturalized English word. In German it means replacement or substitute, and was put into war service by Allied propagandists, with justifiable SCHADENFREUDE, in order to crow about the shortages the enemy people were suffering under Hitler. Ersatz was attached to whatever substance was in short supply and had to be supplanted by, or augmented with, another. It was claimed that German rations included, as a rare treat, "Chicken-and-Horse Paté, half-and-half". Half a chicken to half a horse.

eruption/irruption An *eruption*, from Latin *erumpere*, is a breaking *out*, like the ejection of solid or liquid matter from a volcano, or hot water from a GEYSER, etc., whereas an *irruption*, from Latin *irrumpere*, is a bursting or breaking *in*, incursion or invasion.

eskimo/inuit The traditional name of the *Eskimo* people (sometimes still written *Esquimaux*, in the French manner) has been declared politically incorrect, after someone discovered that in the Eskimo language it meant "eaters of raw fish (or flesh)", so the name was therefore insulting (and clearly that someone was not an Eskimo, as he would have known all

eskimo

along). The word recommended by the equality industry is *Inuit*, the name of an ETHNIC group, though opinion is by no means unanimous and journalists often have to follow their employer's style rules. In August 2002 different papers reported the same news story: *The Times* (and all the others I saw) referred to Eskimos, the *Guardian* to Inuit. See also BLACK, HOTTENTOT, NATIVE AMERICANS and other examples of verbal pussyfooting.

esprit de corps/camaraderie *Esprit de corps* is a French term whose introduction into English is credited to Horace Walpole (1780). It means something between extreme *camaraderie*, a fellow-feeling for a member of one's group or team, or the regard felt by members of a body for its honour. In newspapers it is often written with the first word mis-spelt "Espirit" and the third punned upon. See also SYMPATHY/EMPATHY/ FELLOW-FEELING.

essay/assay An *essay* is a test, proof or experiment, an attempt or endeavour. An *assay*, which comes from the same French word as essay, is also a trial or test – but now used chiefly when determining the quality or fineness of metals, usually coins, bullion or jewellery. Those objects that qualify are given HALLMARKS.

ethnic/foreign/non-white Confusion has beset the word *ethnic* since the dawn of civilization, when Greek *ethnos* meant a nation, but at the same time *ethnikos* was used for a heathen or foreigner. With the rise of Christianity *ethnic* gradually came to denote members of nations or tribes that were neither Christian nor Jewish and were therefore considered heathen or pagan. In modern English – and especially in journalese shorthand – ethnic usually refers to black or Asian minority groups. New shades of meaning are constantly emerging, like "ethnic Albanians", who are often fair-skinned, blond-haired people who look as if they might be tenth-generation Yorkshiremen (and women) but are Muslims living in certain parts of former Yugoslavia. In truth, ethnic is so bothersome a word that it might be better to forget it and specify one's meaning – even if it takes a few extra words.

etymology/entomology An *entomologist* knows about insects, while an *etymologist* knows *why* the entomologist knows about them. The Greek prefix *entomo-* also denotes cutting-up, referring, however, not to cutting up things but to the physical shape of, say, ants, whose bodies appear to be divided, or "cut into segments". The same applies to the Latin *animal insectum*, which refers to the notched or cut-into (*secare*, to cut) shape of many insects. The word *etymology* – the process of tracing the origins and construction of words – is also Greek-based: from *etymon*, the "true, literal sense of a word", a concept for which the civilized old Greeks already had a word when most of the rest of us were still communicating by grunts.

every day/everyday/some day/someday The *Daily Telegraph*, in one of those allegedly special offers, gives readers the chance of winning "a box of Cadbury Wispa Bars everyday"; and "Everyday we mount guard on freedom of expression" – wrote a newspaper editor in a letter to the *Independent*. Another paper's advertisement crowed: "The Arts Page. Everyday in the *Financial Times*." To make the two words *every day* into one word *everyday* changes their function and sense: *everyday*, says the dictionary, is an adjective that means commonplace, mediocre, inferior, that is, *not* special, e.g. everyday clothes as opposed to Sunday best. *Some day* and *some time* have by the same process been contracted to *someday* and *sometime* (though there are distinctions between the latter and some time) and in his *Song Book* Noël Coward hedges his bets by having "Some Day I'll Find You" in the index but "Someday…" as the song title (perhaps to appeal to American usage). In a related blunder British Telecom boasts "We breakdown the charges for these calls…" – mistaking a breakdown for the action of numerically breaking down or analyzing. See also FOREVER/FOR EVER.

every week…/…every week Word order can be crucial. "Five thousand women are raped every week" makes a different statement from "Every week 5,000 women are raped".

evoke/invoke The *Guardian* reported that someone had threatened "to evoke the prices act". It meant to say *invoke*, from Latin *invocare*, to call upon, in the sense of to implore, to call by name; *evoke* is to call forth, to summon up. The difference is small but subtle, and firmly established.

exacerbate/exasperate As one *exasperating* TV weather forecaster said: "Conditions have been exasperated by further rain." What she meant was *exacerbated*, from Latin *exacerbare*, to increase the hurt of a pain, the virulence of a disease, to make worse or AGGRAVATE, whereas *exasperate*, from Latin *exasperare*, means to irritate. Like television weather forecasters…

exact/extract To *exact*, as in exacting revenge, comes from Latin *exigere*, to require or enforce. It is often confused with, or taken as a misspelling of, its near-soundalike *extract*, from *extrahere*, to draw or take something out, like a tooth. The *Daily Telegraph*: "She was coming to extract revenge on this woman who had neglected her children..." But extracting a confession, usually by force, is all too often correct.

exalt/exult Two different actions: *exalt* comes from Latin *exaltare*, to lift up; *exult* from *ex(s)ultare*, to spring up, to leap for joy. Mozart's Motet *Exsultate, jubilate* (with the popular *Alleluia* aria as a last number) will be familiar to many as a delightful musical *exultation*.

excreta/"excretia" *Excreta*, for body-waste, is an unnecessary, pseudo-medical word, for why go into Latin when you can have the homely English, Latin-based *excrement*? Excreta rhymes with Rita, not Lucretia, which is based on the common misspelling "Excretia".

exercise/exorcise/excise Everyone knows what *exercise* is, and most think they don't take enough. But the word sprang from the notion of making *others* do the hard work, Latin *exercere*, "to drive forth tillage beasts, hence to employ, to set to work". That is why, when the armed forces go on exercises, they are set to work with their weapons, not their dumb-bells. *Exorcise* is related, but with a different sense, from a Greek word meaning "to drive out [ghosts, evil spirits, etc.] by casting a spell or oath". *Exorcism* is a pagan act not uncommon among members of Christian churches whose adherents believe this kind of MUMBO-JUMBO to be effective. The procedure involves prayer and, where considered appropriate, holy water; but not a dog-lead, as was suggested in a *Guardian* report: "A priest has been called in to exercise the ghost." But it would be unwise to call the Vicar an *exorcist*, since a famous film ANNEXED that word. *Excise*, as in Customs and Excise, comes from Latin *accensare*, to tax or charge a toll, or (alas erroneously though FORTUITOUSLY apt) *excisum*, something that is cut out, as a surgeon excises bits of flesh. Dr Samuel Johnson's definition of Excise in his *Dictionary* (1755) is: "a hateful tax levied upon commodities, and adjudged not by the common judges of property, but wretches hired by those to whom excise is paid". It seems to be a "difficult" word for new spellers, for it is not unusual to see references in the papers to "customs and exercise" or "customs and exise".

expanded/expansive/extended/extensive *Expanded* means outspread, extended, or made wider, whereas *expansive* is the word for persons (usually men) whose affections, utterances, etc., are effusive or "larger than life" – and may become more so in the course of a fine dinner with plenty of wine and good company. But the Welsh tourist-brochure which enthused over "…an expansive vista from Anglesey in the west to Snowdonia in the east" meant *extensive*; and the music-critic who described as "expansive" a symphony he found tedious or too long should have said *extended*. See also ROTUND/OROTUND.

expatriate/expatriot A person who lives in a foreign country but retains the nationality of, and probably allegiance to, the land of his birth, is an *expatriate*, colloquially *expat* for short. An *expatriot* is a person who was once a patriot but no longer professes patriotic feelings for his country. Hyphenating it "ex-patriot" only makes things worse by emphasizing the split. Perhaps one should make a distinction in the pronunciation – "pay-tree-ate" and "pat-ree-ott". One day a patriotic *expatriate* will sue for being called an *ex-patriot*.

expletive/swear-word Contrary to common belief an *expletive*, as in "The air was blue with expletives", is not the same as a *swear-word*. From Latin *explere*, it means to fill out, which is how most bloody swear-words are bloody-well used, sometimes even in the middle of a bloody word, which is abso-bloody-lutely stupid. It is this – usually senseless – "filling out" that makes them expletives. They are now often more obscene than BLOODY/ BLOOMING/ PYGMALION, but if you were to substitute "jolly well" for every "bloody" above, "jolly well" would also count as an expletive. The technical term for formations like "abso-bloody-lutely" is *tmesis*, from the Greek word for "a cutting", and means "the separation of the elements of a compound word by the interposition of another word or words". Now bloody read on...

explicit/salacious *Explicit*, from Latin *explicare*, to unfold, to make something clear, has become a euphemistic abbreviation of *sexually explicit* or even pornographic. *Salacious*, meaning lecherous, lustful or sexually inspiring, comes from *salire*, to leap or jump – which perhaps also gave us the salad: the Roman food-writer Apicius offered a recipe for a salad containing ginger, pepper, honey and other ingredients and claimed it had aphrodisiac properties. John Dryden (1697) wrote "Feed him with Herbs of generous warmth and of salacious kind." "Spicy" salads? See also INTIMACY.

exposé/exposure *Exposé* is pronounced "ex-poh-say" though when printed is often denied its acute accent on the final *e* and looks annoyingly like the English word *expose*. Like EXTRAORDINAIRE, below, it is an unnecessary French word: all it means is *exposure*.

extraordinaire/extraordinary *Extraordinaire* is another phoney Frenchism, often added to qualify an English noun, e.g. "farmer extraordinaire", which is no better than *extraordinary*.

extrovert/"extravert"/flamboyant *Extravert* is common, but dictionaries say *extrovert* is correct. From Latin *extro-* outwards + *vertere* to turn, it means one who is sociable and perhaps lacking in some accepted restraints, outgoing rather than inhibited (which is from Latin *inhibere*, to hold in). The literal meaning of the French word *flamboyant* is flame-like, also flame-like decorations in art, sculpture and archaeology etc. But from the late 19th century, English writers began to use it figuratively (and often satirically) for anything or anyone they considered floridly or gorgeously decorated or dressed. The *extrovert* Oscar Wilde must have been described many times as *flamboyant*; as is, constantly, the jazz-singer and art critic George Melly. Lawyers, politicians, businessmen and other prominent people qualify for flamboyance as soon as their dress- and hair-styles do not CONFORM to the normal conventions of their profession (their hair being probably longer than usual). Dr George Carey was given the flamboyant label, but only because as Archbishop of Canterbury he often wore a cope and mitre decorated with distinctive, upward-licking flames. Was it his personal fashion statement or did it carry some deeper religious significance? Of hellfire maybe?

F

facing the music/expecting (getting) a reprimand *Facing the music* means facing the consequences of one's actions, usually those which are in some way reprehensible, or disapproved of. Various explanations for the cliché have been suggested. Steve Race thinks it is a reference to the song "Let's Face the Music and Dance", by Irving Berlin – but why should one have to *face* the music when intending to dance? My guess is that when Berlin wrote his song the cliché was already in circulation. Another explanation is that it refers to a traditional British Army ceremony in which miscreants who had been court-marshalled were indeed obliged to face the band that was playing "The Rogues' March" as they were drummed out of their regiment – a custom still occasionally alluded to: every regimental band used to have copies of the march, though today there may not even be a band.... See also (A) CARPETING.

faint/feint *Faint* has meanings of weakness, lack of power and strength. It is related to the verb to *feint* meaning to pretend – best known from its use in boxing, though sellers of STATIONERY have traditionally described *faint* rules on paper as *feint*. Both forms come from the French.

family planning/birth-control/contraception When *contraception* became a subject for public discussion in the early 20th century it was still almost unmentionable, so that polite circumlocution was necessary. At first it was "malthusianism", after T. R. Malthus, who in 1798 advocated population-control in order that there might be enough food for all (and those practising it were from the 1890s said to be "malthusianizing"); then it became *birth-control*, first recorded by the *OED* in 1914; and in 1939 was joined by *family planning* – both coy euphemisms attributed to Marie Stopes, "the great birth-controller", as she was described without a hint of levity (Aldous Huxley in his novel *Crome Yellow* wrote about "the indignation of a convinced birth-controller"). Contraception was a euphemistic technical term that was meant to be over the heads of the common people and juveniles (who most needed to know in simple terms what to do): a contraction of *contra*, against + (con)ception. Today's newspapers have no need of euphemisms, and family planning suggests nothing more intimate (see INTIMACY) than finding somewhere to dump granny while the family goes on holiday.

famous/famed The normal adjective is *famous*, with *famed* as the – usually poetic – alternative. However, journalists decided that by using famed they not only sounded a little grander but could save a syllable. Shakespeare uses the two-syllable form in the first of the following lines, and the one-syllable to make the next line scan: "Were he as famous and as bold in war/As he is fam'd for mildness, peace and prayer", in *Henry VI* (1592).

farrago/mixture/pot-pourri/hotchpotch/gallimaufry *Farrago* is Latin for a *mixture*, originally mixed cattle fodder but figuratively also of words, as in "A strange miscellanie, farrago and hotch-potch of Poperie, Armenianism and what-not" (1637). Lawyers like to say that their courtroom opponents or hostile witnesses tell "a farrago of lies", but if a cliché is called for, a *tissue* of lies might be better. Others are available, most of them borrowed from the kitchen or table. An *olla podrida*, for example, which is a medley, verbal or musical, but originally a rather revolting dish, as an author of 1599 explains: "I desire to know, from whence or why they called it *olla podrida*." Answer: "A rotten or putrified pot. Also a hotchpotch of many meats together." *Olla podrida* is the Spanish for what the French call a *pot-pourri*, also literally meaning "rotten pot" (Latin *putrere*, to be rotten or putrid): "Pot pourri, a pot porridge, a Spanish dish of many seuerall meates boyled or stued together" (1611) – and that was before it referred to dried flowers – or "…an Hotch-Potch" (1725). And a *hotchpotch*, or *hodge-podge*, consisted of "boyled mutton that was nothing but mammockes" (1622) — mammocks being small pieces or shreds. A *gallimaufry* is "a dish made by hashing up odds and ends of food; a hodge-podge, a ragout", or (1623): "That I may neither slovenly chop it into gobbits, nor curiously mince it to a gallamafrie" With the modern spelling it is also "a hodge-podge, confused jumble"). So how about a gallimaufry of lies? Or perhaps a medley or pot-pourri, as described above. Or a *macedoine*? "Mixed fruit or vegetables cut up into small pieces – with reference to the diversity of people in the Macedonian empire of Alexander the Great" (*OED*).

fast lane/overtaking lane The cliché "Life in the fast lane" dates from the second half of the 20th century, when Britons first experienced motorway-driving. The *fast lane* is best left to newspapers and magazines, for police and safety experts never tire of reminding drivers that there is no such thing as a "fast" or indeed a "slow" lane. Only an *overtaking lane* and, having overtaken, the well-trained driver returns to drive on the left.

faux pas/mistake/blunder A *faux pas* is literally "a false step" in French, but in English a *blunder* in etiquette or manners. William Wycherly, in *The Plain Dealer* (1674) must have been among the first to use it as a quasi-English word: "Before this faux pas, this trip of mine, the world could not talk of me."

fazed/phased *Fazed* is a useful and simple little word that has been around since the early 19th century and to be fazed means to be DISCOMFITED, disturbed or put out of countenance. There is no doubt about the spelling (though *feazed* was occasionally recorded). To be *phased* (or more often *phased out*) means to pass through various stages and is unconnected with being *fazed*.

featherbed/subsidize/setaside *Featherbedding*, the action of making comfortable, especially economically or financially, has always been associated with subsidies for farmers. These have been available to them (to the annoyance of the non-farming COMMUNITY), continuously since the early years of the 20th century, when the term was first coined with specific reference to farmers, who perhaps slept in featherbeds made with the down supplied by their own ducks and geese. Another *OED* definition of featherbedding, "getting pay for work not done", would be more appropriate for the practice that arose under European Community laws which some European bureaucrat called *setaside*, that is, leaving fields uncultivated or unharvested so as artificially to adjust and fix prices, enabling some farmers to stuff their mattresses with tons of euro notes.

feisty/raunchy *Feisty* was rarely heard or seen until over-used by columnists, especially female (who may be unaware that in old English it means "a breaking of wind, a foul stink", from *feist*, fart). The *OED* says *feisty* comes from US slang and means "aggressive, excitable, touchy", but in the way it is now used its sense seems to have widened. Not unattractively aggressive women are often so described. The

feisty

pronunciation seems to vary: some say "feasty", others "fice-ty". When *raunchy* was first noticed by the compilers of dictionaries in the 1930s it meant "inept, incompetent, sloppy, unpleasant, contemptible, mean, disreputable, dirty, grubby", which was also how the *OED* saw it, but it is now interpreted in much the same way as feisty, though with additional shades of a bawdy, salacious, smuttily sexy suggestiveness. Like feisty it is often applied admiringly by women to other women (or their writings). For a time feisty and raunchy were almost catch-words of women's broadcasting, e.g. *Woman's Hour* on BBC Radio 4.

fellow-traveller/political sympathizer/stooge Now that Communism is dead and its jargon sounds quaint, we might reclaim the original meaning of *fellow-traveller*: "a person who travels along with another". But from the 1930s it took on political associations, meaning one who *sympathizes* with (almost always) the Communists, fellow-travellers being those was who supported their aims without actually being party members. W. H. Auden, in his *New Year Letter* (1941): "A liberal fellow-traveller ran/With sansculotte and Jacobin/Nor guessed what circles he was in." Like other Communist jargon words (see LIQUIDATE/MURDER) it is a laboured translation from the Russian, in this case *popútchik*, coined by Leon Trotsky to describe non-Communist writers who, he felt, would be sympathetic to the Revolution. In reality the Western Communist fellow-travellers were *stooges*; and a stooge is a conjurer's assistant who acts as a foil to the leading character and is privy to his fraudulent tricks. Fellow-travellers, like lackeys and FLUNKEYS, kept their place in Soviet PROPAGANDA verbiage until the end of Communism and probably beyond. *Sputnik*, the name chosen for the first Russian spacecraft, is another word for fellow-traveller. See also JACOBIN and SANSCULOTTE.

feminist/feminine Far from being synonymous, the two are often mutually exclusive. See also EFFETE/EFFEMINATE.

feral/ferral A *feral* animal is a wild one (Latin *fera*, a wild beast) or sometimes a domesticated one that has reverted to a wild state. The common misspelling *ferral* would suggest one made of iron – for which the Latin word is *ferrum*. No relation to a ferret, however.

ferment/foment A leaflet from a Liverpool exhibition on the Slave Trade contentiously claims that tribal wars in Africa were "fermented" by Europeans – a statement which is doubly absurd. African tribal politics have never needed Europeans to stir up internecine strife; nor would boatloads of yeast have helped. What the writer meant was *foment*: Latin *fovere*, to cherish, encourage. *Ferment* comes from *fermentum*, from *fervere*, to boil. But confusingly the result of *fomented* strife is not a *foment* but may be a *ferment*.

festival/fest *Fest* is the straighforward German word for *festival* but is now often used facetiously and affectedly by arts workers, newspaper diarists and would-be-smart writers: shooting-fest, talk-fest, liquor-fest and film-fest and even f**kfest – all but the last recorded by the *OED* and all from the USA. Sometimes the words are hyphenated, sometimes separate and occasionally two run into one. See also ANGST/ANXIETY/TRAUMA.

fetlock/forelock A school librarian wrote, in a facetious letter to the *Guardian*, "Remind me to touch my fetlock as I go into work this morning." Either she has hairy legs or she meant her *forelock*, the touching of which used to be considered a mark of respect from an inferior (by implication a peasant or worker) to a superior person. A *fetlock* is "that part of a horse's leg where the tuft of hair grows behind the pastern-joint" (*OED*); but a *forelock* is the hair that falls forward between the ears and is found on horses as well as peasants (and presumably school librarians). Fetlocks are part of the parlance of horsemen, but the forelock is usually confined to the act of a servile pulling, or else belongs figuratively to Time, in a cliché that goes back to Edmund Spenser (1594): "The ioyous time wil not be staid/Unless she doe him by the forelock take."

fetus/foetus The word for an unborn baby in the womb is usually given as *foetus* in English, whereas Americans, who always like to reduce spelling to its simplest form, spell it *fetus*. For once – and quite by accident – *they* are right and *we* are wrong, for the ancient Latin for offspring is *fetus*, which only later became *foetus* through a mediaeval misinterpretation of the word. The same applies to *foetal*, which should be *fetal*. See also EFFETE/EFFEMINATE.

fewer/less The difference lies in whether you can count them (whatever they are, e.g. *fewer* sheep) or are faced with an entity (whatever it is, e.g. *less* mutton). To observe this simple rule is not PEDANTRY but logic. The right form sounds natural – neither pseudo-posh nor STILTED

fewer

(as the correct use of WHOM does sometimes) – and no-one will take offence. The editor of the Corrections column of the *Liverpool Daily Post* announced proof-reading changes which "should result in a lot less mistakes finding their way into print". Quite; but then David Blunkett, the Secretary of State for Education at the time, promised: "There will be a lot less memos." In a letter to *The Times* Michael Bird postulated the difference between an editor's "asking his columnists to write fewer pedantic articles and asking them to write less pedantic articles".

fiancé/fiancée A male betrothed has one é, a female two, with an acute accent on the first: -ée. These accents are obligatory; for while "fiancee" might just about pass, "fiance" makes nonsense in the context of betrothal. The old English word fiance (pronounced "fie-ants") means confidence or trust (from French *fier*, to trust). See also PASSÉ.

field sports/blood sports Country folk who support shooting and foxhunting say *field sports,* but those who hate these pursuits, and would like to see them banned, emotively call them *blood sports.* Thus, as with CLOVER/SHAMROCK and DERRY/LONDONDERRY, the word you choose reveals which side you are on.

fiend/buff We seem to have rehabilitated the *fiend* from a near-devil to a lover, or at any rate an amateur in the older meaning of that word. A fiend, in various spellings (*Feind* in modern German), was a foe; but now one reads about "a 100-year-old lady who was a fresh-air fiend". She might also have been a *buff* – or, better, a lover of – fresh air. As a short word, buff has an advantage over most others, e.g. enthusiast, so we get *music buffs, opera buffs, eating-out buffs* and many others. In its original context the word was American and specifically meant "enthusiasts about going to fires" (*Webster's Dictionary,* 1934). As the *New York Sun* explained in 1903, "The Buffs are men and boys whose love of fires, firefighting and firemen is a predominant characteristic" – in other words pyromaniacs by any modern interpretation, including that of Dr Freud. The origin lies in the buff-coloured uniforms which New York firemen wore. See also ANORAK/NERD/ENTHUSIAST.

fin de siècle/advanced/modern/decadent *Fin de siècle* used to be a favourite term of critics (art, theatre and music). It was first spotted in the *Daily Mail* in 1890, when it referred, variously, to movements or manifestations which at the end of the 19th century were considered *modern*, *advanced* or *decadent*. This meaning continued to apply until the 20th but, as that century drew to a close, required qualification as to which century was meant.

fine tooth comb/fine-tooth(ed) comb "Police went through it with a fine tooth comb" is merely ambiguous, but "...a fine tooth-comb" is absurd. Combs have teeth, small or big, widely or closely spaced, and all are tooth combs. What is meant is a *fine-tooth comb*.

fireman/firefighter The politically – and usually factually – correct term is now *firefighter* – just as a policeman must be a police *officer* and a headmaster a head-*teacher* – so as to include the women who perform the same jobs. The fire service admits women to operational duties only if they can carry an unconscious 14-stone man slung over their shoulders without having to make two journeys. See also FIEND/BUFF.

"firstly"/first When one is enumerating points, etc., firstly, secondly, thirdly and fourthly are possible, though unnecessary. However, by the time one gets to fifthly, sixthly, seventhly and eighthly, one begins to realise that these adverbial -*ly* endings are ugly and superfluous. What is wrong with *first*, second, third and fourth, etc? See also "IMPORTANTLY" and "especially importantly" INITIALLY/FIRSTLY/AT FIRST/IN THE BEGINNING.

flair/flare To have a *flair* for something is to show an aptitude, liking or enthusiasm – indeed a *nose* for it, as it comes from French *flairer*, to smell or sniff. The other spelling, *flare*, with which it is often confused, means to blaze up, like a flame, or outwards in shape, like the end of a trumpet or the bottoms of 1960s trouser-legs. It is also a bright light used as a signal. A writer in the *Guardian*, too young to know about World War II, had Royal Air Force bombers landing on a "flair path".

flammable/inflammable/inflammatory This is the only instance known to me of an official change in meaning and usage demanded by a British government body. Officials expressed the fear that people might have misunderstood the *in-* prefix as an *un-*, in other words that *inflammable* material was "unflammable" and fireproof, whereas the *in-* is here an *in*tensifier. *Inflammatory* is now usually confined to abstract use, like an inflammatory speech.

flammable

flaw/floor A pair of homophones – except to English-speaking Arabs and most Scots, who strongly sound the final letter *r*. An advertisement in *The Times* inviting persons to apply for a secretarial post specified "floorless English". Conversely, in *Woman's Weekly*, "My son asked me questions about sex that flawed me", See also FLOOR/GROUND, below.

floe/flow *Floe*, like many words related to snow and ice, is of Norse origin and means a piece of floating ice. This may float on water but is different from *flow*, to glide along as a stream. To confuse matters, a *flow* can also be a watery moss or quicksand.

floor/ground A room has a *floor*, whether this is made of wood, concrete or ceramic; and so has the ocean; but outdoors we walk on the *ground* – earth, sand or mud, pebbles, stones, etc. Had the Bible been written by a modern journalist he would have reported God as saying to Cain (the first murderer), "The voice of thy brother cryeth unto me from the floor", not the ground, as in Genesis 3.10. And on the floor, too, the wicked Onan would have spilled his seed. I suspect that football commentators may have popularized this neologism: "The goalie picked himself up off the floor..." – and here the *floor* is usually made of grass, real or artificial. See also INJURED/WOUNDED and ROCKS/ STONES.

flounder/founder "The *Titanic* floundered off Newfoundland..." according to the *Liverpool Daily Post*. No she didn't – unless she was thrashing about: like a fish out of water (though one can also *flounder* in the mire, as the *OED* helpfully suggests). Maybe it was this that Lewis Smith of *The Times* had in mind when he reported that "the relationship between Sir Elton John and his former lover and accountant [had] floundered". But there is no doubt about the *Titanic*: she *foundered*, "*founder*, to fill with water and sink, to go to the bottom" (*OED*). As did another ill-fated English ship, Henry VIII's *Mary Rose*. Richard Hakluyt wrote in 1600 (of another marine disaster): "Already she had receiued in much water, insomuch that she beganne to founder." See also RACKED/WRACKED/WRECKED.

flout/flaunt "The minister has twice flaunted fair employment rules," said the *Guardian*. Not unless he was waving them about. The writer meant he *flouted* them, meaning contemptuously ignored them. Flouting is related to playing the flute: both Dutch *fluiten* and German *flöten* have derisive (and, in French, also lascivious) meanings. *Flaunting* is of unknown origin, says the *OED*, and was originally what a male bird did with his feathers to impress females, but now members of all three sexes flaunt things ostentatiously, usually their clothes, wealth or other possessions.

flu/flue "Princess Margaret was said to be suffering from flue and has cancelled her appointments," reported the *Liverpool Daily Post*. That would have been *flu* – unless, as a heavy smoker, the late Princess had a fall of soot. *Flue*, the smoke-duct of a chimney, is of uncertain origin, says the *OED*, and possibly related to either fluting or flowing. Flu is short for Italian *influenza*, a word brought from Rome in 1743 when the city suffered an epidemic of *influenza di catarro* and *influenza de febbre* (catarrh and fever – only two of its many symptoms). By 1750 the *influenza* had spread to England, keeping part of its Italian name, in the abbreviated form that is now an English word in its own right. As with other diseases, e.g. the French pox and the German measles, foreigners may be blamed, often with justification, for a certain GERM/VIRUS can sometimes be traced to its first known outbreak, like the Spanish flu after World War I, and the Hong Kong strain after World War II.

flunkeys/flunkies/lackeys The normal spelling for this kind of servant is flunkey, so the plural is surely *flunkeys*, not *flunkies*, certainly by analogy with a plurality of monkeys, not monkies. *Lackeys* (never lackies, note) go back to the 15th century and were always manservants or footmen. Both flunkey and lackey are used as terms of contempt, and the latter was once a favourite weapon in the Soviets' quaint vocabulary of political abuse: "imperialist hyenas and their FELLOW-TRAVELLERS the socialist lackeys…" etc.

flyer/flier Both spellings seem to be current and valid, and when applied to a solo aviator are usually cliché-twinned with LONE. The Americans use both *flyer* and *flier* when they mean an advertising leaflet, especially the interleaved litter that is shed by newspapers and magazines and flies about in the wind, which is how the word flier originated. This practice was established long ago in America. The *Literary World* of 21 December 1889 wrote about "inserting gaily colored advertising fliers into the body of the magazine". Would that the idea had never crossed the Atlantic.

flyer

fondling/cuddling/hugging Charming words which were full of innocence – until ruined by HACKS who gave them salacious connotations: "She then sat on his knee and he fondled her…" The same goes for *cuddling*, which used to be even more innocent, originally meaning "To press or draw close within the arms so as to make warm and cosy…" – except in the tabloids, with their "kiss'n'cuddle" stories. *Hugging* is sometimes allowed to retain its innocence: "To squeeze tightly in the arms, usually with affection; but also said of a bear fatally squeezing a man, dog etc., between its forelegs". Shakespeare, in *Richard III* (1594): "He bewept my fortune, and hugg'd me in his armes." Writers could help to restore the old meanings by using different words when they mean sexual assault.

foodie See GOURMET/GOURMAND.

forbear/forebear To *forbear* (with the stress on the second syllable) means to refrain or abstain, derived an old teutonic word. *Forebears* (with the stress on the first) are ancestors ("usually more remote than a grandfather" – *OED*). See also FORGO/FOREGO.

forced/obliged "Since the withdrawal of the bus-service, children have been forced to walk to school…" Shakespeare's "whining schoolboy with his satchel and shining morning face, creeping like a snail unwillingly to school" may have been taken by the scruff of his neck and *forced* to walk to school, but the children in the report were *obliged* to walk, the only force being that of circumstances.

forcible/forceful A subtle distinction has evolved between these related words. A *forceful* speaker is one who makes his points cogently, effectively and with energy; but a *forcible* act now almost always involves physical and probably violent force – at the very least a bit of arm-twisting.

forever/for ever Few things are *for ever*, but on the rare occasions when something *is* said to last for all time it takes two separate words, "for ever". Only when meaning "incessantly", as a single adverb, is it written *forever*, as in "Why are you forever blowing bubbles?" In spite of persistent misquoters' efforts Rupert Brooke's corner of a foreign field is "for ever England", but the one-word *forever* often turns up in both senses in American English – as does ANYMORE – though poets and clerics have never been averse to the one-word *forever* from as early as the 17th century. Thomas Carlyle even extended it to "forevermore" (one word), which is perhaps a bit much: "Farewell forevermore, ye Girondins" (1871); and Henry Wadsworth Longfellow followed the legal precedent of "heretofore" (1872) in: "Forevermore, it shall be as it hath been heretofore". The poet and wit C. S. Calverley (1831–1884) neatly made it clear:

> Never more must printer do
> As men did long ago; but run
> *For* into *ever*, bidding two be one.

forgo/forego To *forgo* means to do without, to abstain from or relinquish something; to *forego*, to go before or precede, either in place or time. A way of remembering the difference is to notice that *forgo* does without, or forgoes, the *e*. See also FORBEAR/FOREBEAR.

former/one-time *One-time*, in the sense of *once* (as opposed to twice or more times) or as *once upon a time*, is American English, adapted from the German *einmal(ig)*. It can cause misunderstanding, especially when one describes someone as "her one-time lover". It might suggest he managed "it" only once. *Former* lover leaves no doubt.

forte/strength *Forte* is one of many musical terms borrowed loosely to make an English cliché, but this one, unlike CRESCENDO, makes sense. As a musical marking, *forte* does not mean *loud*, but *strong*. Someone's *forte* means, literally, his strength. As an English expression it was first borrowed from the French *fort*, with the same meaning. Thomas Shadwell wrote in 1682: "His Fort is that he is an indifferent good Versificator." Later (1768) Oliver Goldsmith preferred the Italian *forte*, which eventually prevailed. As Pat Ryan, long-serving Principal Clarinettist of the Hallé Orchestra and a great Irish wit, used to say, "My *pianissimo* is my *forte*."

fortuitous/fortunate Both are to do with fortune, but do not share the same meaning. Both come from the Latin *fortuna* (notice that it is a feminine noun – which is why we speak of "Lady Luck"), but whereas *fortuitus* means by chance, *fortunatus* is by good fortune. Football commentators are often heard to cry, "Oh what a fortuitous goal!" when they mean the goal-scorer was lucky.

fracas

fracas/fight/disturbance *Fracas* is a curious archaism meaning a *fight* or noisy *disturbance*, a word of which journalists are unduly fond but which is seldom seen or heard in real life. It may be a throwback to legal French, for in that jargon it does indeed mean a noisy quarrel. However, the three examples the *OED* cites are all GENTEEL: from Lady Mary Wortley-Montagu and Robert Burns – and from W. M. Thackeray's *Vanity Fair* (1848): "A violent fracas took place between the infantry-colonel and his lady." For Thackeray a fracas "took place", whereas in our news language it tends archaically to "ensue". The foreign pronunciation "frack-ahh" is observed, but pronouncing it "fight" or "disturbance" is more euphonious.

frank/honest/sincere To be *frank* is to be (or pretend to be) open, honest and sincere, though people (especially politicians) who habitually preface statements with "Let me be frank with you", or "Quite frankly..." either have something to conceal or are frank only when they announce the fact; or are habitual users of meaningless clichés. *Frank* is also a CHRISTIAN NAME/FORENAME, short for Francis, and a possible source for confusion (see also PAT and HA/HO). John Osborne, in his *Spectator* diary in the early 1990s, wrote: "Maggie Smith came for the day last week. I hadn't seen her for years. Frank, four-square and looking like a plain-dealing goddess..." This seemed to suggest that Osborne had introduced a new character, the effeminate Frank, into his narrative.

frankenstein/monster Contrary to almost universal belief and constant journalistic repetition, *Frankenstein* was not a *monster* but its creator. Dr Frankenstein, the title-character of Mary Wollstonecraft Shelley's horror story (1818) was a pioneer – albeit a fictitious one – of spare-part transplant surgery and electric-shock therapy: he collected organs and other bits and pieces from corpses he stole from dissecting-rooms and graveyards, assembled them, then electrified them into life. In the story this unlikely procedure worked, giving the corpses everything except a soul. Today's tabloids, ready to coin a catch-phrase for every occasion, have given us "The Frankenstein organ scandal", etc., as well as "Frankenstein food" to describe genetically modified crops grown from specially bred plants or cloned animals. Since Frankenstein was the *creator* of the monsters it is wrong to call some poor, misshapen animal "a Frankenstein"; and the *Daily Telegraph* was wrong, too, to accuse the African National Congress in 1971 of having "created a political Frankenstein which is pointing the way to a non-white political revival".

In German-speaking lands Frankenstein is an aristocratic surname, and thanks to Mary Shelley's creation Dr George Frankenstein, the pre-World War II Austrian Ambassador to the Court of St James's, was given a hard time. But in spite of the jokes he had to endure, and took in good part, he had the good sense to remain in England when Austria was annexed by Hitler. He was eventually given an English knighthood for, among other good deeds, his musical patronage. See also DRACONIAN.

frequent/frequent

> The auld wife sat at her ivied door,
> (Butter and eggs and a pound of cheese)
> A thing she had *fre*quently done before
> And her spectacles lay on her apron'd knees.
> > C.S. Calverley (1831–1884): *Ballad*.

> Myself when young did eagerly fre*quent*
> Doctor and saint, and heard great argument
> About it and about: but evermore
> Came out by the same door as in I went.
> > Edward Fitzgerald: *Rubaiyat of Omar Khayyam* (1859).

friar/frier/fryer/fryable/friable A *friar*, from the Latin (later also French) word for brother, is a member of a religious order. One who *fries* (usually fish, perhaps also chips) is a *fryer*, alternative spelling *frier* – a kind of back-formation from "fries", or fried potatoes. French fries have no connection with the euphemised English FRIES/TESTICLES below, although these, like bacon, sausage and tomatoes or whatever is capable of being fried, are *fryable*. That which is easily crumbled, like fresh bread or soil, is *friable*, from Latin *friare*, to crumble into small pieces.

fries/testicles Even in these EXPLICIT times the *testicles* of domestic animals when sold by an old-fashioned butcher (and never found in a supermarket) are described coyly as *lamb's fries* or *pig's fries*.

frisson/thrill/shiver *Frisson* is French for a shiver – what Arnold Bennett in *The Truth about an Author* (1903) called "the cult of the literary frisson", and this is exactly what it seems to give: an emotional *thrill*, with or without an actual *shiver* – just "a certain frisson of excitement".

frisson

from hell/bad/deplorable/unpleasant Hell is seldom far from the MEDIA. Interviewees who have come through a bad experience claim to have been "to hell and back" (and may add that now all they want is to "get on with the rest of their lives"). In popular writing, anything considered unpleasant is claimed to have emanated *from hell*. A takeaway that made them sick? "A kebab from hell". A woman-columnist's dinner-party tale of a bad *au-pair*? "Nanny from hell". Even the *New Scientist* had "a research project from hell". Ophelia might have described her increasingly unstable Hamlet as a "boyfriend from hell", though Shakespeare made her say it more prettily: "...a look so piteous in purport/As if he had been loosed out of hell" (like the bat which the *OED* first noticed coming "out of hell" in 1921). Shakespeare's *Richard III* (1594) has an exclamation that could be quoted in Parliament by an Opposition member: "Avaunt, thou dreadful minister of hell"; but in *The Merchant of Venice* (1596) there occurs a line so baldly modern that theatre producers change it rather than provoke unseemly laughter – for once Shakespeare sounds un-Shakespearian: "Oh hell! What have we here?" A cliché, perhaps?

fudge/smudge/fake/botch To *fudge* means to *fake*. There is also political or financial fudging ("To fit together in a clumsy, makeshift or dishonest manner ... to make a problem look as if it had been solved by altering figures..." – *OED*), which became a late-20th-century cliché. The old authors had prettier ways of using the word, e.g. Nathaniel Fairfax, in his *Treatise of the Bulk and Selvedge of the World* (1674): "They may be fudged up into such a smirkish liveliness, as may last as long as the Summers [sic] warmth holds on." In politics, fudging produced a much-quoted but unexplained statement in 1997 from the Chancellor of the Exchequer, Gordon Brown: "We are against fudging convergence." This was something to do with Europe but as it did not have the Churchillian resonance of "We shall fight on the beaches" was remembered only because of its incomprehensibility. *Smudging* is distantly related to *fudging*, and this, too, can mean "to bungle, make a mess of something" (*OED*); or, in drawing, to rub an image so as to make it less clear. *Botching* something is to repair it badly or clumsily. But a *fudged convergence...*? Britain quickly tired of political fudge and reverted to what most people have always understood by it: a boiled-together mixture of milk, sugar, butter, possibly chocolate, and a few drops of vanilla extract, left to set and cut into small pieces.

furor/furore *Furor* is an old English two-syllable word (from Latin) for fury, rage, madness or anger. It was used by William Caxton in about 1470 and remained thus in all subsequent centuries until the 20th, when the Italian three-syllable version *furore* became the preferred one. There is no good reason for the change, except perhaps for emphasis and euphony.

galore/plenty *Galore* is one of the few Irish borrowings into English (though some claim it was Scottish-Gaelic before the Irish adopted it). It means an abundance, or plenty – from the Irish *go leór* (or if you prefer the Gaelic, *gu leór* or *leóir*) – and is older than the Spanish import BONANZA. Henry Teonge's *Diary* (1675) speaks of plenty thus: "Provinder, good store, beife…chicken, henns, gallore".

gamine/tomboy A *gamine*, from French *gamin*, is "an attractively pert, mischievous or elvish girl or young woman, usually small and slim". Not to be confused with a *tomboy*, a kind of gamine with a masculine streak but not necessarily of small stature or slight frame: "A girl who behaves like a spirited or boisterous boy; a wild romping girl; a hoyden". Shakespeare has "tomboyes" in *Cymbeline* (1611), but tomboys appeared earlier still. Priests in particular hated them, no doubt feeling that short-haired, mannish young women were a threat to their authority. John Calvin in 1579: "Sainte Paule meaneth that women must not be impudent, they must not be tomboyes, to be shorte, they must not be vnchast." T(homas) Stoughton (1622): "Of such short-haired Gentlewomen I find not one example, either in Scripture or elsewhere. And what shall I say of such…Tomboyes?" An *OED* source of 1657 even comments on their characteristically unfeminine walk: "(a) stradling kind of Tomboy sport".

gamut/gambit *Gamut* is an obsolete musical term which eventually came to mean the musical scale, hence its most common figurative use, "running the whole gamut", the whole range of things or ideas. Charles Dickens acknowledged its musical origin when he wrote in *A Tale of Two Cities* (1859): "The sounders of three-fourths of the notes in the whole gamut of crime"; and the critic and wit Dorothy Parker said of Katharine Hepburn's performance in a Broadway first night: "She ran the entire gamut of her emotions from A to B." It should not be – though it often is – confused with *gambit*, which was originally an Italian wrestling-term, *gambetto*, tripping the opponent's heel, hence the gambit in a game or sport with which a player tries to obtain some advantage over an opponent.

gaol/jail Two words with the same pronunciation and meaning, and of the same provenance, but with different spellings: *gaol* probably survived only because it was the spelling used in old English legal documents in preference to *jail*. In all other respects gaol causes confusion – to spell-check computer programmes as well as to foreigners who, being more familiar with football than law, tend to see it as a mistyping of "goal". One of the alternative English spellings was "gayhole", which could lead to spurious ETYMOLOGIES.

gauge/gouge A *gauge*, from an old French word *gauger*, to measure, can be either a measuring-device or else a fixed standard of size or thickness (e.g. of sheet-metal or paper). To *gauge* means to ascertain (sometimes estimate) such measurements, also feeling, opinions, etc. It is confusingly pronounced "gage", and often mis-spelt "guage". A *gouge*, which looks as if it should be from French *gouge* but in fact is "probably of Celtic origin" (*OED*), is a kind of chisel with a rounded cutting-edge (instead of the more common flat one) with which to make rounded grooves or holes, in wood or stone. It is pronounced with an "ow" sound.

geezer/geyser A travel-writer gushed in the *Daily Telegraph* that she had "enjoyed some ancient geezers" in Iceland. There is no accounting for taste: "Geezer is a term of derision applied to men, usually *but not necessarily* elderly..." (*OED*). Thank you for that. But in Iceland a *geysir* is a hot spring, a natural phenomenon which, incidentally, in 1878 gave an English firm of plumbers the idea of patenting *Maughan's Patent Geyser*, a bathroom contrivance "so constructed that any quantity of hot water can be drawn from it with the utmost facility". *Geezer* apparently comes from Northumbrian slang for a rough actor or mummer.

genteel/gentile/gentle Up to around World War II every middle-class person would have been pleased to be described as *genteel*, that is, of superior rank, whereas today the word is often used SARDONICally. There are, for example, "genteel" ways of holding a table-knife: like a pencil, the little finger delicately crooked and pointing outward. *Gentile* occurs in the Vulgate for members of tribes other than the Jewish ones (see also ETHNIC), and simply meant heathen. It comes from the Latin *gens*, a nation, *gentilis*, of a nation (and in the French *gentil* has developed a different meaning – *très gentil*, very nice). In modern use gentile has shed the "heathen" insult but still exclusively denotes non-Jews. When the *Liverpool Daily Post* described shops of the John Lewis Partnership as "rather gentile stores", it meant "genteel", of course – but was accidentally correct: the largely Welsh 19th century founders of the John Lewis Partnership were gentiles whereas their contemporary, David Lewis Cohen, philanthropic "Friend of the People" and founder of the rival Lewis's, was not. *Gentle* is not only related to genteel but originally meant the same: well-born, springing from a family "of position", hence the description of "gentleman". Like many mediaeval words (see NICE), gentle has had several meanings, including "enchanted or haunted by fairies". When fishermen speak of their *gentles* they mean the maggots they use for bait.

geriatric/gerontic In its strict sense *geriatric* describes those who are both old *and* sick, or at any rate old and attended by a doctor. The word is constructed from the Greek prefix *ger-* (*geras*, old) and *iatros*, a physician. To describe old age on its own, whether the person is sick or not, the appropriate word is *gerontic*, from *geron*, an old man.

gibbets/giblets "Highwaymen were hanged from the giblets..." claimed a reporter in the *Leicester Herald and Mercury*. Unlikely – unless they were strung up with chicken entrails. *Gibbets* came from the French *gibet*, gallows. *Giblets* were also originally French and meant a stew or ragout – into which presumably all manner of otherwise useless meat was thrown.

gigolo/giglet/toyboy/cicisbeo/poodlefaker The *cicisbeo* is of uncertain origin, says the *OED*, but possibly an inverted corruption of an Italian endearment, *bel cece*, beautiful chick; or, surely more likely, uninverted, from the French *chiche beau*. In Italian a *cicisbeo* is a "a knot or ribbon, such as may be worn by a *cavalier servente*, fastened to his sword-hilt or walking-stick, etc." – so perhaps the *cicisbeo* is named after the fashion accessory he affected (and could thus serve also as a word for the at-present-nameless little support-ribbons people wear to display their solidarity with some cause, minority or grievance – different colours for different areas of support). Anglicized as *chichisbee*, it was an object of contempt – or envy: Lady Mary Wortley Montagu, in a letter of 1718: "The custom of cecisbeos...I know not whether you have ever heard of those animals." The *cicisbeo* was replaced first by the *gigolo* and later the *toyboy* – but whereas a toyboy implies a younger man, a cicisbeo can be an escort of any age. A gigolo is a supposedly handsome, elegant (possibly but not necessarily effeminate) man who cultivates the company of older, usually married, women; or is kept by one. The OED has gigolo as the masculine counterpart of a *gigole*, French for a tall, thin woman, charmingly anglicized by Shakespeare as a *giglet* – though this is, in turn, explained as "a lewd, wanton, empty-headed girl, given to vapid remarks and giggles"; and in 1885 *Chambers's Journal* asked, with NICE prescience, "Why should female clerks in the postal service consist of pert giglets hardly out of their teens?" It was in use from the 14th century until late Victorian days, when the statutory hiring-fairs for serving-girls were still known as "Giglet Fairs". (*Giglet* would make a welcome change from the done-to-death *bimbo*). Arnold Schoenberg wrote a cabaret song (yes, a *cabaret* song) which he called "Gigerlette". Finally, a *poodle-faker*, in English late 19th/early 20th-century officers' slang (briefly revived in the Royal Air Force in World War II) was "a man who cultivates female society, especially for the purpose of professional advancement; a ladies' man, a socialite; also, a young, newly commissioned officer"; later it acquired suggestions of effeminacy (*OED*). In other words, a poodle-faker was a military version of the gigolo. More liaison-fodder will be found under CATAMITE.

gild/guild/guilt To *gild* is to cover with gold, and that which is so covered or plated is *gilt* or *gilded*. These words have nothing to do with *guilt* (as opposed to innocence), e.g. "Princess Diana's guilt dressing-case"; nor with *guilds*, like the ancient associations of trades and crafts. Frequent punning by headline-writers does nothing to help us to sort out the difference.

go/goeth See YE/ OLDE/THE OLD.

go missing/disappear Before, during and after World War II, some unfortunate people were reported missing, were lost, or simply *disappeared*. They did not consciously *go missing*, as they might go shopping or pub-crawling. A former Labour minister and the fictional Reginald Perrin in a TV series intentionally faked their disappearance but they, too, did not go missing. Reports like "She went missing after going shopping at Tesco" are penned as if they were nothing out of the ordinary. It is a tiresome kneejerk news cliché. If newsmen had had anything to do with it, Janacek's opera *Diary of the Man who Disappeared* would have been named in English *Diary of the Man who Went Missing*.

googly/gooly/google As every cricket BUFF knows, a *googly* is "a ball which breaks from the off though bowled with apparent leg-break action", and is an attempt by the bowler to deceive the batsman. *Goolies* may also figure in the game, but only accidentally and painfully, when struck by a ball, for they are the testicles. This is not merely cricketing usage but long-established school and general slang. The word comes from *gooly*, Hindustani *goli*, a bullet, ball or pill. The successful internet search-engine "Google" may have been named after the cricketing googly, defined in Baker's *Dictionary of Australian Slang* (1941) as "an awkward question which a person would rather not answer". Like bowling a googly.

gopher/gofer/goffer An article in the *Independent on Sunday* reported the appointment as Professor of Music at Cambridge University of a composer called Alexander Gopher. Circumstantial evidence and a little foreknowledge suggested that this previously unknown musician was probably the distinguished composer Alexander Goehr. Perhaps the writer ran his copy through a computer spell-check, which had never encountered "goehr" and suggested "gopher" instead. When the Lord, according to Genesis 6.14, ordered Noah to make himself an ark He specified "gopher wood", though Biblical areas of the world seem not to grow it: the nearest appears to be the American yellow-wood tree, *Cladrastis tinctoria*. According to *Webster's Dictionary* a *gopher* is also a burrowing rat – not to be confused with *goffers*, which are frills on a lady's bonnet made with a goffering-iron; nor with a *gofer* (sometimes incorrectly written "gopher"), a menial worker in films and TV who runs errands – sent out to "go for" things needed in the production. See also TWOFER.

gourmet/gourmand/foodie Both *gourmets* and *gourmands* are lovers of food, but whereas the gourmet is (or claims to be) a food expert, talks at length about it and does much sniffing, squeezing and tasting, the gourmand is a glutton who just eats it – lots of it – taking the enjoyment to excess without necessarily informing himself of recipes, ingredients or other niceties. Wise William Caxton in 1491 warned, "Take none hede to gourmans & glotons which ete more than is to theym necessary." See also under GRUMMET/GROMIT for a gourmet who is an expert on wine. If there had been no *junkies* in the 1960s and 70s there would have been no *foodies* in the 80s, when this term was first spotted, in *Harpers and Queen* ("one who is particular about food, a gourmet"). See also BULIMIA, under ANOREXIA/BULIMIA.

graduate/postgraduate/graduand "Dear Sir–I am a postgraduate in English Studies…" opens many a letter sent daily to potential employers. Suggestion for a pompous reply: "Dear Applicant–I am a pedant. When you began your university course you were an *undergraduate*. When you lined up to shake hands in exchange for your degree diploma, you were, briefly, a *graduand*. As soon as you got it – God knows how – you became a *graduate*. You were never a *postgraduate*. The only person who can be called "a postgraduate" is a dead graduate. However, should you decide to study for another degree you would become, not a postgraduate, but a postgraduate *student*. Is that clear?" See also ALUMNUS/SOPHOMORE,

grand/grandiloquent A celebrity magazine-writer, searching for a grander adjective than plain *grand*, gushed about "Princess Margaret in her grandiloquent drawing room…" If only those walls could speak — for *grandiloquent*, from *grand* + *loquus*, speech (also sometimes *magniloquent*), means speaking grandly, though what is now usually meant is pompously. See also ROTUND/OROTUND.

great grand/great-grand When used as a designation of kinship, e.g. great-grandfather, great-great-grandmother, great-uncle, etc., this always needs at least one hyphen, unless written as one word, like grandfather. This avoids confusion between someone's great-uncle and his great uncle – thrusting greatness on him – or attributing size and grandeur to his great grand mother, unless she was a lady who was both great and grand. A columnist on *The Times* compounded this nonsense with eccentric mispunctuation, "…the great, great, granddaughter of the first Earl of Oxford".

gregarious/egregious One of Mrs Malaprop's favourites. At a quick glance the two words look alike – and curiously both are related to sheep, lambs or other animals that con*gregate* in flocks. A *gregarious* person is fond of company – from Latin *grex*, a flock or herd, and hence *gregis*, inclined to associate with others of one's kind. The herd, on the other hand, might shun him because he does not fit in, is perhaps of the wrong colour, is taller, has an extra leg or is in some other way unacceptable. He is therefore *egregious*, from Latin *e-* out (of) + *grex*, flock – for he stands out from the rest. Later usage made *egregiousness* pejorative – for after all outstanding people often find themselves unpopular with the herd – but early examples from the Bible, Shakespeare, Marlowe and others confirm that it was first a compliment. Thus Sir Thomas Hobbes (1656): "I am not so egregious a mathematician as you are".

gremlins/little people The *OED* suggests that *gremlins* got their name by analogy with goblins, or *little people*, which if true would agree with Charles Graves who, in his book *The Thin Blue Line* (1941), says of a World War II pilot "...the Little People – a mythological bunch of good and bad fairies originally invented by the Royal Naval Air Service in the Great War...those awful little people, the Gremlins, who run up and down the wing with scissors going 'snip, snap, snip', made him sweat." After World War II gremlins were demobilized and entered civilian life with a vengeance, joining the firm that practises MURPHY'S LAW – motto: "If anything can go wrong it will." A *Daily Telegraph* columnist: "Gremlins were at work in this column last week..." ; and in broadcasting many a technical mistake or unplanned HIATUS is attributed to them.

grill/grille/grid "The Sheik's wives peeped out from behind a grill..." claimed *The Liverpool Daily Post*. Not unless they were slaving over their master's kebabs (Western habits are springing up everywhere), for *grilles* are gratings or screens, and have an *e*, whereas *grills* are for cooking and have none, though they might have some sort of metal *grid* to let the fat drip through. See also BARBECUE/BARBEQUE/BARBEQ etc., and BOIL/BROIL.

grim/gruesome *Grim* means savage, harsh, daring, determined, stern, unrelenting, merciless, etc. But because it seems like almost a contraction of *gruesome* it has become the all-purpose, snappy news adjective to describe anything to do with the aftermath of death ("the grim reaper") especially by violence – often the discovery of mutilated victims of accidents or murder; particularly the exhumation of corpses. The current vogue-term "body parts" often figures in such reports. Whenever police are called in to investigate, or gravediggers to exhume corpses, the words "grim task" leap to the page as if by reflex action.

grisly/grizzly/gristly *Grisly* describes something that causes horror, terror or fear; like GRIM/GRUESOME, above, it has been in use since the Middle Ages – one of Chaucer's favourites. But the *Guardian* described a "grizzly, detailed exploration of [a gruesome murder]", and elsewhere, conversely, a "gristly bear". Bears and babies are *grizzly*, that is, grey-coloured, as in Shakespeare's *Antony and Cleopatra* (1606), "To the boy Caesar send this grizzled head", or grumpily grumbling. *Gristly* is appropriate only for tough tissue or cartilage found in meat – and cookery columns.

grummet/gromet/gromit/washer "A gromit is a tiny tube that is inserted into the opening of the eardrum..." claimed Susan Clark, Health Journalist OF THE YEAR, in the *Sunday Times*. The object a doctor inserts into a glue-ear is a *grummet*, which in engineering applications can also be a kind of *washer*. *Gromit*, along with Wallace, is a character in a series of films by the AWARD-WINNING Nick Park – and a cleverer choice: in Sussex dialect a *gromet* or grummet is an awkward boy; in sailors' slang a cabin-boy; and in the vocabulary of the GOURMET/GOURMAND a wine-taster's assistant. A possible etymological connection between a gromet and a (small) groom has also been suggested.

guidelines/guides/rules Guidelines were originally real lines – also known as guide-ropes – which have existed in specialist applications since the 19th century. The abstract and figurative guidelines, now so common in daily journalism they are hardly noticed, are a literal translation of the German *Richtlinien*.

— H —

ha/ho/ha-ha/hey/huh/right? etc. *Ha* is "an exclamation expressing surprise, wonder, joy, suspicion, indignation, etc."– depending on the intonation used; and much the same applies to *hey* and *ho*. When reduplicated, *haha* represents laughter, as does *hoho* (convention insists that Father Christmas utters hearty cries of it). These syllables (being echoic) go back to the Greeks and Romans and occur in early English. Shakespeare was fond of the exclamation "Ho!" – and in *King Lear* (1608) the line "Dinner, Ho, Dinner!" has given rise to the suggestion that the King had a Chinese cook (for Hamlet's Irish friend, see PAT). As a hyphenated noun, *ha-ha* is a sunken garden-boundary invented by 17th-century French landscape-designers (occasionally seen also in English gardens) to afford a view uninterrupted by fences. "Hey!" must find a place here as a new, trendy interjection over-used by columnists ("but *hey! that's fashion!*"). *Huh?* is interrogatory and often occurs in fictional dialogue, as though a speaker were calling for reassurance. The same effect is produced by slipping the occasional *right?* into the conversation – habits associated with American speakers, right? The *Canadian Journal of Linguistics* in 1972: "Whatever its origin and history, *huh?* is currently in widespread use in the United States." To where, the writer might have added, it could have been carried by the Pilgrim Fathers, especially if they took a copy of Thomas Middleton's *A Mad World, My Masters* (1608): "There's old for thee! huh, let her want for nothing, master doctor."

hack/flack/flak *Flak* is the German acronym of **F**lugzeug**a**b**we**h**r**k**a**none and nothing else (the word means anti-aircraft gun, literally "defence gun against flying things"). Members of the British armed forces adopted this abbreviation into service slang, from where it passed into general use. It even acquired a secondary slang meaning, as in "taking the flak", taking blame or punishment (a meaning not known in German). The spelling *flack* is wrong for both these senses: an American derogatory word for a press publicist or journalist, as *hack* is in English. See also ERSATZ.

haemorrhage/bleed/blood loss *Haemorrhage* comes from the two Greek words for blood and raging respectively. It is medically appropriate only for a calamitous and probably life-threatening loss of blood, but for lay persons and HACKS has become a cliché – making ordinary *bleeding* sound more dramatic. Also, figuratively, for concepts such as the dramatic depletion of manpower, funds, etc. Unfortunately news words based on scientific terms soon enter would-be-posh popular language, where they sit incongruously. A Liverpool woman went to her GP and said, "Doctor, I'm haemorrhaging", though she showed no outward sign of blood loss. The doctor said, "Where are you bleeding from?" She replied, "Oh, from Knotty Ash, doctor!" See also ARTERIES/VEINS

hair's breadth/"hare's breath" *By a hair's breadth* may figure in an account of a narrow escape, that is, by a very small margin, no bigger than the breadth of a hair. A *hare's breath* would be of no help. The confusion is made worse by the fact that many people pronounce breadth and width "breath" and "with", without sounding the *d*. Breath may also be BATED, but not baited.

haj/pilgrimage *Haj* is Arabic for a pilgrimage, specifically to MECCA. It is not suitable for devotional jaunts to Lourdes, Walsingham or Canterbury, which are *pilgrimages* – a word that occurs in many languages and various forms, and is almost as old as Christianity itself. The spelling *hajj* is also valid.

hallmarks/signs Almost daily statements like "Police say the shooting bears all the hallmarks of a gangland killing" make one wonder if they are crime-stoppers or silversmiths. Life in the outside world gets ever more EXPLICIT, yet PC Plod clings to his old euphemisms – see also ELEMENTS MALES, TARGET, and ESSAY/ASSAY.

hangar/hanger Coats are hung (not HANGED, see below) on *hangers*, but aircraft are housed in *hangars*. The purpose of a *Guardian* headline

HANGARS AROUND

for a picture of airport surveillance-men in which no actual hangars were shown, would have been to invite groans from colleagues – or confuse shaky spellers.

hanged/hung Ian Herbert in the *Independent*: "The men...were believed to have been hung for their crimes in the village's Hangman's Lane..." Pictures and game are *hung*; people, regrettably, *hanged* (and Parliaments, committees and juries can also be hung, i.e. undecided). Men described as "well hung" are supposedly (sexually) well-endowed. To say or write, "He hung himself" is as absurd as "She brung me a present". The *Daily Express* headline"

QUEEN MOTHER TO BE HUNG IN GLAMIS CASTLE

meant her portrait, not the late Royal CENTENARIAN.

have/of The fact that this unequal pair finds a place in this book is a reflection of the calamitous dumbing-down English has suffered. The *Independent* magazine carried a full-page advertisement for Philips Dictation (!) Systems containing the interesting sentence: "In the time it took Dickens to write *A Tale of Two Cities* he could of told us a dozen more." A correspondence followed, most letters deriding the advertising agency that produced such a solecism. But one trendy educationist wrote: "Pupils who write *could of* are applying good phonic principles of writing because they always hear the unstressed 'have' of 'could have' reduced in pronunciation" (someone should have told him that one of the delights of English is that what you hear is not always what you get). Then the Managing Director of the agency responsible weighed in, to grovel. He apologized "most sincerely" to readers and to his clients, Philips Dictation Systems, explaining: "'Could of' was simply a typesetting error that slipped *passed* the keenest eyes [My italics]." It would of been better for him to of kept quiet.

havoc/devastation/disarray/disorder *Havoc* has its origin in a mediaeval French word, *havot*, then used by the French in the phrase *crier havot*, a war-cry which in the Middle Ages was a military order for troops to pillage and massacre without quarter. As *crier havoc*, the earliest use, in legal Anglo-French, is dated 1385 by the *OED*. It was Shakespeare who kept "crying havoc" alive for all time (with the famous quotation you will find under DOGS OF WAR). To journalists havoc is a convenient and emotive death-and-disaster word ideal for reports of earthquakes and floods. *Havoc* is usually wreaked; more rarely and less happily, wrought; but in earlier times, before clichés ruled the jobbing writer, people exercised greater choice: they *played* havoc, *created* havoc, *made* havoc (with...) See also DOGS OF WAR/MERCENARIES.

head/headmaster/headmistress/head-teacher *Head* as an
abbreviation of *headmaster* used to be considered disrespectful and would
not have been uttered in a headmaster's or headmistress's presence.
Today it is their preferred description, being non-discriminatory. Indeed
headmaster and *headmistress* have been declared politically incorrect, with
head-teacher an acceptable compromise. See
CHAIRMAN/CHAIR/CHAIRWOMAN/CHAIRPERSON.

heel/heal The *Guardian* wrote of an editor of the fashion magazine the
Tatler: "…there are plenty who would like to stick the knife, the boot and
a stiletto heal in"; and the same paper also described someone as "well-
healed". Both writers meant *heel*, but this is not only the back of the foot
(or shoe): it is also slang for a rotter, a disreputable, untrustworthy
person, invariably male. But to be well-heeled one needs to be more than
simply well-shod (and not "down-at-heel"): generally well equipped and
supplied, with money as well as necessities and comforts – which would
include decent shoes only incidentally. When Mark Twain asked, in a
letter dated 1866, "Are you heeled?" he meant armed with a pistol,
which is still the understanding in US slang: "well-heeled" in full.

heir/heiress Whereas *heir* is normally used in the proper way, e.g. to
indicate family succession and, possibly but not necessarily, a man's
expected inheritance (of money, property or a title), *heiress* is often brought
out by journalists as shorthand code meaning "the daughter of a very rich
man". At any rate they *assume* him to be rich; since the MEDIA are unlikely
to be privy to any testamentary arrangements he might have made: for all
they know daddy might be leaving all his money to his cat, and the cat to
his mistress. Qualifications are common, e.g. "Gold Heiress" for a metal-
broker's daughter; or "Turkey Heiress" for a Miss Matthews, whose father
made a fortune selling this particular type of poultry.

helpmate/helpmeet Of *helpmate* the *OED* says that the word is "chiefly
applied to a wife or husband" and it has indeed been a favourite for
memorial inscriptions to (usually) wives, since the 18th century. In 19th-
century usage the word erroneously became *helpmeet* through a misreading
of the passage in the Bible where the Lord declared, in Genesis, that man
should not be alone: "I will make him an helpe meet for him" (which,
incidentally, the updated *New English Bible* of 1970 with exquisite political
correctness changes to "I will provide a partner for him"). The *Authorized
Version*'s "An helpe meet for him" meant *meet* or *mete*, meaning proper,

125

suitable, as in Chaucer's "There nis no womman to him half so mete". More MEAT/MEET/METE confusions under this heading.

hero/veteran/ex-soldier A *hero*, from Latin and Greek *heros*, is one who shows or has shown extraordinary courage, usually in time of war and in the face of mortal danger. One who merely *took part* in a campaign, whether as hero, coward, unwilling foot-soldier or deserter, is a *veteran*, from Latin *veteranus*, old – a "vet" in the USA (confused in British English with vets who are animal-doctors – US veterinarians). But that is not good enough for the MEDIA, which like to elevate and dramatize anyone who was merely present to "World War II Hero" or "Gulf War Hero", not simply "a former soldier". In Zimbabwe during the 1990s, Robert Mugabe's teenage thugs who were not even born when he took power were officially called "war veterans".

hiatus/hiccup/lacuna/mistake A *hiatus* is neither a *hiccup* (in the popular sense of a small error or accident), nor a *mistake*, but is the Latin word for a gap, opening or hole, usually one that should not be there (exemplified in medicine by the *hiatus hernia*, a protrusion through a wrong opening). A short, unplanned silence, whether on the radio or during the course of a play or musical performance, might be called a hiatus (for which GREMLINS are usually blamed) or a *lacuna*, Latin for a hollow or gap; but when a music critic wrote, "There was a slight hiatus in the wind section when the first oboe played a B flat instead of a B natural," he intended to tell his readers that the note was wrong, not missing – though most of all he wanted to tell them that he *noticed*, even if they did not.

highly suspicious/deeply suspicious At first thought the two appear to be interchangeable, but usage seems to suggest a subject-object distinction, in that a person may be *deeply* suspicious of something that he finds *highly* suspicious.

him/his One does not have to be a poet, or know about such old-fashioned technical terms as "possessive gerunds", to *sense* that the lines

> The manner of his leaving of the room
> Was a matter of his going to his doom.

would sound absurd as "the manner of *him* leaving" and "a matter of *him* going". An example of today's dumbed-down usage.

hindi/hindu *Hindi* is the language, principally of Hindustan in Northern India, but its people are *Hindu*.

hoard/horde "The mediaeval Viking-style boat found in the River Severn…will reveal a whole horde of secrets about mediaeval history" – the *Guardian*. "Hoards of students are arriving at Lime Street by every train" – the *Liverpool Daily Post*. Wrong way round. *Hoard*, a Teutonic word for a store or secretly hidden material; but *horde*, from Turkish *orda*, a troop or band of soldiers, usually thundering across the plains on horseback. If uncertain which is which we might try store instead of a hoard, crowds instead of hordes. See also CACHE.

hoi polloi/the people *Hoi polloi* is Greek for the majority, the people, the common herd, LUMPEN and the various other terms under that cross-reference. Usually used as "the hoi polloi", which is a tautology, as *hoi* in Greek means "the".

holocaust/shoah At the height of World War II, when Enigma-decoded messages revealed for the first time the systematic murder of millions of Russians, Poles, Jews and others, Winston Churchill said, "We are in the presence of a crime without a name." Unbeknown to him, on 5 December 1942 the *News Chronicle* had already named it, though the term was not to catch on until the 1950s: "Holocaust… Nothing else in Hitler's record is comparable to his treatment of the Jews. The word has gone forth that the Jewish peoples are to be exterminated… The conscience of humanity stands aghast." Then, on 23 March 1943, *Hansard* reported a certain peer as saying, "The Nazis go on killing. If this rule could be relaxed, some hundreds, possibly a few thousands, might be enabled to escape from this holocaust." They were prophetic words, for at that time the Allies knew about the extermination-camps but not the gas ovens – and *holocaust* comes from the Greek *hol-*, all + *kaustos*, burnt, or burnt whole, referring to the Greeks' sacrifice-by-fire. After a popular book that was made into a film the word entered the language, though many Jews prefer the more accurate Hebrew *shoah*, catastrophe.

home counties/southern-english counties The *home counties* are supposedly those nearest or near to London. What sheer, naked metropolitan arrogance. Home is where the heart is – and many hearts – mine, for a start – prefer to beat elsewhere in England. To avoid giving offence to touchy northerners (not to mention the people of Cornwall, Devon, etc.), one could specify Surrey, Kent, Essex, Hertfordshire, Buckinghamshire, Berkshire or Sussex and what used to be Middlesex.

homophobia/anti-homosexual *Phobia* is Greek for fear, and *homophobia* means fear of man, as shown by an animal that runs away at the approach of a human. What people now mean by *homophobia* is a *dislike* of, or prejudice against, homosexuals; not *fear*.

hoodoo/voodoo Both refer to superstitious matters or behaviour, and indeed *hoodoo* is a variant of *voodoo*; but while the first is used in general terms and in much the same way as JINX, voodoo is more specifically a form of witchcraft, originally African, practised by people in the West Indies, especially Haiti.

hoops/whoops Laughter comes in onomatopoeic *whoops*, not *hoops*. Hoops are rings or bands that go round the staves of a barrel, or enclose the skirts of 18th-century ladies.

hoover/hoovering/vacuum-cleaner/vacuuming *Hoover* is now a generic term for a vacuum-cleaner, *hoovering* for vacuum-cleaning, with *vacuuming* an unsatisfactory alternative. The first Hoover was produced in 1908 by the Hoover Suction Company and Adrian Room's *Dictionary of Trade Name Origins* reveals that W. H. Hoover (1849–1932) did not invent but merely bought and marketed the cleaner, which in fact was the work of J. Murray Spangler, a caretaker in an Ohio department store. Room suggests that "Spangler" and "spangling" would have made a better word for a cleaner and its action, in view of its association with "glittering" and "sparkling". Unlike the firms that sell formica and Y-fronts, Messrs Hoover seem not to object when their name is applied to other products of the same kind.

host/hostage/hostile/hospitable A writer in the *Cambrian News* (from an extract quoted by the *Guardian*) expressed "...gratitude to the twinning committee and the people of Saint Brieuc for the exceptional hostility shown to us during our recent visit". Blame the similarity of the Latin roots for that: *hostis* was always an enemy while *hostage* derives from *obsidio*, meaning a siege and thence *obses*, a one caught in a siege; but *hospis* could mean either a stranger – who could turn out to be *hostile* – or else a *host* offering *hospitality* to a stranger – and the word *guest* is also derived from *hospis*. It became not merely a two-faced word but one that spawned numerous meanings: a host can be a company of armed men, or a peaceful multitude of angels – the heavenly host; the Lord God of Hosts as well as the bread consecrated in the Eucharist (which believers regard as the body of Christ), or simply a large crowd, whether friendly or hostile; as well as a host of other things. Arab people are known for their hospitality to strangers and are truly hospitable – but they also developed the ancient Middle-Eastern practice of hostage-taking of unspeakable cruelty.

hotel/pub/hostlery Historians studying 19th- and 20th-century street-directories of northern-English industrial towns have expressed astonishment at the disproportionately large number of hotels available in places where few tourists set foot. The answer lies in a north-south semantic divide. What northerners call a *hotel*, the southern English know as a *pub*, or public-house. Although northern-English drinkers also call them pubs, their formal description as hotels is an echo of old laws that obliged innkeepers to provide rooms for travellers, if necessary in the landlord's own quarters. These obligations remained in force long after the Rose and Crown, the Great Eastern Hotel or the King's Arms were catering only for drinkers, not travellers; and numerous pubs in the north of England to this day genteelly prefer to call themselves hotels. The related word *hostelry*, which implies accommodation, has largely been annexed by facetious newspaper columnists, who "repair thither" to "sample mine host's powerful brew", etc.

hottentot/khoi-khoin Seventeenth-century travellers returning from Africa gave the nicknames *Hottentots*, meaning stammerers, to members of the Khoisanid race they had encountered – "on account of their clucking speech". This "clucking" must be an early reference to what modern speech experts call the "Xosa click", which is required for the authentic pronunciation of their now more acceptable name, *Khoi-Khoin*. See also ESKIMO/INUIT and other cross-references to the politically correct renaming of natives.

hue-and-cry/ "hugh and cry"/tally ho *Hue*, from old French *huer*, from the 1300s meant a shout or hoot, an outcry or cry of pursuit, in hunting or war. "Why dost thou me pursue with cry of hounds, with blast of horne, with halloo and with hue?" wrote George Turberville in *The Noble Art of Venerie or Hunting* (1575). As *hue-and-cry* it became the standard expression for the hunting of supposed felons, and if necessary was cried aloud by an aggrieved party or a constable (who later used his whistle or rattle to reinforce the noise). "Tally ho!" was presumably reserved for fox-hunting. The *English Police Gazette*, containing notices of wanted criminals, was subtitled *Hue-and-Cry* and distributed nationally and internationally, the precursor of today's computerized communications. *Hugh and Cry* is a nonsensical misreading. The mediaeval word hue relating to colour seems to be unrelated.

human/humane Both come from Latin *humanus*, relating to something belonging to man, but the two forms have acquired different shades of meaning expressed by a difference in spelling, stress and pronunciation.

humour/humorist/humorous/humor *Humour* loses its second *u* when modified to *humorous*. There seems to be no particular reason for this, though both *humourous* and *humourist* look cumbersome and wrong. The same applies to other word modifications, like glamour/glamorize, vapour/vaporize, etc. Americans avoid the problem by spelling nouns like *humor* and *glamor* without the *u* near the end of the word, just as they duck out of having to make a PRACTICE/PRACTISE decision by using the same spelling for both. It can be only a matter of time before we copy them. From duck-out to cop-out.

hunchback/kyphosis/kyphotic The problem of what to call certain medical conditions without giving offence has been brought to the fore by the need for political correctness. The medical name for an outward curvature of the spine is *kyphosis* or *cyphosis* (pronounced the same but written differently, according to the writer's preferred way of spelling anglicized Greek). The traditional but crude *hunchback* is surely better avoided when speaking of living persons; also doctors' informal name "Dowager's Hump" for a similar condition that afflicts elderly women. (Inward curvature, curiously enough, is called *lordosis*, but has no connection with dowagers or lords). None of this justifies meddling with history – as an English theatre company did by changing the play known in English as *The Hunchback of Notre Dame* to *The Bellringer of Notre Dame*. This leaves Australian surfers in a quandary, as they perform "a quasimodo – a surfing feat performed in a crouching position".

hurdy-gurdy/barrel-organ/street-piano/hurly burly Several confusions exist and are daily repeated and compounded. The commonest error is to describe *all* handle-turned instruments as hurdy-gurdies. The *hurdygurdy* (both the one-word and hyphenated forms are correct) is a stringed instrument "bowed" with a rosined wooden wheel instead of a hand-held bow; and playing it requires a great deal more skill than merely turning the handle attached to the wheel. The *barrel-organ*, too, is played with a handle, but has organ-pipes, not strings, to produce the sound. The *street-piano*, miscalled both barrel-organ and hurdygurdy, is a kind of keyboardless piano whose hammers are activated by turning a handle, a pinned barrel taking the place of a keyboard. This may also be – accurately – called a *barrel-piano*. None of the above is related to the *hurly burly*, a pleasing reduplication word which the *OED* says means "commotion, tumult, strife, uproar, turmoil, confusion," adding "formerly a more dignified word than now". It has been known since the middle of the 16th century, and seems to have started life as *hurling and burling* – but confused an estate-agent, who complained of "...the hurdygurdy of modern life" on BBC Radio 4.

hurl/throw The old Germanic word *hurl* has all but disappeared from ordinary speech: people prefer simply to *throw*, chuck, lob or toss things. But hurl is alive, if only in news prose. Where we throw stones, MEDIA people habitually report ROCKS being hurled; and people are hurled to the FLOOR where ordinary folk are merely thrown to the ground. This is one of many examples of the way news English fossilizes or falsifies the language. As in the next paragraph, for example.

hurtle/fall *Hurtle* is another archaically STILTED news-word seldom used by ordinary people, just as falling people or objects plunge or plummet, anything that goes upwards SOARS and what is thrown is HURLED (above).

hypo/hyper/hypocrite *Hypo* is the Greek prefix meaning below or lower, whereas *hyper* means above, over or higher (see also next entry). But although someone who is *hypercritical* is over-critical, a *hypocrite*, confusingly, is not sub-critical but comes from a different background – from the Greek stage, where the hypocrite was the actor who played the goody-goody on the stage, but reverted to his own wicked ways when not on stage. And see below.

hypothermia/hyperthermia In the simple old days unfortunate people died of cold, or froze to death. They still do, but newspapers call it *hypothermia*, though sometimes they misprint it *hyperthermia* – which would mean too *much* heat.

I

i/me/myself Like WHO/WHOM this and related constructions are often used with a false gentility, being also known as Nobs' Pronouns. Nobs tend to say and write "...from my wife and I" because they feel that "me" is vulgar. If they think away the wife they realise that "from I" is absurd; so they play safe with "from my wife and myself" – and in church probably sing "Abide with Myself" and go on to see *The King and Myself*. But it is a genteelism well worn by time: John Gerard in his *Herball* (1636 edition) says "[Crane's bill] prevaileth mightily in healing inward wounds, as my selfe have likewise proved".

icon/role model *Icon* is Greek for a picture or image, also a religious artefact that usually shows Jesus and/or the Virgin Mary. Today's alleged icons are more accurately *role models*. The word went into common use from about 1980, when some imaginative computer programme designer applied it to the now familiar small, symbolic picture that appears on a screen to represent a particular option. Thanks largely to this, not the Greek Orthodox religion, we now have gay icons, fashion icons, sporting icons, etc.

illegible/ineligible/intelligible *Illegible* is a common sports malapropism – especially among football commentators: teams may "field an illegible player". Illegible, from Latin *legere*, to read, is that which cannot be read. What they mean is *ineligible*, from Latin *eligere*, to choose, which refers to someone who is not allowed to be chosen. *Intelligible* is what most footballers are not when they speak, and comes from Latin *intellegere*, to understand.

illusion/delusion Both are concerned with deception, Latin *illudere*, to deceive, which gave us *illusions*, unreal attributions of reality, false beliefs, etc., – as well as the *illusionist*, another name for a conjurer (see also IMPRESSIONIST). *Deludere*, to fool, cheat or mock, resulted in *delusions*. The two are often used as synonyms or ALTERNATIVES, but better to be under one's own *illusion* than be *deluded* by someone else.

imaginary/imaginative A fairy-story is *imaginary*, but the person who wrote or told it would have been *imaginative*.

immanent/imminent/eminent *Immanent*, from Latin *im + manere*, to dwell, means inherent, present or abiding; *imminent* from *im + minere*, to impend, to be about to happen (even to hang over, e.g. over one's head, as a threat). *Eminent* comes from *eminere*, to stand out, either physically, like a mountain peak or a six-foot-eight basketball player, or metaphorically, like five-foot-nothing Franz Schubert or Albert Einstein. See also EGREGIOUS.

immured/inured *Immured*, from Latin *im+murus*, means walled in, entombed or shut off. To be *inured*, (usually followed by "to"), from *in + ure*, is to be accustomed, immune or habituated to something.

implacable/impeccable The *Daily Telegraph* claimed that "Lady Pulbrook [had] implacable good taste" – *twice* in the same article, as if to make sure readers knew it was a howler, not a mistyping. *Implacable* is that which cannot be appeased, irreconcilable, inexorable; the opposite of the now rare placable – from Latin *placare*, to please – capable of being pleased, appeased or pacified. What the writer meant to say was that the lady's taste was *impeccable* – from Latin *peccare*, to sin or err, with a negative prefix *im-* – not to be faulted.

implement/implement Marcellus in Shakespeare's *Hamlet* (1602) speaks presciently of the "foreign mart for *im*plements of war" – known today as the international arms trade. Any measures to counter the trade would have to be impl*em*ented.

important/"importantly" Some things are important, others more important or less important, some most important and some unimportant. *Nothing* is "important*ly*". The *OED* recognizes this by calling "importantly" a "quasi adjective". Any statement beginning "More importantly" – and we hear and see this nonce-word every day in all the MEDIA – should be regarded as suspect. "Importantly" is valid only as an adverb, as perhaps when describing a person's exaggerated sense of his own importance – for example, a pompous man like a dictator or DIGNITARY who struts "importantly". It is not an adjective, which is why people never say, "More unimportantly"; just as they would not say of a NICE thing "This is very nicely". See also

DIRECT/DIRECTLY, FIRST/"FIRSTLY" – and INITIALLY/FIRSTLY/AT FIRST/IN THE BEGINNING for a way in which a modern Bible might open the Book of Genesis.

impressionist/impersonator To a moderately well-read person an *impressionist* is a member of the school of French painters active from the 1870s, such as Monet and Manet; or a composer (usually but not always French) belonging to a certain group exemplified by Claude Debussy. However, to the avid television-watcher an impressionist is a comedian whose act consists of doing "impressions", or impersonations, of well-known personalities. The same fate has overtaken the famous furniture-makers Chippendale and Sheraton, who are now known chiefly as dancers and hotels respectively. "Madonna and Child" would be a pop-singer and her offspring; and BIG BROTHER a television show, not a character invented by George Orwell.

in extremis/in extreme circumstances/as a last resort A letter from one Robert Pace to Cardinal Wolsey, ca 1530: "Mr Dean off Paulis hath lyen continually synst Thursdaye *in extremis* and is not yit dedde" – which means the poor Dean of St Paul's was in his last THROES, at the very point of death. What it does not mean is as an extreme measure, or *last resort*: a government spokesman, defending the Prime Minister Tony Blair's fleet of cars, wrote of his "people carrier", "Because the Galaxy has folding seats at the back you can actually pack it with eight people *in extremis*." Though in those circumstances an ambulance would be better.

incense/incense Both come from Latin *incendere*, to set alight, which is what one does when burning *in*cense, stressing the first syllable. One can also set feelings alight, figuratively, perhaps to make someone "burn with rage", when the second syllable is stressed and one is in*censed*.

inchoate/incoherent/inarticulate *Inchoate* is derived from Latin *inchoare*, to begin, and means something at an early stage, immature or as yet unformed, but ambitious graduates of the Malaprop College of Journalism like to press it into service as a would-be elegant portmanteau variation of *incoherent* and *inarticulate*, as in "He was inchoate with rage". *Incoherent*, from Latin *in* + *cohaerere*, is that which fails to stick or cling together; *inarticulate* that which is not jointed and, when applied to speaking, is unintelligible. See also COHERENT/COHESIVE.

135

incubation/quarantine *Incubation* is the action of sitting on an egg in order to hatch the young, which is generally performed by birds or reptiles; also the process or phase through which the germs of disease pass between INFECTION/CONTAGION and the development of symptoms. *Quarantine*, from Latin *quarentena*, forty [days] is the time of isolation necessary for being presumed free of the disease. And see below.

incubus/succubus The difference is postural. Latin *in* + *cubare* means to lie *upon*, whereas *sub* + *cubare*, is to lie *underneath* (in fact Latin *succuba* came to mean a whore). An *incubus* was a sexual nightmare that manifested itself as a male spirit or devil that lay upon a sleeper (female, unless presumably special circumstances applied); and a *succubus* a nightmare apparition that lay beneath – both in order to have or attempt to have sex with the sleeper. That, at any rate, was the explanation or excuse given on waking, from either an erotic dream or a real event which the sleeper would wish (or pretend to wish) had not happened. So when in doubt, they said it was all a dream – or else blamed the devil. The naming of the *succubae* proves that there was a "missionary position" before there were missionaries.

incunable/incurable An obituary in the *Daily Telegraph* described a deceased man as an expert on *incurables* although the context made it clear that he was a bibliophile and not a medical man. The writer had probably put *incunables*, but was "corrected". Incunables is the anglicized form of *incunabula*, applied to books printed before 1500 (the word is Latin for swaddling-clothes, and refers to the earliest stages or first traces of anything – in this case the "nappy stage" of printing).

indefensible/undefendable "During the War the Channel Islands were indefensible", a man said on the BBC. This statement is true only in the sense that some of the islanders treasonably collaborated with the occupying Germans: actions that were *indefensible* – that is, unjustifiable and morally inexcusable. What the writer meant was that the Channel Islands were *undefendable*, i.e. incapable of being defended against the invaders. The British legal system insists that even the most indefensible criminals are not undefendable. Only in archaic usage were the two forms sometimes treated as synonymous.

indigent/indolent *Indigent* is used rarely now, usually in tandem, as "the indigent poor" – surely a tautology of sorts, as it comes from Latin *indigere*, to lack, to be destitute? And yet perhaps there is some sense in it, for now we have the oxymoronic "affluent poor" – who exploit (THE) SYSTEM for all they are worth but are officially unemployed. After all, indigent is occasionally employed as if it were the same as its near-soundalike, *indolent*, which means lazy or averse to work.

inequity/iniquity *Iniquity*, a straight translation of Latin *iniquitas*, is wickedness, unrighteousness, and in this sense occurs dozens of times in the Bible. It gradually merged its meaning with *inequity*, also from *iniquitas* but meaning unfairness, gross injustice, unequal treatment, inequality or public wrong. Two words which, while remaining much the same, developed different shades of meaning.

infected/infested The traditional distinction seems to be a matter of size: *infected* with BACTERIA/GERMS but *infested* with rats, mice, lice, fleas, worms, beetles, etc.

infectious/contagious Dr Andrew Boorde, in his *Dyetary of Helthe* (1542), writes: "When the Plages of the Pestylence or the swetynge [sweating] syckenes is in a towne or countree...the people doth fle from the contagious and infectious ayre". *Infectious* comes from Latin *inficere*, to imbue something or somebody with some quality, to dye; but *contagious* from *con + tangere*, to touch together. Hence the wisdom that contagious diseases are transmitted by touch, infectious ones by proximity: the idea of invisibly transmitted micro-organisms like BACTERIA/VIRUSES was not understood until much later.

infer/imply A common inward/outward confusion. To *infer*, from Latin *inferre*, to bring or carry something in, is to draw a conclusion, either from evidence or from known or perceived facts. To *imply*, from *implicare*, to unfold, is to assert or express something that is not formally stated. In other words, one *draws* an *inference* (inwards) and *makes* an *implication* (outwards).

infighting/squabbling *Infighting* is a boxing term which means getting so close to one's opponent that he cannot take a swing. It has been annexed by the news MEDIA (and is often preceded by "political") to mean *squabbling* within a group or political party, usually one engaged in INTERNECINE conflict or strife.

infinite/infinitive/inordinate *Infinite*, from Latin *infinitus*, means unbounded, without end. An *infinitive* is the simple form of a verb, i.e. *to love*, without inflexion or indication as to who is loved or doing the loving. To say "He took an infinitive length of time to make up his mind" may be trying to sound posh but is actually plain wrong. The speaker probably meant *inordinate* – excessive, immoderate or, in a modern sense that is pleasingly redolent of the Latin root, "out of order".

informer/informant Both sorts of persons *inform*, but meanings have diverged. An *informer* in archaic English was in fact a teacher, one who informed his pupil by imparting information (it was formerly an element in newspaper names, like the *Newtown Informer*). An *informant* also informs, but can no longer be called an informer, as this now suggests the clandestine giving of information, to the police or other interested parties. In the press "my informant" simply means someone who gave information, e.g. about a news story.

initially/firstly/at first/in the beginning *At first* and *in the beginning* are better than *initially*, which can sound stilted and would-be posh – perhaps one of the now outmoded "Gasping Adverbial Openers". During the last three decades of the 20th century, journalists' developed an obsession with starting sentences with an adverb followed by an unnecessary comma (in broadcast speech, a gasping breath). This made sentences sound lame and laboured. Such adverbial scene-setters ran the whole GAMUT from A to Z, from "Amazingly" to "Predictably", from "Happily" and "Gloriously" to "Startlingly" and "Unconscionably" (though not "Verily", which had a good run in the Bible but never caught on among secular folk). In my *KEEP TAKING THE TABLOIDS* (Pan Books, 1983) I proposed a *Bible According to Fleet Street*, the Book of Genesis beginning, "*Initially*, God created the heaven and earth. *Basically*, the earth was without form, and void. *Noticeably*, darkness was upon of the face of the deep. *Reportedly*, the spirit of God moved upon the waters. *Loftily*, God said Let there be Light. *Predictably*, there was Light. *Brilliantly*, God called the light Day and *additionally*, the darkness He called Night. *Curiously*, God created man in His own image. *Startlingly*, male and female created he them. *Thankfully*, God saw everything that He had made and, *interestingly*, it was good. *Subsequently*, the evening and the morning were the sixth day…" etc. Mercifully this fad is no longer fashionable. See also "IMPORTANTLY", IRONICALLY and BASICALLY/WELL; and cross-references.

injured/wounded People hurt in civilian events like road-accidents, fights, duels or by cutting themselves with a kitchen-knife, are injured, though their injuries may be described as *wounds*. In battles or other serious warfare they are *wounded*. Even in street battles or violent demonstrations, participants are injured rather than wounded. This is a matter of convention, not rules. See also FLOOR/GROUND and ROCKS/STONES.

insidious/invidious Both have nasty connotations. The Latin *insidiosus* means cunning, deceitful, lying in wait (*insidiae*, ambush), sly, underhand, ARTFUL, stealthy; even a disease can be insidious if it takes one unaware. *Invidious* comes from Latin *invidia* and means ill-will, animosity, envy, giving offence to others, and some even worse things.

in situ/in place *In situ* is Latin for "in (its) (original) place" but is sometimes misunderstood. Overheard: "They said they'd cleaned the carpets in Situ. Well, I don't care where they did them – all I know is they made a lousy job of them." See also PENURY.

instigate/initiate *Instigate*, to urge, cause or incite, spur or stimulate, from Latin *stigare*, to prick. *Initiate*, to start something, from Latin *initium*, the beginning. As Dr Andrew Boorde warned in his *Dyetary of Helthe* (1542): [Too much sleep] "doth instigate and lede a man to synne".

institutionalized/widespread/common *Institutionalized*, now almost invariably coupled with racism or HOMOPHOBIA, and possibly sexism, or some other sort of ism perceived by the speaker or writer, came to the fore after the publication of a report which famously but fatuously ascribed "institutionalized racism" to the police. What it meant was that racialist prejudice is *widespread*, or *common* in any place or group where supposedly macho men congregate – in the police as in the armed forces, in pubs and working-men's clubs. To be institutionalized it would have to be specifically organized.

internecine/brotherly *Internecine* is usually coupled with fighting or warfare, specifically between brothers or members of the same group such as a trades union. Its real meaning is mutual killing, from *inter-* + *necare*, to kill; or "mutually assured destruction" as might happen in a NUCLEAR war. See also INFIGHTING.

intimacy/sex *Intimacy* comes from the Latin *intimatus*, innermost, deepest, as perhaps in a profound or close friendship: a fine, positive and pretty word. Too positive and pretty for prurient Victorian newspaper reporters, who turned it into a euphemism for sexual intercourse. The *OED* traced this use to the *Daily News* of 23 January 1889: "The defendant did not, however, have intimacy with her. He had never been intimate with her"; and the *Westminster Gazette* of 14 December 1907: "She stayed the night with Wood at his father's house… Intimacy took place on that occasion." The euphemism remained in use until about the 1970s, when newspapers started to print EXPLICIT details of sexual encounters, but has rather spoilt the "decent" use of the word, for example an historian's innocent statement that "Disraeli was intimate with the entire Royal family".

into/in to Like ONTO/ON TO, *into* and *in to* have separate functions, as a *Guardian* writer failed to see when reporting a juvenile offender who had "turned himself into a policeman". No, he turned himself *in* – gave himself up – to a policeman.

inveigh/inveigle From a book review in the *Daily Telegraph*: "Shelley appears as a political figure in a long poem inveigling against the Peterloo Massacre." To *inveigle* is to cajole, or persuade someone by guile. The writer meant *inveigh*, which means to speak vehemently against or strongly to denounce something or somebody and is nearly always coupled with "against". It is an alternative spelling of *invey*, to invade, from Latin *invehere*, to carry, bear to or bear into.

ionic/ironic Alas, once again it was a sub-editor on my favourite newspaper, the *You-Know-Who*, who thought he knew better than the architect-author, turning some pillars into "Ironic columns".

ironically/(co)incidentally In statements like "Ironically, forty years later I was standing on the same spot…" irony is not usually involved – more likely coincidence; and the same goes for paradoxically. POIGNANTLY is also often misused in such a context.

it's/its *It's* is the abbreviated form of it is. *Its* is a possessive pronoun, like *his* and *hers*, *ours* and *theirs*, and takes no possessive apostrophe – unlike Tom's, Dick's and Harry's. See also THERE'S/THEIRS/"THEIR'S". The confusion is widespread and time-stained: a 1923 election poster reads: "GREET THE DAWN:GIVE LABOUR IT'S CHANCE".

— J —

jacobin/jacobean/jacobite The *Jacobins* were a group of subversive Paris intellectuals active around the time of the French Revolution. They got their name from the old convent of the Jacobins in Paris, where they secretly met to propagate the ideas of democracy and equality and, by implication, affirm their opposition to royal and clerical tyranny. They would also have supported the sansculottes (see LUMPEN). The description of Jacobin is now often loosely used by political commentators and applied to anyone with anti-royalist views. *Jacobean* (from the Latin *Jacobus,* James) refers to the literature, architecture, etc., of the reign of James I of England/VI of Scotland (1603-1625), whereas *Jacobites* were the adherents of James II who sought to restore him to the throne after his enforced abdication in 1688. The name was later – reasonably enough – applied to supporters of James's son the Old Pretender, also James – and less reasonably to those of *his* son, the Young Pretender, also known as Bonnie Prince Charlie. See also SOCIALITE/SOCIALIST.

jekyll and hyde/split personality Defence lawyers trying to claim that their client had suffered a personality change are fond of invoking the title characters from Robert Louis Stevenson's *The Strange Case of Dr Jekyll and Mr Hyde* (1886): "My client is a Jekyll and Hyde character whose personality completely changes when he has had a drink." Split personality is a popular lay term for schizophrenia (see SCHIZOPHRENIC), which is made from two Greek word-elements, for "split" and "mind" respectively. Other figures from the past commonly called up in court to help a "sympathy" defence are Robin Hood and Walter Mitty.

jewellery/jewelry Both are equally correct and have existed side-by-side for centuries: with *iuelrie* appearing in the 1300s; *jowalre* in about 1470; *jewelry* in the 1880s but *jewellery* not until the 1890s. The modern pronunciation of both seems to be the two-syllable "joolry".

jingoism/chauvinism/blind patriotism *Jingoism*, a form of bellicose *chauvinism*, is derived from the music hall song, "We don't want to fight, but by Jingo if we do, /We've got the ships, we've got the men, /We've got the money too." This is often quoted as an example of the national feeling that preceded World War I; but although the Jingo Song was much sung in the music halls at that time (recordings survive) this was a later adaptation. Jingoism dates from 1877, when Russia declared war on Turkey, and Britain, under the premiership of W. E. Gladstone, threatened to send an expeditionary force to protect Britons and other Christians who were being given a hard time by the Turks' ruling muslims. "By Jingo!" was a substitution for "by Jesus!" to avoid swearing by a sacred name, as "gosh" and "golly" are for "God". Chauvinism comes from the French counterpart of jingoism, named after a soldier, Nicolas Chauvin. He was lauded by his officers for blind and unquestioning devotion to Napoleon, idolized by nationalists but ridiculed by his fellow-soldiers. He, too, appears in song, the *vaudeville* (1831) "Je suis Français, je suis Chauvin".

(high)jinks/jinx *High jinks* are "various frolics formerly indulged in at drinking-parties…[and] mostly consisted in deciding by the throw of a dice who should perform some ludicrous task for the amusement of the company…" This *OED* definition is now a little outdated; as is its revelation that *jinking*, or "moving quickly to and fro", was yet another euphemism for sexual intercourse (as if we needed any more). From this comes the jinking in sports like rugby football or soccer – a quick movement to elude an opponent. The *jinx* that brings bad luck (see HOODOO/VOODOO) is American and no older than the early 20th century.

jostling/jousting "Racing yachts are *jousting* for position", said an ITN news-reader, and the simultaneous subtitles confirmed that it was in his script. Repelling boarders with lances, were they? No, they were *jostling*. As often happened with lookalike words, both once shared a meaning, but after mediaeval tournaments went out of fashion, *jostling* gradually parted company from "joustling" and took its modern spelling and modern, non-equestrian, meaning – that is, pushing and shoving, to contend for a good place.

joy-riding/car-stealing *Joy-riding* is one of the most foolish, thoughtless press euphemisms, for it makes *car-stealing* that often brings death and injury sound like a harmless recreation. It was originally an American "sport" defined as "a pleasure-trip in a motor-car, aeroplance, etc. often without the permission of the owner of the vehicle". Clichés of this kind are INSIDIOUS: during the 1999 Balkans conflict Robert Fisk reported in the *Independent* that a Serbian secret policeman who was shot dead had been "joy-shooting", that is, celebrating by firing shots into the air.

jumbo/big *Jumbo* meaning *big* is probably related to the West African MUMBO-JUMBO, but in its English use for anything of great size (now especially in commerce, with jumbo jets, jumbo hamburgers, jumbo-sized packets of this and that) goes back to mid-Victorian times, when the London Zoological Gardens owned an African elephant that became a children's favourite and almost a mascot to the people. Even more so after February 1882, when P. T. Barnum's self-styled "Greatest Show on Earth" bought the elephant from the Zoo and exhibited it nationwide, further spreading its fame – and its name, which was Jumbo. This is how jumbo became a synonym for big, though the animal itself might have got its name from Swahili *jambo*, meaning hello.

jungle/bush/rain-forest *Jungle*, from Hindi *jangal*, desert, wasteland or forest, and Sanskrit *jangala*, dry ground, is wild and uncultivated land in, usually, India. In Africa the same kind of terrain is called *bush*: for on that continent jungle is as rare as the tiger. What used to be called the "South American jungle" is now almost always described as *rain-forest*. The reason is partly semantic but mostly because it sounds more ecologically friendly, as these fascinating areas are under threat from tree-fellers, builders and other predators. The slogan "Save the Jungle" would not have the same resonance. *Rain-forest* (1898) is a straight translation from a German explorer's *Regenwald* – dense tropical forest in an area of high rainfall and rich variety of wild-life, plant species, etc.

justify/defend As with REFUTE/DENY, the two are not the same. A man may try to *defend* his actions but may not succeed in *justifying* them.

— K —

kafkaesque/nightmareish "There we were queuing in a dingy corridor for half an hour – it was Kafkaesque…" said a frustrated traveller, interviewed on TV about a holiday FROM HELL. Another man, thwarted by municipal officialdom, also invoked the Austro-Czech writer Franz Kafka (1883–1924), whose works often portray perplexing and threatening situations: "It was like something out of Kafka" – though it is a fair assumption that both were more familiar with the cliché than with Kafka's works. See also PINTERESQUE.

kick-start/start Merely *starting* something is not good enough for MEDIA folk. They have to *kick-start* it. The expression originated with motorbikes – and became a cliché just as these began to be fitted with electric self-starters that removed the need for kick-starting.

killed after/killed when/died When the *Guardian* reported that a member of the American Kennedy family "was killed after hitting a tree while skiing…" a reader asked, pertinently if a little tastelessly, "*How* was he killed? Did they stamp on him?" In fact the unfortunate man had *died* instantly. Another reporter wrote, just as absurdly, "Two people were injured *after* a car COLLIDED with a lamp-post." Road-rage? BBC radio news: "…a child has been seriously injured after being savaged by a dog." *The Times*: "The SAS soldier was fatally wounded after being hit in the stomach during a heavy exchange of fire." What next? "A man was killed after he was decapitated"?

knighted/benighted "Paul was beknighted in 1997…" wrote a *Liverpool Daily Post* man, thinking he was cleverly ringing the changes. If Paul was *benighted* (the *k* is as unjustified as many a K) then this happened earlier than 1997; for *benighted* means overtaken by the night, and usually refers to intellectual or spiritual darkness or ignorance: "He that hides a dark soul and foul thoughts/Benighted walks under the mid-day sun" – John Milton, *Comus* (1634). See also LABOUR/BELABOUR and RATE/BERATE.

knobs/nobs When the *Guardian* wrote "...what working-class people would call the knobs" it meant *nobs*, a 19th-century slang word for the *nob*ility, but which now simply means well-to-do, educated or "posh" people. When working-class people speak of *knobs* they mean something else, and not only doorknobs.

kosher/halal/correct *Kosher* comes from the Hebrew *kasher*, right, *correct*, genuine, appropriate, and has been so thoroughly anglicized as to be almost universally understood. I have seen a Roman Catholic priest describe – without irony or a smile on his face – something he thought not quite right with his Church as "not quite kosher". During the 1999 Balkans conflict Group Captain Glenn Edge of the Royal Air Force said of Serbian FLAK: "It wasn't one man lying on his back firing his kalashnikov. It was the kosher gear". Both the priest and the RAF officer were correct in their English parlance, though in strict Jewish use it refers to food prepared according to rabbinic law. The Muslims' equivalent to *kosher* is *halal*, but as far as I know they use this only for their meat, not their machine-guns. The Jewish opposite, i.e. non-kosher, is *trayf*, pronounced to rhyme with safe, though this has not yet caught on in non-kosher circles. It comes from Hebrew *teref*, torn to pieces, meaning the flesh of an animal killed by another animal and without religious ritual.

kow-towing/obsequiousness *Kow-tow* was brought back from China by 18th-century English travellers and is now used – often with SARCASM – for someone who shows undue and probably undeserved respect by his *obsequious* behaviour – Latin *obsequiosus*, compliant, obedient. Chinese *ko + tou*, knock the head, in effect means "head-banging" – from the Chinese custom of touching the ground with the forehead as a mark of respect, submission or worship. Pope John Paul II used to kow-tow by kissing the ground on arrival in all the many foreign countries he visited – though some said it was because he flew Alitalia.

kudos/cachet/brownie points *Kudos* is Greek for praise, glory or renown, and its anglicization began with English public-school boys who would have learned the meaning in the classroom. *Cachet* is French for a seal, meaning one of approval; and the imaginary award of *Brownie points* is a tedious and over-used cliché for the earning of real or imaginary "points" by way of praise. Brownies are, among other things, young Girl Guides who receive rewards for the well-accomplished tasks their leaders set them.

kudos

labour/belabour An Independent Television News reporter from Washington thought he was using an elegant variation when he said, "They are not belabouring this point…." To *labour* a point is to argue it strenuously and probably with difficulty. To *belabour* something (or someone) means to beat or thrash it (or him). The same trap lurks in KNIGHTED/BENIGHTED and RATED/BERATED.

lama/llama In Tibet and Mongolia are found priests called *lamas*, *dalai lamas* if they are chief priests, noted for their outward calm and professional serenity. In South America there are *llamas*, ruminant quadrupeds which are said to spit when angry. It is one *l* of a difference, as tabloid journalists would say, although the anglicized pronunciation is the same for both kinds of mammal.

large/largely *Large* is an adjective denoting size, but the adverb *largely* means abundantly, in large measure, to a great extent. *Writ large*, meaning written in large or big letters, has a pleasingly archaic-poetic ring to it ("new Presbyter is but Old Priest writ large" – John Milton, 1608–1674): trying to improve it by adverbial gentrification as "writ largely" is absurd.

laud/lord A *Guardian* columnist deplored the way "…the north of London lauds it over the south". Latin *laudare* is to praise, hence *laud*, to speak – even sing – the praises of something or someone, anyone, from God downwards: indeed its earliest use in English usually implied an act of worship. *Lording* (usually followed by "it"), which is what the writer meant to put, is to behave in a high-handed and supposedly lordly manner. Shakespeare's *Henry VI Part 2* (1592): "I see them lording it in London streets".

laudable/laudatory That which is praiseworthy is *laudable*, an adjective derived straight from its Latin equivalent, *laudabilis*; but an expression of praise is described as *laudatory*. The person who does the praising is a laudator, a noun once common but now old-fashioned, which is also a direct adaptation from Latin *laudator*. None of the three has any connection with lords – see above.

laughably/laughingly A displayed advertisement in *The Times* for a Corby trouser press claims that "… with it's [sic] unique stretcher system it is laughingly [sic] quick and easy to use…" So now we know: the pianist Liberace went *laughably* all the way to the bank. *Laughably* means something that is laughed at, *laughingly* the action of laughing.

laver/lava/larva *Laver* (or *Laver Bread*) is an edible Welsh water plant, *Porphyria umbilicalis*, which was known to the Romans and is eaten boiled in salt water or fried in oatmeal. It has nothing to do with volcanic *lava*; although this is how it often occurs in cookery books and newspaper cookery columns. Nor has it anything to do with *larvae*, though it has appeared in shops as Larva Bread – suggesting baked weevils.

lay/lie/laid/lain Reporting a law-case in which an American woman unsuccessfully claimed she had been raped, *The Times* wrote "…the woman undressed herself, laid on the bed and offered him her body". What promiscuity! Latin *promiscere*, to mix up; and goodness how people mix up *lie* and *lay*, *lying* and *laying*, *lied*, *laid* and *lain*. Here are some examples which, however confusing, may be taken as correct. The woman in the story did not deny that she and the man had previously *lain* together, so she doubtless *lay* on the bed – and might even have *laid on* (meaning supplied) the bed, just as she could have *laid on* the wine, or the venue for their tryst. But then she *laid* a complaint. One of the two must have *lied*, but if she did *lay* down her honour, your Honour, even if the boy *laid into* her, he has now *laid off* her. Hens, m'Lud, may be good *layers*, girls good (or easy) *lays*. A *lying-together* may result in a *lying-in*. The resulting baby should be *laid* on his back so he can *lie* safely, happily gurgling (and has *lain* like that all day). The *laying-on* of hands is the province of healers; the *laying-off* of workers that of bosses. I was *laid up* with sciatica the other day. Now I *lay* me down to sleep. This home-made doggerel may make a useful mnemonic:

> A tearful American maid,
> Weeping openly, claimed she'd been laid.
> She had lain on her bed
> With a young man, she said,
> But she lied that he laid her, the jade.

The confusion is widespread, now that newspapers are produced by writers who have never been readers and as students are no longer required to study authors who knew their craft. Thus a leader-writer on the *Guardian* saw nothing wrong with the following sentence: "One of New Labour's least appealing traits is its willingness to lay down with Mr Murdoch". Shakespeare always got it right. To quote from several of his works: "Full fathom five thy father lies" – "This skull has lain in the earth three and twenty years"– "Well said, that was laid on with a trowel" – "O sleep, thou ape of death, lie dull upon her! And be her sense but as a monument, thus in a chapel lying..." And he also teases us: "[Virginity] is a commodity will lose the gloss with lying."

legendary/mythical/famous A *legendary* person is part of legend, in other words, fictitious, but in MEDIA usage it has come to mean very *famous*. *Mythical* has gone much the same way. Under the headline

MYTHICAL FALLS FOUND

The Times reported, mysteriously, "Explorers have discovered a mythical 100ft high waterfall in the Himalayan mountains of Tibet...a previously unexplored five-mile gap in the Upper Tsangpo Gorge..." Had it been mythical they would not have been able to find it, except in the imagination. Another *Times* writer gushed about "the legendary volcano Vesuvius". See also UNKNOWN.

liar/lyre As homophones go, *liar* and *lyre* are not likely to be confused except by facetiously inclined headline-writers for a weak headline joke. But I swear (and can prove) that the *Guardian* employed someone who *without trying to be funny* wrote about "Orpheus and his liar".

lick/defeat/conquer In its literal meaning, *lick*, the passing of the tongue over something, has been in use since the beginning of Teutonic and English languages; and the other sense, of beating, thrashing or *defeating* someone or something, from as long ago as about 1500. A glossary of 1567 defines it as "*Licke*, to beate". Thus Fanny Burney's *Diary* (1775): "As for your father, I could lick him for his affected coolness and moderation"; Thomas Hughes, in his famous book on public-school life, *Tom Brown's Schooldays* (1857):

148

"Say you won't fag – they'll soon get tired of licking you";
Spurgeon's *Sermons* (1879): "America in the olden time, when every man was free to lick his own nigger"; and the bullying Tom in Mark Twain's *Tom Sawyer* (1876): "'I'll dare you to step over that [line] and I'll lick you till you can't stand up'." None of that prepares one for this extract from an American Army medical journal: "Dr O. C. Wenger, the famed doctor, who licked venereal disease in the army during World War II ..."

lightning/lightening Both forms are connected with light, but over the centuries the spellings diverged. The *Psalms* in Wyclif's translation of the Bible (1382) had "Thi lytnying is schyneden [shining] to the world", whereas Capgrave's *Chronicles* (1425) preferred to give it the extra syllable: "The moost horribil thunderes and litynnyngis that evyr ony [ever any] man herd". Now that separate spellings have been agreed, *lightening* means to lighten, to make lighter, in shade, illumination or weight, while *lightning* strikes. Another interesting definition of *lightening* fell into disuse in the 19th century: "That exhilaration or revival of the spirits which is supposed to occur in some instances just before death"; and indeed many writers who have had near-death experiences have described being aware of bright lights. Shakespeare wrote in *Romeo and Juliet* (1592): "How oft when men are at the point of death, have they been merry? Which their keepers call a lightening before death".

limbo/uncertainty *Limbo* is a region that supposedly exists on the border between heaven and hell, where the recently deceased (and unbaptized infants) must wait while it is decided which way they are going. Today it is either a cliché for a state of uncertainty or a West Indian dance in which the dancer bends backwards and passes under a horizontal bar raised only a few inches off the ground – trying not to fall over. See also BEATIFY/ BEAUTIFY.

limpid/limp "The performance was marred by a rather limpid performance from [a well-known pianist]", wrote a well-known music-critic in the *Daily Telegraph*. The context revealed that he meant *limp*, and was trying to say that the performance had been lacking in firmness. *Limpid* means clear, transparent, pellucid, and is also used by music-critics.

149

linchpin/"lynch-pin" A *linchpin*, or *linch*, is driven through the end of the axle-tree of a wagon to stop the wheel from falling off. It may be either hyphenated or written as one word. Motor-cars use a more complicated method of keeping their wheels in place, so the term has gone out of use, except in a figurative way to describe something essential to a case, lawsuit or argument etc. *Lynch-pin* is an incorrect spelling, suggesting it has something to do with the Lynch Law named after the odious Capt. William Lynch (1742–1820) of Virginia. Those who look for racial insults where none is intended have written impassioned words against a non-existent slight when they read "lynchpin". The same applies to DERACINATE and NIGGARD(LY).

lineage/linage *Lineage* is pronounced "linny-age" and refers to lineal descent from ancestors; *linage*, pronounced "line-age", means the number of lines in printed matter, especially classified advertisements.

lineament/liniment *Lineament* is a contour or distinctive feature, as on a map or drawing; *liniment* (from Latin *linire*, to smear), an embrocation or ointment.

liquidate/liquidize/murder/assassinate *Liquidate*, in the sense of stamp out, wipe out or kill (usually by the state) is one of many sinister words we owe to the Soviets, although some were originally German. *Likvidirovat* was first spotted by the *OED* in *Pravda* as early as 1924; later the Nazis used it in German as *liquidieren*, from which it was eventually anglicized, still with its deadly meaning. Perhaps that is why when, in about 1950, the familiar electric kitchen implement was introduced it was called a *liquidizer*, not *liquidator*. A little less sinister but still feared is the liquidator appointed to wind up a company and ascertain what liquid assets may be left over for creditors.

liquorice/lickerish/liquorous *Liquorice* is produced by evaporation from the liquorice root, *Glycyrrhiza glabra*, and has from ancient times been used as a sweetmeat ("His love is al so swete, y-wis, so ever is milk or licoris", ca 1300) as well as a medicine ("Lycuresse is good for the voyce", 1519). Many people pronounce it – and therefore some writers write it – *lickerish*, although this has nothing to do with liquorice. Lickerish is an adjective altered from *lickerous* and also known since the Middle Ages (ca 1275), meaning "sweet, tempting, attractive, pleasant to the palate". *Liquorous* is different again, the adjective of *liquor*, whether alcoholic or not.

literally/really etc. *Literally* is an adverb indicating that an idea expressed must be taken in its literal sense, but it is more commonly used as a meaningless, intensifying filler, often nonsensically: "Her eyes were literally glued to mine" appeared in a soppy article in a women's magazine; even the celebrated Vladimir Nabokov, author of *Lolita* and an acknowledged master of English, wrote in *Invitation to a Beheading* (1960): "...with his eyes he literally scoured the corners of the cell"; the *Good Food Guide* included an alarming report about a seafood restaurant: "Crabs and lobsters are literally found crawling round the floor waiting for an order"; and even more alarmingly, a speaker on BBC Radio 4 said of an adventurer-turned-lecturer, "Grey Owl could rivet an audience to their seats, literally."

little-known/little known "We have chosen little known people..." said the publicist's hand-out, implying they had chosen small, known people. *Little-known*, hyphenated, makes things clearer.

loathe/loth/loath To *loathe* is to show a strong dislike or aversion, but being *loth* (alternative spelling *loath*) is to show merely reluctance or an unwillingness. A pre-17th-century English popular song, "Loth to depart" (on which several composers wrote variations), probably helped to keep that expression alive, while loathing developed separately.

lobby/entrance/lobbyists In largely rural old England a *lobby* was a small enclosure for cattle in or near a farm-yard, but by around 1600 Shakespeare was already using the word in the urban sense, for the *entrance* hall or vestibule of a dwelling. The Parliamentary lobby, too, is older than one might think dating from about 1640, when it was "one of the two corridors to which members retire to vote when the House divides" – an apparently effortless translation from the farm-yard to Westminster. For after all, the party whips who herd Members of Parliament into voting-lobbies were originally called "whippers-in", which is from hunting parlance. Parliamentary lobbies and corridors have traditionally also been used for interviews between members and "persons not belonging to the House" – namely the unlovely *lobbyists* who lobby MPs for favours, in return for money paid to them (usually the lobbyists but sometimes clandestinely the MPs) by people with a collective sectional interest.

lobby

loft/attic *Loft* is derived from variants of *Luft*, meaning air or sky in old Germanic and other Nordic tongues; also therefore an upper room. The *attic*, or in full attic STOREY, is named after a classical Greek architectural feature placed at the top of a building. Until the early1990s only pigeons and impoverished poets lived in lofts or attics – converted roof-spaces normally used for storing LUMBER. However, thanks to a trend for the conversion of disused warehouses into apartments, "loft living" has become fashionable among city-dwellers.

lone/lonely/solo/lonesome/loner *Lone*, solitary, having no companions, is one of the most poetic words in English, but also a stilted press cliché-term for actions undertaken by a single person which are normally done by two or more, i.e. lone sailor, lone walker, lone explorer, etc. In reports of funerals or other memorial occasions, the press likes to be able to report a lone bugler playing the Last Post, or a lone piper a Scottish lament, as if they were pathologically *lonely* (except for an accidental misprint in the *Lancashire Evening Post* which referred to "a lone bugger sounding the Last Post"). As a musical cliché it seems to be restricted to those functions and instruments. Yehudi Menuhin, standing all alone on the huge platform of the Royal Albert Hall and playing a *solo*, or unaccompanied, Bach Partita on his violin, was never a lone fiddler. Lone is also used in the context of solo achievements, e.g. by a lone flyer, or lone rower. Headline-writers find the lone/loan pun irresistible, which so confused an obituarist in *The Daily Telegraph* that he described a deceased person as "… something of a loan wolf". Better than a loan shark, any day. *Lonesome* has acquired shades of usage all of its own, probably derived from a popular song asking, "Are you lonesome tonight?" Whenever a murderer, rapist or other serious miscreant is caught and his neighbours are buttonholed by the MEDIA, he is nearly always described as a *loner*. "He kept himself to himself" (or, in the obituarists' stock phrase, similarly applied, "He was a very private person").

lord's/lords/lourdes *Lord's* is the cricket ground, the home of cricket itself, and the headquarters of Marylebone Cricket Club. It was opened by Thomas Lord in 1780 and remains a place of pilgrimage for cricket-lovers. It is still "his", needing the possessive apostrophe *Lord's*: without it, as *Lords*, it is short for "the Lords", the House of Lords, or Upper House of the British Parliament. For *Lourdes* see under HAJ.

low key/softly/unobtrusively/restrained The intended meaning of *low key* is that something is muted, *restrained* and perhaps of modest ambition, as in "CAREFULLY ORCHESTRATED in a low key" (nothing is ever "carelessly orchestrated in a high key"). Like other misused music-based clichés, *low key* makes no sense to the musician. There is no such thing as a "low" key in music. The scale, say C – D – E – F – G – A – B – C, repeats itself all the way up the keyboard, so that an F may be lower than a C. The cliché arose from a misunderstanding of the way 19th-century music publishers issued thousands of songs transposed into different keys: sopranos could buy a song in the key of C, contraltos the same song but in the key of F below – high voice and low voice respectively. The words *High Key* or *Low Key* were printed on the cover. When people stopped buying sheet-music the allusion ceased to mean anything. See also CRESCENDO and ORCHESTRATE.

lumbar/lumber *Lumber* gets in one's way – in the form of clutter such as disused articles with which one is *lumbered*; and the word also means roughly sawn or hewn timber (perhaps by a lumberjack). *Lumbar* is the adjective derived from Latin *lumbus*, loin, and should strictly refer to that part of the body, or perhaps to a medical procedure involving the spinal CORD in the lumbar region.

lumpen/the great unwashed/sansculottes/proletarians/proles
Lumpen is a curious immigrant of a word, beloved of political and social commentators, who have turned it into an English adjective. It is a German noun meaning rag or rags, and in its socio-political context is based on *Lumpenproletariat*, coined by Karl Marx to describe the lowest, most unenlightened and stupidest members of society (*his* words). In German the word *Lump* also means a scoundrel, and has nothing to do with poverty and lack of enlightenment, nor with the English word "lump". Shakespeare, incidentally, uses "patch" in the same way, transferring the raggedness of the wearer's clothes to the person: "A crew of patches, rude mechanicals…" in *A Midsummer Night's Dream* (?1595/6) and numerous other plays. Marx's *Lumpenproletariat* had its English equivalent in what the upper classes, with their habitual daily bath, called *(the) (great) unwashed*. This phrase probably originated with W. M. Thackeray, who wrote in *Pendennis* (1850): "There are individuals still alive who sneer at the people, and speak of them with epithets of scorn. Gentlemen, there can be but little doubt that your ancestors were the Great Unwashed." Shakespeare may have inadvertently

lumpen

started the idea that working-people are dirty – in *King John* (1595): "Another leane, vnwash'd Artificer...."

Across the Channel, whatever the French Revolution abolished it was not class discrimination: the *sansculottes* (*sans*, without + *culottes*, knee-breeches) were the lowest class of revolutionaries, despised by the WELL-HEELED and well-dressed JACOBINS just as they were, later, by the middle-class Marxes and Engelses. Contrary to a widely held view, the sansculottes did not have to revolt in their underpants. The name simply meant that they were too poor to buy the latest knee-breeches fashionable among the bourgeoisie. To call someone a sansculotte was as much a fashion statement as a political one, perhaps like commenting in the 1980s that Michael Foot, MP, still wore his 1960s donkey jacket, flares and solid brogues, when his Islington comrades had gone into Armani suits with narrow trousers and winklepickers. English political commentators still use sansculottes when they mean ragged-trousered revolutionaries – which Robert Tressell had in mind when he wrote his influential *The Ragged-trousered Philanthropist* (1914).

Proletarians were a legacy of the Romans, for whom a *proletarius* was a citizen of the lowest class, fed and clothed by the state and encouraged to produce offspring to swell the Roman legions. (Hitler and Stalin copied this kind of national breeding programme, and the Soviets honoured super-fertile women as "Stakhanovite Mothers", after a – presumably equally fertile – Russian miner). *Proletarius*'s pleasures were not aesthetic but orifical – food and sex – and he was conditioned to respond to a monotonous drum-beat. Much like today's proles, except that *they* are part of an affluent underclass that wields economic power. The abbreviation *proles* may have been invented by George Bernard Shaw: at any rate he is recorded by the *OED* as the first known user of the word, in a letter dated 1887: "We call the working men proles because that is exactly what they are." Later George Orwell immortalized proles in his novel *Nineteen Eighty Four* (1949).

luncheon/lunch/dinner The formal word is *luncheon*, seldom used in speech but more common in print, on invitations. Most people automatically say *lunch*, which is also a verb (never "ladies who luncheon"). The *OED* quotes an author of 1829 who noticed the change, attributing it to London's most select assembly rooms, in King Street, St James's: "The word *lunch* is adopted in that 'glass of fashion', Almack's, and *luncheon* is avoided as unsuitable to the polished society there exhibited." Lunch could be taken at any time of the day, and was a lighter meal than luncheon, just as a trunch is shorter and lighter than a truncheon. *Dinner* is now the traditional evening meal, except in the north of England, where it still means lunch.

lurgy/germ A suspected infection for which the writer/speaker has no explanation may be blamed on a *lurgy*: "I must have picked up a lurgy somewhere", more facetiously a "dreaded lurgy". It was popularized by a BBC radio comedy programme: "A fictitious, highly infectious disease invented [?] and made a byword by the Radio Goons", says the *OED*, but draws attention to a possibly related word for malingering workshyness, "feverlargie", defined in 1808 in terms that fit the modern Social Security scrounger: "Two stomachs to eat, and none to work".

luxurious/luxuriant/luxuriate/sybarite When Auberon Waugh in the *Daily Telegraph* described the late comedian Jimmy Edwards as "having a luxurious mustache" he meant *luxuriant*. In Latin *luxus* means abundant and sumptuous enjoyment, as luxury does now, but dirty-minded mediaeval clerics equated enjoyment with sex, so that in Chaucer's time *luxurious* was the same as lascivious, lecherous and unchaste – the "foule lust of luxurie" (in *The Man of Law's Tale*, ca 1386); and *Anon.* in 1450, "Leude touchinge and handelynge [made] the folke falle into the orible synne of luxurie". Dr Andrew Boorde in 1542 advised patients that "Cucumbers restrayneth veneryousnes, or lassyvyousness or luxuryousnes". But luxury eventually reverted to the meaning of extravagantly comfortable living that is still current (see also DELICIOUS for a comparable change). *Luxuriant* is about neither sex nor luxury, but abundance: it is something profuse or excessive, and today is most often applied to hair; more rarely, to florid or exuberant speech. One *luxuriates* in – always in – luxury, mostly a bath. *Sybarite* referred to natives of Sybaris, an ancient Greek city of southern Italy, voluptuaries "who were traditionally noted for their effeminacy and luxury". However, the supporting quotations given by the *OED* suggest that this "effeminacy" would have been no more than a lazy languidness. See also NICE.

luxurious

— M —

magnate/magnet Yasmin Alibhai-Brown in the *Independent* wrote about "a Chinese newspaper magnet". She meant *magnate*, which comes from Latin *magnus*, great, and later *magnas*, a great man – today usually a wealthy one and probably an industrialist to boot, but not necessarily one with magnetic qualities. A *magnet*, from Latin *magnes*, the Magnesian stone, or lodestone, is the thing that physically attracts metals such as iron and steel.

mail/post Purists who try – usually in vain – to protect the English language from American influences have been heard to condemn the use of *mail* for *post*. *Mail* was the normal English word for a collection of letters or packages which only later became the *post* – and that was long before there were any English-speaking Americans. From about 1200 AD *mail* was, first, a bag or sack, and then specifically a sackful or packet of letters. Numerous examples occur from the early 17th century. The *London Gazette* in 1684 reported "Our Pacquet-Boats put to Sea yesterday with the Mails for Calais…" So it was the Pilgrim Fathers who took the mail to America.

marinade/marinate A *marinade* is a liquid in which foodstuffs like meat, vegetables, etc., are soaked before cooking, to make them tender or imbue them with flavour. It would originally have been salt water, or brine from the sea (hence the *marine* element), but a variety of flavours is now assumed. The stuff which is in the marinade is now, by general custom, *marinated*, though *marinaded* (as some prefer) cannot be wrong.

maritime/naval *Maritime* refers to that which is connected with the sea, whereas *naval* specifically refers to the maritime armed forces, in Britain the Royal Navy.

marmite policy/small doses A member of the (English) Refugee Council, objecting to the dispersal of IMMIGRANTS across Britain, was reported in the *Independent* as saying: "This threatens to become exactly the Marmite policy of thinly spreading asylum-seekers that we were trying to avoid." The reference is to a well-known proprietary yeast-extract (first manufactured in England in 1902), which is delicious when spread thinly on buttered toast but less palatable in heavy concentration. Although pronounced "mar-might" in the English way, the name comes from the French word *marmite*, a stew-pot, a specimen of which is illustrated on the label (a *marmiton* is a French scullion or kitchen drudge). See also SOFTLY SOFTLY etc.

maths/math *Maths* is the colloquial abbreviation of mathematics, long-established in the British education system and in schools, though in decline. Americans prefer to make even short words shorter, so they say *math*. This had its own meaning from early mediaeval times, namely the amount of grass or crop mowed (also *mowth*); hence also the *aftermath*, for a second mowing.

may/might When used in present-tense or implied-future applications "might" and "may" are often interchangeable, though with subtle differences, e.g. "I might speak to her/I may speak to her". Hesitancy may also be a factor: "May I have a word with you?" and "Might I have a word with you?" have faintly different nuances, as "I may" can be taken as permission having been granted. But the may/might difference becomes crucial when what has happened is in the past: "Had he studied more he *might* have passed his exam" implies that he was lazy and did *not* pass. But "…he *may* have passed his exam" means that the speaker is unsure whether the candidate did or did not pass. So "Had he studied more he may have passed" is nonsense. The following examples come from the news-MEDIA.

> Angela Phillips (the *Independent*): "Had Virginia been at university today…she may never have become a Bottomley…" Is the writer *doubting* that Mrs Bottomley married Mr Bottomley? We *know* she did. There is no "may" about it.

> Stephen Cape (BBC News) about a boat from which all passengers were rescued: "Some passengers may not have survived." But as he had told us a moment earlier, all *were* taken off and all survived.

may

Hilary Finch (*The Times*) about a concert: "Norrington may have done better to remind himself of Mahler's…metronome marks…" This postulates the *possibility* that Norrington followed Mahler's directions: what she means is that he did not but ought to have done.

BBC News: "A number of [jail] suicides may have been avoided." Yet the item was about jail suicides that *had* happened and had *not* been avoided.

BBC reporter: "Had there been a proper search, the bomb on the [Lockerbie] airliner may have been detected." The whole world knows the tragic outcome, because the bomb was not detected.

Liverpool Daily Post: "A blaze victim who died in a bedsit above a disco may have had precious minutes to escape if a fire alarm had not been disconnected."

Emily Davies in *The Times*: "…her daughter may have lived if she had not gone to hospital." The child unfortunately did *not* live, as the story made clear.

In each of the examples given above, "may" should have been "might". There is not an iota of doubt about it; and all educated writers would, without question, have put "might". But during the 1990s a craze arose among unconfident users of the language to treat "may" as a kind of GENTEEL inelegant variation. It saves no time, sounds no better – and conveys a different sense from that intended. Consider also these exchanges : 1) "Mum, can I go to the pictures?" – "Yes, you can, but you may not." 2) "Might I go to the pictures?" – "Yes, you might, but you may not if you don't eat your supper."

maybe/may be *Maybe* is an adverb and means possibly, perhaps; *may be* indicates a possibility differently expressed ("what may be may possibly be") in two separate words.

mayhem/chaos *Mayhem* was formerly a legal term (from an Old French word that also gave us *maim*) for the crime of inflicting a bodily injury upon a person "so as to make him less able to defend himself or annoy his adversary". The offence is "malicious injury to the person" and surgeons who remove a healthy limb or a man's healthy organs may still lay themselves open to such a charge. *Chaos,* according to the Chambers Dictionary, was originally "the state of matter before the universe was reduced to order", and in Greek mythology it was the disordered void from which sprang Gaea, mother of all things earthly and divine. Today's usage makes the two words loosely interchangeable and less specific, referring to any state of disorder, whether cosmic (see ASTRONAUTS) or otherwise.

meat/meet/mete We know what *meat* is, and *meeting* people; but the other spellings are more obscure and may confuse. To be *meet* (with) is to be even or quits: Shakespeare in *Much Ado about Nothing* (1599): "You tax Signior Benedicke too much, but he'll be meet with you." Something that is fitting or becoming is usually written *mete*: as in the *Book of Common Prayer, Communion* (1548/9): "It is mete and right so to do"; and to apportion praise or penalties, is to *mete out* punishment. Simply meeting people is for many no longer enough. They have to "meet with" or even "meet up with" them – an Americanism some English critics dislike. "Meeting out punishment", as a *Guardian* writer insisted, should have been *meting*. See also BOIL/BROIL and HELPMATE/HELPMEET.

mecca/place of pilgrimage/desirable place etc. *Mecca*, Arabic *Makkah*, in what is now Saudi Arabia, is a place sacred to Muslims, who regard it as the birthplace of Muhammad. Millions of worshippers go there for their annual HAJ, or pilgrimage. It has became a byword for any place allegedly desirable to visit – and in this context is generally written in lower-case often inappropriately used. A travel-writer enthused about "Eilat in southern Israel, the mecca of English sun-seekers". Mecca Dancing was an early attempt at commercially exploiting the name, but certainly the most incongruous, as the Muslim religion forbids mixed-sex dancing. IRONICALLY it was a Jewish enterprise.

medium/media When people speak of *the media* they mean the *news* media, COMPRISING the *print* media (plural because there are several: newspapers, magazines, etc.); the *sound* and *visual* media (radio and television); or the *mass* media in general, including advertising. A multiplicity of media, which any reasonably well-read person would as a matter of course treat as a plural noun: "the media *are*..." But from the 1980s, when most English schools had abandoned the teaching of grammar and Latin, a few media people (who had no benefit of such teaching) began to treat the word as if it were singular: "The media is..."

This absurdity now trips effortlessly off most media persons' lips and few eyebrows are raised. For example, when ITV Television News said, "The media are withdrawing" its BBC rivals, relentlessly down-dumbing, said of the same story, "the media is withdrawing". The dwindling band of those who still care are free to continue saying "The media are…" but may get the funny looks reserved for PEDANTS, who have conceded defeat. It is an excellent example of how Gresham's law affects usage: "Bad coinage drives out good". As James Cope suggested in a letter to *The Spectator*, "those who cannot stop themselves from using 'media' in the singular should adopt the spelling 'meeja' and leave us pedants in peace". Much the same applies to CRITERIA.

memento/"momento" A General of the British Army, writing in the *Daily Telegraph*, complained that although he was able to find Napoleonic memorabilia in a shop at the site of Waterloo (the battle, not the station) he "searched in vain for a suitable momento bearing the victor's effigy". *Momento* is Italian for a moment; what the General intended was *memento*, from the Latin for a warning or admonition (as in *memento mori*, a reminder of death), later meaning a souvenir. The confusion is widespread, not helped by bad diction. As early as 1951 even Dylan Thomas succumbed to it, enclosing "a momento" in a letter to a friend. Perhaps in jest. The confusion did not make him a less good poet, nor the General a worse soldier.

metal/mettle The *Daily Telegraph* claimed in a leader that someone had been "put on his metal". The intended word was *mettle*, which means of a good quality or hard disposition. But both spellings formerly had the same ferrous meaning – another instance of divergent spellings fixed by usage. This is why we have the curious term "metalled road" – a road made with hard material, not containing *metal* as the word is now understood. Mettle, incidentally, means much the same as fettle, as "in fine fettle", or in good trim. It is a Lancashire dialect expression dating from the 18th century.

meteoric rise/spectacular rise "Hitler's meteoric rise to power", wrote The *Guardian* and so did probably every other paper. Meteors do not rise: they fall.

meter/metre A *meter*, often used as a suffix or in combination, is a mechanical or electrical device that measures something, as for example the thermometer, mileometer, taxi meter, tachometer, gas or electricity meter. A *metre* is the measurement itself, as in kilometre, centimetre or millimetre, which European bureaucracy is forcing upon a reluctant British people. Americans confuse the issue with one of their "simplifications", using meter for everything.

metrication/metrification *Metrification* is verse constructed in metre. *Metrication* is measuring in metres, centimetres and other decimal units.

milestones/millstones/landmarks *Milestones* were ancient small stone pillars set in the ground at the side of highways to tell travellers the distance in miles to (or from) the next (or last) place along the road. Most have either been uprooted and destroyed, or remain unnoticed by the speeding motorized traveller. But metaphorical milestones are part of our lives: many things, like advances in medicine, sports or engineering, are compared to them. As a motoring-editor of the *Daily Telegraph* wrote of a car, "This new model is something of a milestone." *Millstones*, too have largely been forgotten: instead of grinding corn they are mercilessly used to grind out clichés, like "a millstone round the neck". No wonder then that a CARTOON in *The Oldie* confused matters, showing two stone-age men standing by three big, circular millstones, each with a hole in the middle. They were arranged like a table and two seats, and the caption read: "Believe me, it's a *milestone* in the history of patio furniture." Another travellers' aid, the *landmark*, too, survives only as a cliché. This also originally was a stone (or stones) set in the ground, marking a land boundary, or as a conspicuous object visible from the sea, to guide sailors in navigation. Hence all our landmark measures, meaning important ones. A landmark decision is a legal one that creates a precedent.

militate/mitigate *Militate*, from Latin *militare*, to serve as a soldier, and therefore to fight, conflict with, or be inconsistent with something; which is why it is always paired with "against". *Mitigate*, from Latin *mitigare*, to make better or alleviate, to improve, needs no pairing, least of all "against". "Although the distant period mitigates against my absolute certainty…" wrote Julie Wheelwright in a book-review for the *Independent*.

(to) minister/administer/administrate Difficult as it is to believe if you look at members of the Government, their fleets of big cars, their grace-and-favour mansions and other perks, the Latin word *minister* actually means a servant, the exact opposite of *magister*, master. What

Ministers, as public servants, are supposed to do is *to minister*, or serve. The *Guardian* absurdly had the young Mussolini (ever the bureaucrat?) "administering to sick animals". To *administrate* now has bureaucratic shades of meaning, none of them opprobrious: just efficient administrative practices.

mink(s)/minx "How do minks have babies?" asks the old chestnut. Answer: "In the same way that babes have minks". And a *minx*, says the *OED*, is "a pert girl, a hussy, a lewd or wanton woman". This goes back to the 16th century and at first meant a beloved pet dog: "...little mynxes, or puppees that ladies keepe in their chaumbers for especiall iewelles to playe withall" (1542).

minefield/danger area/landmine *Minefields* were at first exclusively naval – parts of the sea where mines were laid in World War I and also World War II. It became an over-used figurative cliché ("a veritable minefield of political correctness") only after the end of World War II. During that war a *landmine* was a large bomb dropped by parachute. Only later did it become the stock word for an explosive device or booby trap buried in the soil.

minuscule/"miniscule" Latin *minusculus* means very small, a diminutive of *minor*, and was formerly used for very small letters in printing – and from this it became the word for unimportant or insignificant matters. But *minusculus* is not the same as Latin *minimus*, the least, or smallest, so that miniscule is an erroneous formation – though not as erroneous as the schoolboy-howler translation as "a kindergarten, or mini-school".

miracle/remarkable *Miracles* are not only rare but, when encountered, usually fraudulent. The delightful *OED* definition should be writ large in places where they are thought to manifest themselves: "*Miracle* – a marvellous event occurring within human experience, which cannot have been brought about by human power or by the operation of any natural agency, and must therefore be ascribed to the special intervention of the Deity or of some supernatural being; chiefly, an act (e.g. of healing) exhibiting control over the laws of nature, and serving as evidence that the agent is either divine or is specially favoured by God". In the press, however, miracles are nothing more than hyperbole for *remarkable* events; for example, "miracle babes" are born – and survive – with quite unmiraculous frequency.

missile/missive/letter/missal Both *missile* and *missive* come from the same Latin word, *mittere*, to send, but a *missive* is a letter, usually a very formal directive, as from an ecclesiastical establishment, or else a facetious one, as perhaps between schoolgirls. A *missile* can be more deadly – and is either thrown or fired. The long-established distinction did not trouble a young BBC Reporter who, speaking from Israel, reported that "A gas cylinder filled with explosive [had been] made into a deadly missive…" The American pronunciation of *missile* sounds like *missal* (Latin for "of the Mass"), which causes further confusion for English-speakers, who do not know whether it will be thrown, fired, or used for saying Mass.

moat/mote As every schoolboy knows, a *moat* is a protective ditch round a castle (from a mediaeval English word for an embankment, *motte* in Norman French). The even older *mote* (dating from at least 1000 AD) means a tiny particle of dust, especially "one of the innumerable minute specks seen floating in the sunbeam" (*OED*), which comes from St Matthew, 7.3, "Why beholdest thou the mote that is in thy brother's eye, but considerest not the beam that is in thine own eye?" – in other words, observing a small fault in another person while ignoring a greater one of one's own.

mogul/tycoon/magnate/mandarin For many decades the English word most readily coupled with *mogul* was "movie", to refer to the chief, boss or owner of a Hollywood film company, but Britain now also has press moguls, media moguls, food moguls and others. It is Indian of Persian/Arabic origin and denotes the ruling class or royalty, like the Grand Mogul, Emperor of Delhi. *Tycoons* come from Japan, where *taikun* means a great lord or prince; and someone in 1861 called Abraham Lincoln one, albeit facetiously. *Mandarin* was a generic name for a Chinese person of much importance, a government official, facetiously westernized, chiefly into "Whitehall mandarins". See also PUNDIT/GURU.

momentarily/in a moment The Americans do much to refresh the language, and numerous Americanisms are to be welcomed into mainstream English. But there is no doubt also that many changes were introduced by IMMIGRANTS to the USA with an imperfect knowledge of it. This is an example which, though it has gained unquestioning acceptance in American dictionaries, DISCOMFITS British ears. In British

English *momentarily* means *for* a moment, for a very short time, whereas to North Americans it means *in* a moment. An English traveller with an American airline was alarmed to hear the Captain announce: "Please fasten your seatbelts. We shall be taking off momentarily."

moneys/monies/money/sums The first of the two plural forms of *money* is right, the second wrong. If there were a rule it would be that words ending in *-ie* singular become *-ies* plural, e.g. scottie/scotties, but *-ey* singular becomes *-eys* plural, as in FLUNKEY/flunkeys or monkey/monkeys. As for *moneys/monies*, both are avoidable and should be left to accountants, solicitors and money-lenders. Is a plural needed at all? Just *money* usually suffices. Or else *sums* should do the trick.

moonlight/moonshine Both forms are ancient, and Shakespeare famously liked both: in *The Merchant of Venice* (1596): "How sweet the moone-light sleepes vpon this banke"; and in *The Merry Wives of Windsor* (1598): "Pinch him and burne him, and turne him about, till Candles and Star-light and Moone-shine be out." *Moonlight* is now the preferred form, perhaps because *moonshine* is associated with smuggled or illicitly distilled spirits. But there is the "moonlight flit", when tenants flee without paying the rent. The Germans have always preferred *Mondschein*: Beethoven's Piano Sonata Op.27 No. 2 became known as the *Mondschein Sonate* but in English the "Moonlight", not "Moonshine" Sonata.

moot/mute In ancient England a *moot* was an assembly of people, a court or council discussing or dispensing justice, hence the many mediaeval moot halls. That which is debatable or can be argued is therefore a *moot point* – not a *mute* one, as it is sometimes written, for this would be a silent one, from Latin *mutus*.

moreish/moorish Food described as *moreish* is claimed (usually by those that made or sell it) to be so good that one wants more. It is part of the "yum-yum" vocabulary of advertisers, food-writers and columnists, but they did not invent it. Jonathan Swift in 1738 has this exchange: "How do you like this Tea, Colonel?" – "Well enough, Madam; but methinks it is a little more-ish." On the other hand those who advertise Selfridges' ready-made dishes as "Rich, creamy and moorish" by their misspelling suggest an Arabic/North African connection.

more/new/fresh Not only are the three words often confused but they can mislead. For example, when "She said she liked nothing more than a bacon sandwich", did she mean there was nothing she liked better, or that it was all she wanted – a bacon sandwich but nothing *more*? *Fresh* talks could be more talks (more talks than what?) or renewed talks: more does not necessarily mean *new*, and new does not necessarily mean fresh. A common example: "Three weeks after the earthquake fresh bodies have been uncovered…"

morganatic/civil marriage The word *morganatic* emerged from obscurity at the time of Edward VIII's abdication and marriage to the divorced Mrs Simpson – and it keeps hovering on the edge of a revival whenever a comparable event is postulated. Morganatic has nothing to do with Mr and Mrs Morgan (nor with a royal mistress of that name, as has been suggested) but everything with the morning-after-the-night-before. The German *Morgen*, (Old German spelling *Morgan*) means morn or morning, and refers to the traditional "morning gift" the groom would give to the bride after their first night together. In the highest circles it was not necessarily a mere trinket: "He has wooed the young countess an' given her for her morning-gift Strathboggie and Aboyne…" (Maidment's *North Countrie Garland*, 1824). The legal provisions of the Latin *matrimonium ad morganaticum*, says the *OED*, were that in "a marriage by which the wife and children that may be born are entitled to no share in the husband's possession beyond the Morning Gift…she remains in her former rank and the issue of the marriage have no claim to succeed to the possessions or dignities of their father". The gift might have come from a married commoner or an unmarried philandering prince wanting to express his gratitude for the delights he had enjoyed, so the recipient was not necessarily a lawful bride: it might have been a one-night arrangement. Wagner's *Siegfried Idyll* was a morning gift to his mistress Cosima, played by an *ad hoc* band on the stairs leading to her bedroom. Confusingly there were in Victorian times also *mourning-gifts*, presented to mourners by the dead person's family, often made of jet and containing a small lock of the deceased's hair.

mourning/morning *Mourning*, feeling (or showing) grief or sorrow, now generally at someone's death, is from an old Teutonic word that had wider meanings of sadness, at any rate as it was used in Chaucer's *Canterbury Tales* (ca 1386): "I shal make thyn herte for to morne ffor wel I woot thy pacience is gon" and appears to have no connection with French *mourir*, to die. *Morning*, the part of the day before noon, comes from Middle English *morwening*, and is related to the German *Morgen*. The left-wing politititian Ken Livingstone, who considers a dinner-jacket capitalist apparel, was reported in the *Independent* as having attended a solemn commemoration "wearing his morning suit". He was quick to point out that it was not a *morning* suit (which would have consisted of a cut-away "penguin" tailcoat and striped trousers) but an ordinary black lounge-suit that might have been called a "mourning suit". (In the Liverpool dialect, one's best suit is called a "bezzie" or "funeral suit"). The difference in spelling is, of course, relatively modern: but confusions arise when morning and mourning are treated as homophones – as they are by nearly all speakers (though not in the home of my fussy first in-laws-once-removed [by divorce], where anyone who did not clearly say "moor-ning" was reproved).

mozartian/mozart-like/mozartish "The splendid drawing-room resounded to the strains of the Mozartian concerto." Later in the *Times* article it became clear that what the writer had heard (and knew he had heard) was indeed a concerto by Mozart, not one that merely *sounded* like music by this composer. Had it been a concerto by his pupil Hummel it might have qualified for the description of *Mozartian*. See also SHEEPISH/SHEEPLIKE.

mrs/miss/ms Since the late 17th century (the *OED* suggests 1670) the abbreviation MS has stood for manuscript, originally Latin *manuscriptum*, something written by hand, plural MSS. But in 1952 the authors of *The Simplified Letter*, published by the National Office Management Association of Philadelphia, USA, advised secretaries to "use the abbreviation Ms for *all women* addressees [their italics]. This modern style solves an age-old problem." Many writers see no problem, because *Miss* Sally Jones and *Mrs* Jane Smith may take no offence at being addressed as plain Sally Jones or Jane Smith. Other women, both married and single, use *Ms* as if to say: "My marital status is my own affair." (partner serves much the same purpose). Yet as early as 1754 *The Connoisseur* "...could not help wishing that some middle term was invented between Miss and Mrs. to be adopted...by all females not inclined to matrimony". See also COMMON-LAW(HUSBAND/WIFE)/MISTRESS/LOVER/CONCUBINE.

mugging/robbing *Muggers* already posed a threat in colonial India, but were called muggers only by the British, in a punning sort of way with reference to their jaws, as a soundalike for the Hindi *magar*, the broadnosed crocodile, *Crocodilus palustris*. On the other hand, in

Liverpool scouse "I'll mug yer" until the mid-1960s was not a threat but a promise, meaning "I will treat you and buy you a drink". But it was always a bit of a two-faced word – three-faced if you include "mugging up" for intensive learning or swotting. Charles Dickens (1855) used it in the sense of "making grotesque faces", but in the *Swell's Night Guide* (1846) it already meant fighting, striking someone in the face (i.e. his "mug"), also "to beat up and rob". Which brings us to the present day – but confounds those who claimed mugging was of Afro-Caribbean origin: an assumption based on the fact that in New York mugging was always black street-crime.

mumbo-jumbo/gobbledygook Objections to the pleasant reduplication of *mumbo-jumbo* have been raised on grounds of race, but they might equally well be based on feminist thinking. For the *OED*, citing a source of 1738, postulates a Congolese origin, and (quoting an 18th-century traveller called Moore) says it was "a grotesque idol said to have been worshipped by certain tribes or associations of Negroes" and was "a dreadful Bugbear to the Women, call'd Mumbo-Jumbo...a Thing invented by Men to keep their Women in awe". *Gobbledygook* dates from World War II and was coined by American servicemen to pour scorn on Washington's pretentious verbiage that was high-sounding but made little sense. See also JUMBO/BIG.

murphy's law/sod's law Both are usually explained as demonstrating that "If anything can go wrong it will". The earliest example found by the *OED*, in the *Nation* (USA), says, "There is an old military maxim known as Murphy's Law which asserts that wherever there is a bolt to be turned, someday there will be someone to turn it the wrong way." That is dated 1958, but it must be older, and is probably British. In 1952 the astronaut John Glenn confidently stated that "Murphy was a careless, all-thumbs mechanic [in the US Navy] who was PRONE to make such mistakes as installing a propeller backwards". Murphy's Law is also known as *Sod's Law*, defined in the New Statesman (1970): "Sod's Law is the force in nature which causes it to rain mostly at weekends, which makes you get flu when on holiday, and which makes the phone ring just as you've got into the bath." Sod and Murphy often work hand-in-glove with the GREMLINS, who may take the blame for human errors. In the USA, where there are more Murphys than in the whole of Ireland, North and South, the equivalent expression is "Shit happens". See also GREMLINS/LITTLE PEOPLE.

muscle/mussel HOMOPHONE troubles sometimes strike in places one might think they could never reach. A press release issued on behalf of the Reverend Ian Paisley (a Northern Irish politician) complained that "the Irish Language Body has been given mussels to enforce the public practice of the Irish Language in Northern Ireland". Oh no! not the dreaded orange-and-green-lipped mussels!

musical chairs/jobs (benefits) allocation *Musical chairs* is a Victorian parlour-game in which a number of persons walk round a smaller number of chairs while music is being played. When the music stops, each tries to secure a chair and sit down on it. The person left without one pays some kind of forfeit. The game is all but forgotten, together with most other parlour games (except in the form of a race to get to the seat with the best view of the television); but the term is used with reference to the allocation of, or competition for, jobs or other benefits. Among senior executives of the BBC the rules of musical chairs have traditionally been that when the music stops they put out another chair. See also NEPOTISM/CRONYISM/PLACEMAN.

— N —

naiveté/naivety A good English word *naivety* has been available since at least 1708, yet writers and speakers still prefer the French word *naiveté*, meaning the quality of being artless.

narcotics/opiates/drugs *Narcotics* is often used by the MEDIA as if it meant illicit *drugs*. They are sleep-inducing substances, and most are legal. The word comes from the Latin and Greek for drowsiness or stupor. *Opiates* are derived from opium and are usually legitimate painkillers. Chaucer knew them both in the *Knight's Tale* (ca 1386): "With nercotikes and opie of Thebes fyn"; while a surgical textbook by Traheron (1543) is more specific: "Opiate medicines [ass]swage payne, howbeit it is onely after the maner of palliation". A drug can be any substance used as a medicine, so a "drugs haul" could consist of a million aspirins.

native americans/red indians A generation ago most people would have considered the two terms synonymous, but sensible political correctness has reminded us that American Indians are neither *red* nor are they *Indians* (a misnomer apparently based on the flawed navigation of Columbus), which would vitiate the term, as well as its absurd portmanteau "Amerindians". *Native Americans* is both factual and colourless. As for their tribes, terms like Sioux are also frowned upon (like ESKIMO), for Sioux means "deadly poisonous snake". Instead, "Dakota people" is recommended – at any rate in Rosalie Maggio's allegedly bias-free word finder, *A Dictionary of Nondiscriminatory Language* (see POLITICALLY CORRECT) – which, incidentally, also frowns on "cowboy" as insufficiently gender-inclusive, so that the game of Cowboys and Indians would become Cattle hands and Native Americans. Also prohibited are 18th-century American terms like Indian Gift or Indian Giver, which refer to a gift whose donor expects it to be returned or reciprocated (in the UK probably with a life peerage). See also CAMP/TOWNSHIP/RESERVATION/GHETTO/QUARTER.

native americans

natives/indigenous people The politically correct have decided that the word *native* is insulting, demeaning and patronizing, especially in facetious phrases like "the natives are friendly". It should, they say, be replaced by *indigenous people*.

naturists/naturalists/nudists/textiles the *Liverpool Daily Post* excitedly reported that police had spotted *naturalists* on the sand dunes at Ainsdale. There is indeed some rare and interesting fauna and flora in that area, but the context of the story made it clear that they were *naturists*, a time-worn, self-awarded euphemism for *nudists*. These quaintly call wearers of clothes *textiles* ("There are textiles coming to have a look").

naught/naughty/nought *Naught* means "nothing", often used in phrasal or poetic ways, for example something that "came to naught"; or "Say not the struggle naught availeth", in the poem by A. H. Clough (1819–1861), so memorably quoted by Winston Churchill in World War II. A *nought*, confusingly, is the figure zero. *Naughty* formerly had connotations of "bad" or "rotten", as in the "verie naughtie figes which might not be eaten", in the Bible, Jeremiah 24.2, and the same applies to Portia's candle which shines like "a good deed in a naughty world" in Shakespeare's *Merchant of Venice* (1596). Since the 17th century it has also been applied to children (in the way parents might affectionately call their offpsring "wicked"), but previously had stronger meanings, especially sexual ones: "doing the naughty" was to have sexual intercourse or be sexually promiscuous. It was this behaviour (not that of wayward children) which caused the final decade of the 19th century to be called the *Naughty Nineties* (it became a MEDIA cliché only later, from the 1920s). Brewer's *Dictionary of Phrase and Fable* says the Naughty Nineties were the time "when the puritannical Victorian code of conduct gave way to a growing laxity of sexual morals, a growing cult of hedonism, and a more lighthearted approach to life" (the decade was also briefly called the "yellow nineties" after naughty Oscar Wilde and the "Greenery-Yallery" of the Yellow Book). But although this perceived moral decline quickened in the new century the years 1900-1909 were never designated the "naughty noughties". The 1920s saw much greater moral laxity than that which had coloured the nineties, with their unbridled ragtime "and all that jazz"; when women's hemlines rose, free-range bosoms acquired a life of their own, and flappers started to smoke cigarettes – yet the twenties, too, escaped the "naughty" label. Later in the 20th century, not even World War II, with all its horrors, gave any name to the 1940s (the "roaring forties" would have been a ready-made gift but had been appropriated by sailors). The introduction of the contraceptive pill did give rise briefly to the permissive "swinging sixties", but as things became ever more permissive towards the end of the 20th century and beyond it into the new millennium, people seemed to give up coining such facile terms.

nauseous/nauseated That which is loathsome, disgusting, sick-making or indeed nauseating, is *nauseous*. A person affected by such qualities is *nauseated*. Latin *nausea* and Greek *nausia* both had *nau*tical origins and literally meant seasickness. See also AD NAUSEAM/TOWARDS REVULSION.

naval/navel Few writers have a problem with *naval* which, as everyone knows, pertains to the navy, from Latin *navis*, a ship; nor with their *navel*, from a Teutonic word that gave the Germans the *Nabel*. The Greek word *omphalos* has had little influence on our tummy-buttons – it also means the hub of a wheel, or a centre-point, and gave its name to Omphale (who with Hercules made up the most interesting cross-dressing couple of Greek legend), but medics prefer the Latin *umbilicus*. Compulsive headline punsters can never resist jests like "Navel Bases". This led to confusions, as in the *Guardian's* non-accidental "naval-gazing".

né/née French for "born", used in English to give the premarital or birth-name of a person, usually a woman, and written in small letters, *née*. As men do not usually change their name upon marriage, the masculine form *né* is seldom seen.

nepotism/cronyism/placemen In Latin *nepos* is a nephew; and also the standard euphemism, since the Middle Ages, for the bastard sons of Roman Catholic clergy. When it came to jobs or perks, the "nephews" were sure to get preferment before other aspirants (Latin *preferre*, to advance or put forward). *Nepotism* also benefited grandchildren and other relatives – and later still, *cronies*. In the UK these came into their own from May 1997. For as soon as Tony Blair became Prime Minister he embarked on a programme of political appointments on a scale unprecedented in British political history, the recipients of these honours inevitably being dubbed "Tony's cronies". In the USA *cronyism* had been recorded as early as 1840: "The appointment of friends to government posts without proper regard to their qualifications", but Samuel Pepys was already favouring his friends a couple of centuries earlier: in 1665, in his *Diary*, he mentions "Jack Cole, my old school-fellow, who was a great chrony of mine". (Could Pepys's spelling provide a clue to a possible derivation – from Greek *chronos*, time, i.e. a contemporary?) Another old English word for such beneficiaries is *placemen*. In a quotation from the House of Lords of 1741 these are defined as men who "hold an appointment in the service of the sovereign or state; almost always with depreciatory or hostile connotation: [a *placeman* is] one who is appointed to such positions from motives of interest, without regard to fitness". It is a way of buying loyalty – in much the same way as African or Arab dictators guard against COUPS by appointing to high office only members of their own family or tribe.

nice/niceness/nicety *Nice* has had many meanings, beginning with foolish and stupid; then, in the Middle Ages, it meant vapid, wanton and loose-mannered: "Nyce she was, but mente noone harme... but only lust and jolyte", wrote Chaucer in *Romaunt of the Rose* (before 1366). A century later it was used of dress, to mean flaunting, extravagant, elegant and smart; but Coverdale's Bible translation of 1535 had, in Ecclesiastes 43.27: "...straunge wonderous workes, dyuerse maner of nyce beestes and whall fishes". In 1573 it meant what is now miscalled "gay", in Florio's *Paranimphia*: "An effeminate, nice, milkesop, puling fellow"; also coy, shy, reserved or affectedly modest, reluctant; fastidious, difficult to please (from the 16th to the 19th centuries); also, in parallel periods, precise or strict, punctilious, etc. – which led to what is now looked upon as the second meaning after the all-too-common, all-embracing, all-purpose adjective of approval. And very nice, too. But *niceties* never made this modern transformation (nor did "a nice difference", meaning a precise one), so a SPIN DOCTOR was mistaken in saying that "Mr Blair was in no mood to exchange niceties" with his French counterpart (intending "pleasantries"?) when the two prime ministers were pictured undiplomatically glowering at each other. A nicety today is a minute distinction, whereas the government spokesman meant the minister was in no mood to be nice to the Frenchman. Further confusion has been brought about, needlessly, by the formation of the National Institute for Clinical Excellence, a body charged to oversee the effectiveness of prescription drugs; why should so learned a body stoop to make silly acronyms? But spokesmen and newsreaders drop in the word NICE without further explanation of its meaning.

niggard(ly)/niggle/nigger *Niggard* has no connection whatever with *nigger*, but comes from Scandinavian languages – *njugg, nögg, nigla*, a miser (the *OED* also postulates an early French source). Numerous early English texts confirm this: Geoffrey Chaucer in his *Romaunt of the Rose* (before 1366) has the line, "A fulle gret fool is he, ywys, / That bothe riche and nygart is"; and in 1483 William Caxton's *Cato* gives the proverb, "Men saye comynlye that the nygarde expendeth more than the lyberalle." And so it goes on, down the centuries, the noun and its related adjective and adverb always denoting miserly, mean, parsimonious and grudging people unwilling to spend their money. But this cut no ice with the Government of Washington, District of Columbia, USA, whose watchdogs were informed (in January 1999) that a Mr David Howard, Director of Constituent Services, had told his staff he was *niggardly* over spending government funds. In spite of widespread protests from literate Americans, Mr Howard was dismissed. However, after a week or two it emerged that as a self-declared homosexual his sacking could have been seen as discriminatory, so he was reinstated – albeit for the wrong reason. It was a cunning ploy to save the face of his accusers, who were not obliged to admit they had made asses of themselves. However, in the same week a White House lawyer denounced some "legal MUMBO-JUMBO" (which could indeed be interpreted as racist) with not a whisper of protest being heard. Other words that should be avoided in case they cause offence to the ignorant include LINCHPIN and DENIGRATE; even *niggling*, from *niggles*, which are petty, trifling complaints, has come under suspicion. See also DERACINATE.

nine-eleven/eleven-nine Americans abbreviate dates by putting the month before the day, so that the outrage of 11 September 2001 is referred to in America by the abbreviation *9/11*. If the British were given to using such snappy spoken abbreviations this would be the ninth of November, though regrettably a few English journalists have adopted the American form when referring to this shocking event. Some, however, still find the time – and respect – to say "the eleventh of September". Although the US practice predates the invention of the computer, it is more computer-efficient and may therefore eventually be adopted worldwide. For a date such as 01/09/11 (year-month-day) is chronologically sortable on a PROGRAM, whereas 11/09/01 would give a false reading. Even the Bible, in Genesis 7. 11, appears to endorse the American date-order when it reported an earlier calamity to befall mankind: "In the six hundredth year of Noah's life, in the second month, on the seventeenth day of the month...were all the fountains of the great deep broken up and the windows of heaven were opened." In other words the Great Flood occurred on 2/17.

no-one/no one *No-one*, as in "no-one is to blame", means nobody is to blame. "*No one* [person] is to blame" means no one, separate, single person (and "noone", which is also sometimes seen, is a non-word). English can cope with the loss of colons and semi-colons, but hyphens are often essential to conveying the intended meaning.

normalcy/normality Americans say and write *normalcy*, Britons prefer (a state of) *normality*, which both looks and sounds better. In the Classical world *norma* was Latin for a carpenter's or stonemason's square, which therefore became a pattern or rule for that which conforms. See also ENORMITY/ENORMOUSNESS.

nuclear/ "new-kew-lar" "New-kew-lar" or "new-kee-lar" are common mispronunciations arising presumably from a confusion of the spelling – so common that it is shared by a number of otherwise excellent radio and TV reporters and presenters, as well as President George W. Bush of the United States of America, who can launch a nuclear device but is incapable of pronouncing (and probably spelling) what he may launch.

nude/naked In spite of its honourable association with Classical painting and scuplture, *nude* has fallen victim to tabloid sleaze and usually suggests salacious nakedness: nude is rude, whereas *naked* is factual and neutral. (Yet children are seldom nude, even in the grubbiest tabloids, but naked.)

— O —

o/oh The two exclamations seem to be interchangeable, but *O* is chiefly associated with poetry, while *Oh* is more appropriate for what the *OED* calls "pain or terror... shame, derisive astonishment, or disapprobation". Here intonation is everything.

oblivious/forgetful/absentminded *Oblivious*, often intensified with "totally", now usually means a complete lack of awareness, perhaps even that caused by a loss of consciousness; but its early "correct" meaning was related only to *forgetfulness*, from Latin *obliviosus*, forgetful. According to *Punch* (see RECUPERATE/RECOVER) Americans who wanted to sound English and posh would say "obliviate" in place of forget (and presumably sent little posies of obliviate-me-nots). In an older sense of *absentmindedness* it occurs in a delightful, pre-1644 quotation from one J. Capgrave, offered by the ever-watchful *OED*: "This emperour Claudius was so obliuiows that, sone aftir he had killid his wyf, he asked why sche cam not to soper."

odious/odorous *Odious* comes from Latin *odiosus*, hateful, repugnant, disagreeable and offensive, though not specifically to the nose. Shakespeare's *Othello* (1604) has "You told a Lye, an odious damned Lye". The cliché "comparisons are odious" had become a proverb by the 1400s, e.g. with Lydgate's "Odyous of olde been comparisonis/And of comparisonis engendyrd is haterede" (ca 1430). *Odorous*, from Latin *odorus*, fragrant, at first meant only a *good* smell, as in Shakespeare's "Odorous Chaplet of sweet Sommer buds" in *A Midsummer Night's Dream* (?1595/6), but the bad-scented meaning eventually drove out the good (Gresham's Law applies also to words). The malapropism "comparisons are odorous" also comes from Shakespeare, in his *Much Ado about Nothing* (1599), where the Constable Dogberry uses proto-policespeak.

odious

official/officious Although minor *officials* can be the most officious, this is just a happy coincidence, as the two words have different origins. *Official* comes from Latin *officium*, office, adjective *officialis*; *officious* from *officiosus*, obliging, dutiful – a definition which would be wholly welcome were it not for the fact that some officials are overzealous and may enjoy misusing their power, often to the detriment of courtesy. This secondary meaning is almost as old as the NICE one. William Warner in *Albion's England* described Cardinal Wolsey (1602) as "…that slye, officious, and too Lordly Cardnall" [sic].

of the year/approved of *Of the Year* awards are an invention of the publicity industry and recipients are almost always those put forward by members of a professional group, like film-makers or TV producers. The nonsense started in the 1960s, with the "election" of a "Pipeman of the Year" (courtesy of the tobacco industry). Then came a "Tieman of the Year", a "Margarine Cook of the Year", a this-that-and-another thing of the year. And each time publicists set up a contest the public falls for it. The BBC runs the praiseworthy but fatuously misnamed *Young Musican of the Year* competition, which invites voters to judge the disparate and uncomparable (though often incomparable) skills of trombonists and percussionists against those of trumpeters and violinists. See also AWARD-WINNING/ALLEGEDLY GOOD.

-ography/-ology The *-(o)graphy* element in English words comes from the Greek *graphein*, to write, but *-(o)logy*, also from Greek – *logos*, a word or reason – has come to be used as the "knowledge" suffix. So, for example, the *radiographer* takes the x-ray pictures but the *radiologist* knows how to interpret them. Radiologists would not wish to be called radiographers, though theirs is also a highly skilled job. To give another example, *graphology* is the knowledge, interpretation, etc., of writing. But often things go wrong, as when 18th/19th-century quacks, claiming to be able to interpret bumps on the head, optimistically named their theory "phrenology". This means knowledge of the mind when, at best, they should have called it "craniology", knowledge of the SKULL.

orchestrate/organize/score In music, *orchestration* is the disposal and setting out of the separate instrumental parts of an *orchestral* composition (you don't *orchestrate*, say, a string quartet or violin-and-piano sonata, you *score* them). Nor can you orchestrate, say, a speech unless you first set it to music with instrumental accompaniment, though in 1936 a perceptive critic wrote of Gerard Manley Hopkins's "subtlety and variety of verbal orchestration". But apart from skilful and imaginative use, pressing orchestration into non-musical service is sure to produce a cliché. For further raids on the musical cliché cupboard see CRESCENDO and LOW KEY.

orientated/oriented/orienteering The word for an abstract inclination towards a certain goal or aim is *orientated*, not *oriented*, which if it means anything is "facing the Orient", i.e. East. The same applies to disorientated/ disoriented. *Oriented* is a mainly American abbreviation. *Orienteering* is only remotely connected with either, a mid-20th-century, purpose-invented word for the sport of finding one's way across rough country with the aid of a map and COMPASS. Literally it would mean "finding East" – and presumably the skill lies in working out the other compass points from it.

overweening/"overweaning" A writer in the *Independent* decribed Sir William Beveridge, the founder of the British National Health Service, as "overweaning". Some say the Welfare State has been nannying us – but not to the extent of breast-feeding. What the writer meant was that Beveridge was *overweening* – which means conceited, arrogant and with too high an opinion of oneself (from *ween*, Old English for opinion, belief). *Weaning* a child is to accustom it to the loss of its mother's milk (German *entwöhnen*, to disaccustom), so it is difficult to see how a baby can be "overweaned". By coincidence a *wean* in Scots dialect is a small child, a contraction of "wee ane".

oxymoron/contradiction *Oxymoron(ic)* is now often used, as in this book, in its modern superficial meaning of a *contradiction in terms*, an incongruous conjunction. Its literal meaning, from Greek *oxys* = sharp (wise) + *moros* = dull (foolish), is "a wise fool", and was originally "a rhetorical figure in which contradictory or incongruous terms are conjoined so as to give point to a statement or expression" (see also SOPHOMORE): bitter-sweet, cordial dislike, gentle violence, etc. The Bible and other poetry are full of apparent oxymorons, like "Let the dead bury their dead" (St Matthew 8.22) and Wordsworth's "The child is father to the man".

177

— P —

pace/in spite of/pardon me... The Latin *pace* (rhyming with Saatchi, not with face) is an abbreviation for *pace tua*, by your leave, root-word *pax*, peace – in other words, "Don't be cross if I say this...", though often intended as a sarcastic aside: "*Pace* Fowler, a split infinitive is always ugly". It introduces a disagreement with, or polite rejection of, someone's statement or opinion – but is often erroneously used as though it meant "in spite of". The *OED* cites a second Latin tag, *pace tanti viri*, "by the leave or favour of so great a man", which can serve to emphasize either the deference or the sarcasm.

paean/paeon A *paean* is a hymn or chant, usually of praise or thanksgiving, originally addressed specifically to Apollo but now available to just about anybody or anything the writer or speaker considers worthy of one. A *paeon* is a metrical foot of four syllables, one short followed by three long, which would be expressed as · – – – in morse code. Just to confuse, paeans were composed in the paeon metre.

paedophile/child-molester/pedophile/pederast *Paedophile* is one of the most wicked misnamings of the 20th century – false on all counts – but unfortunately we are stuck with it. They even have a collective noun – they come in RINGS. The word was first coined in 1906, as the more correctly Greek-based *paidophile*, by Havelock Ellis, a writer about sexual abnormalities. It is made from the Greek words for *children* and *love*, respectively, and was hardly ever heard until adopted in ca 1970 as a self-description by a band of *child-molesters*, who insisted that they loved children and did them no harm. It was an attempt to legitimize their activities – indeed make them seem desirable – for should we not all love children? In the pre-Internet 1970s the group set up a notorious register, calling it the "Paedophile Information Exchange", approachably acronymed PIE. The ringleaders were convicted and imprisoned, but their coinage remained and was widely adopted, even by law-makers. The

American simplified spelling *pedophile* is gaining ground in the UK, even though it is a false etymology (Latin *pes, pedem*, foot), thus inadvertently shifting the sexual interest from children to feet (Havelock Ellis had a term for *this* aberration, too: foot-fetishism). Yet *pederast* suffered a similar modification from *paederast* and survived, though its meaning is more user-specific: "Pederast, a Sodomite, a buggerer" (1730) – and for the last-named word see under CATAMITE/SODOMITE. In England, whenever there is some HUE-AND-CRY about *paedophiles* it is paediatricians who get their windows broken by the slow-reading underclass; and so great is the hysteria attending cases of child-molesting that the university faculties of paediatrics have suffered a loss of entrants. Some judicious name-changing seems overdue.

pallet/palate/palette A trio of confusibles that seems to flummox many writers. Thus a wine correspondent of the *Daily Telegraph* (whose very livelihood depends on his *palate*) wrote about imbibers and their *palettes*, while a *Times* obituarist lamented the loss of a flautist's "rich pallet of sound". A *pallet*, from French *paille*, straw, is a kind of rough mattress (see also POUFFE); the palate, from Latin *palatum*, is the roof of the mouth; and a palette, derived from the diminutive of the Latin *pala*, a shovel, is a French word, adopted into English, for a board on which painters mix their pigments.

pants/shorts/underpants/drawers/trousers An American man's *shorts* are a Briton's *underpants*, and what the American calls his *pants* the Englishman calls *trousers*. *Pants* is a comparatively new word (originally short for *pantaloons*) even for Englishmen. Pre-Edwardian men wore *drawers* under their breeches (and drawers were worn by both sexes, though 17th–19th-century women normally wore none, as their skirts were voluminous enough to keep their charms hidden). In pre-textile use, pants would have suggested an agitated bosom poetically heaving: "As if the earth in thick, fast pants were breathing" (Coleridge, *Kubla Khan*, ?1798).

parameter/perimeter/boundary/limit *Parameter* is a scientific term that means "the third proportional to any given diameter and its conjugate or, in the parabola, to any abscissa on a given diameter and the corresponding ordinate... etc." as the *OED* makes clear. It does not mean what politicians and others think it means, namely *limit*, *perimeter* or the line or lines forming a *boundary*, etc. When scientific or artistic terms become clichés, meaning is almost inevitably mangled.

paramount/tantamount *Paramount*, from Old French *par à mont*, means above, higher, in motion, position or importance; *tantamount*, also from Old French *tant amunter* and Italian *tanto montare*, to amount to as much, to be equivalent.

passed/past/pastimes/past times *Passed* and *past* are related homophones with different functions, often depending on whether qualified by *is* or *has*: "She is *past* 50 this year" but "she has *passed* 50". Conversely, "Another year has *passed*" but "the worst is now *past*". *Times* that *pass* become *times past* – or *past times*; but not *pastimes*, which means pursuits that pass the time: they were by 1490 known to William Caxton, in his *Eneydos*: "The fayr passe-time that they take thereat". The *Guardian's* statement "The unreformed House of Lords finally past into history" was wrong: it *passed* into history. Is that clear?

pat/paddy/irishman/patsy/stalking-horse/stool-pigeon *Paddy* is the affectionate and ancient nickname for an *Irishman*, also *Pat* (both are short for Patrick), which not even the most politically correct have reason to condemn as RACIST. Sir Walter Scott in 1825 referred to "youthful Pats and Patesses" as "decent and comely". Someone giving a prompt answer might "have it (off) pat" and it is also an expression or exclamation meaning smartly, promptly or "just like that" – so when Hamlet muses about killing his uncle it sounds as if he has an invisible Irish accomplice: "Now might I do it, Pat, now he is praying"; and in *A Midsummer Night's Dream* (?1595/6) Quince appears to tell a phantom Irish friend of a good venue: "Pat, Pat; and here's a marvellous convenient place for our rehearsal." In *King Lear* (1608) Pat is bad news: "And Pat he comes like the catastrophy of the old comedy." (But see also Lear's Chinese cook, under HA/HO; as well as Maggie Smith's effeminate friend FRANK). The Irish-American *patsy*, says the *OED*, is "a person who is ridiculed, deceived, blamed or victimized"; or, in court, one who considers himself to have been blamed for another's misdeed, "framed", or "fitted up": "I was just a patsy, your honour..." A *stalking-horse* was at first a real horse, "trained to allow a fowler to conceal himself behind it in order to get within easy range of the game without alarming it", though today the reference is usually to a little-known politician who allows himself to be put up as a spoiler candidate in an election he has no hope of winning. The presence of a stalking-horse always portends intrigue, deception or subterfuge. A *stool-pigeon* is "a person employed, especially by gamblers, as a decoy" (*OED*), though for lovers of American crime ficition is also a police informer, in which case it may be abbreviated to *stoolie*.

pate/paté/pasty The *pate* is the head, especially the top, whether bald or not, and has been around much longer than the *pâté*, to wit since at least 1300 AD: "He smot him with a ston behynde in the pate that al the scull to-daschte the brayn ful out therate." A *pâté* is a paste – fish-paste, liver, ham etc. – brought from France around the beginning of the 18th century (the *circonflex* replacing an s). It was anglicised as *pasty*, but this now usually means a small pie containing meat and potatoes, which is almost invariably – whatever its geographical origin – described as "Cornish". The *circonflex* has now been abolished even in France, but the acute accent on the *é* saves confusion.

pathos/bathos *Pathos*, the Greek word for suffering, was taken into poetic English from the 15th century, and thence into medical language in relation to diseases and their study, to describe various morbid or abnormal mental or physical conditions and disciplines, like pathology, etc. By the 19th century it had been taken over by philosophers, and by the 20th the general public made free with it, hence our "pathological liars" etc. *Bathos* is Greek for depth, the lowest point or bottom, and is not heard as much as *pathos*, which is why it is sometimes wrongly "corrected" to *pathos*. In 17th- and 18th-century rhetoric and literary criticism *bathos* denoted a ludicrous descent from the grand or elevated into the commonplace, or a "come-down".

peal/peel Together with PEDDLE and PEDAL (below) *peal* and *peel* are long-term residents in the *Guardian*'s retirement home for tired old puns and inadvertent HOMOPHONES, e.g. "peel of bells".

pedant/pedagogue Originally a *pedant* was a teacher, from French *pédant*, Italian *pedante*, a schoolmaster; probably from Greek *pais*, a boy (whose teacher would have been a *pedagogue* — and sometimes unfortunately a PAEDOPHILE. See also DOMINATE). Teachers like us to get things right and may show impatience if we don't. This is the *OED* definition of *pedant* in full: "A person who overrates book-learning [*can* anyone?] or technical knowledge, or displays it unduly or unreasonably; one who has mere learning untempered by practical judgement and knowledge of affairs; one who lays excessive stress upon trifling details of knowledge or upon strict adherence to formal rules; sometimes, one who is possessed by a theory and insists on applying it in all cases without discrimination, a doctrinaire". A *pedagogue*, from Greek *pais*, boy (child) + *gogos*, leader or teacher, is literally "a leader of boys"; and could

pendant

therefore be a scoutmaster as well as a schoolmaster. The emphasis on *male* learning and teaching was characteristic of the Classical period and should not be taken as a slight on present-day girls.

peddle/pedal A *pedlar* is one who goes about carrying small goods for sale, which he *peddles* – and his single *d* seems to be there just to confuse uncertain spellers (*peddler* is an accepted alternative spelling). Bicyclists *pedal* their machines – and get an extra *l* when *pedalling*.

penal/penile *Penal*, from Latin *pœna*, penalty, *penalis*, of or belonging to punishment; but *penile* from *penis*. The two are sometimes confused, especially as Americans pronounce both the same, speaking of "pen'l servitude" as well as "pen'l intercourse".

pendent/pendant As with DEPENDANT/DEPENDENT, both words come from Latin *pendere*, to hang, but a difference in spelling has arisen between the noun and the adjective. By convention the thing or object that hangs is pendent, but is itself a pendant. Not so in an article in the *Tatler* about a society wedding between a rich old peer and a young society beauty, though it did not affect the ambiguity of the statement. Listing all the wedding-gifts, as was common in more leisurely days (see also DEPENDANT/DEPENDENT and MORGANATIC/CIVIL MARRIAGE) the *Tatler* reported that "the groom's present to the bride was an antique pendent". And see the footnote to CAVALRY/CALVARY.

peninsula/peninsular *Peninsular* is the adjective (as in Peninsular Wars), *peninsula* the noun – a piece of land nearly surrounded by water and therefore almost an island: Latin *paene*, almost + *insula*, island.

penny/pennies/pence/pee Writing about the publication of Princess Diana's will, a columnist in the *Independent* asked, "why, with a total bequest of £21,711,486, not a single pence was earmarked for charity." Before UK decimalization we spoke of a single, singular *penny* and several, plural *pennies* (or *pence*); also *tuppence, thruppence, fourpence*, etc. In 1971 the "pee" entered the language – at first facetiously and then as the standard way of the clueless majority, although no-one ever said "six dee" for 6d (*d* stood for Latin *denarius*). Pee for your thoughts? Half-a-pound of two-pee rice?? Sing a song of six pee??? Perhaps the *pee* was introduced as a harbinger of the Euro, pronounced "uro".

penury/poverty Living in *penury* means subsisting in STRAITENED circumstances, from Latin *penuria*, need, want, poverty – though not to a writer on the *Liverpool Daily Post*, who thought it was a place: "Jacob Epstein lived during his early years in Penury, near London." A reader spotted: "The English drown their chips in salt and vinegar. This cannot possibly happen in Lucullan, France..." (Lucullan, adjective, a reference to Lucullus, a Roman famous for his sumptuous banquets). See also IN SITU.

perform/carry out They mean much the same, though there may arise subtle differences. Thus routine surgical operations may be *carried out*, or simply done, but lengthy, complicated and probably newsworthy ones, like a transplant, are invariably *performed*. Politicians perform metaphorical u-turns, whereas motorists are more likely just to "make a u". More surprisingly, journalists prefer the grander form when reporting sexual activity; as in "She then performed a sex act on him", apparently elevating it to the status of a performance and almost implying the presence of cameras, lights and an audience. See AURAL/ORAL.

person/penis *Person* in the context of human anatomy is an absurd and coyly old-fashioned legal term for the *penis*, as in "The accused exposed his person to an elderly female", or in its archaic legal form, "with the intent of insulting any female" – which many lawyers and police officers have been obliged to intone solemnly in court (though the exact nature of the insult would have been open to interpretation). Modern frankness of speech and some efforts to reduce legal jargon eventually made this euphemism obsolete. See also INTIMACY.

phylacteries/phylloxera The writer who asserted in the *Liverpool Daily Post* that "Jewish men prayed with phylloxera on their heads" confused two near-soundalikes. The small leathern boxes containing biblical texts which male Jews bind to their foreheads for prayer are *phylacteries*. *Phylloxera* are the dreaded vine-lice that sometimes infest grape-vines and ruin wine crops.

picaresque/picturesque The two are unrelated. *Picturesque* is obviously about pictures, but *picaresque* comes from Spanish *picaresco*, roguish or knavish, from Latin *pica*, a magpie, the bird often accused of being a thief (Rossini's opera *La Gazza Ladra*, or *The Thieving Magpie*, is only one example). *Picaresque* is a French adaptation later adopted into English, usually by literary critics: "a picaresque novel...", originally applied only to works with a Spanish theme.

pickpocketing/pocketpicking Light-fingered miscreants go picking pockets, not pocketing picks, yet the false back-formation *pickpocketing* has been in use since the end of the 18th century. It should of course be *pocket-picking* (hyphenated or as one word), dating from at least 1662, still used by the Victorians before being supplanted by the absurd *pickpocketing*. However, *pocketing* is a recognized verb among journalists, especially gossip-writers, who are doing their silliest best to replace it with the trendy "trousering", as in "he trousered a large cheque".

piebald/skewbald/brindled The maligned magpie gets the blame again: *piebald* usually describes a cow, horse, dog or other animal having black and white patches like a magpie. Brown (or other colours) and white patches are *skewbald*, both from around 1600; and *brindled* means striped or streaked, like a brindled cow. An earlier form is *brinded*.

pigeon/pidgin/pidgeon *Pidgin* (or *Pidgin English*) is a quaintly simplified South East Asian dialect, a form of English with elements of Chinese, though consisting mostly of near-English words, like "baragap" for broken and "blong me" for mine. It has nothing to do with the *pigeon*. Pidgin is a corruption by Chinese-speakers of "business" – hence the expression, "That's *your* pidgin" (not the nonsensical "your pigeon"), meaning "That's *your* business". A travel-writer on the *Daily Telegraph* who reported "...haggling over the price in pigeon Greek" was miles out – thousands of miles – in every way. *Pidgeon* is a family name, or else a misspelling.

pinteresque/silence The adjective *Pinteresque* (more rarely *Pinterish*), from the name of the playwright Harold Pinter (b. 1930), refers to platitudes separated by long, studied silences, in reference to his perceived style. If these are rather nightmareish they could also be KAFKAESQUE. Since the plays of George Bernard Shaw have suffered a decline we hear fewer references to things Shavian, an adjective he coined in 1903: never slow to appreciate his own genius he latinized himself "Shavius". Ibsen's (or his imitators') work is simply Ibsenish; and Oscar Wilde's Wildean – usually meaning epigrams that rather predictably turn truisms upside-down.

pint-sized/small In English slang a small person is sometimes described as *pint-sized*, perhaps with reference to beer, a pint of which the practised drinker may consider a small amount (and which seems to have survived

METRIFICATION). But since Imperial measures are no longer taught to schoolchildren, a young reporter was able to write in the *Guardian*: "Farmers are facing ... [a] threat in the form of the pint-sized but destructive Colorado beetle." Some beetle... Conversely, a serious news-item in the *Liverpool Daily Post* began, "A pint-sized schoolboy..." Some schoolboy, some pint.

plaintiff/plaintive "Then, to the plaintiff sound of the piper's lament, the coffin was borne..." reported the *Guardian*. Litigious to the last? No, the paper is evenhanded, so it also gave us "The plaintive will have had a period of sickness..." A *plaintiff* is one who brings a civil action in a court of law, during which he may give evidence *plaintively*, that is, in a complaining, grieving or lamenting manner. Both words have the same origin, but when spelling was more or less standardized early in the 19th century, the complainant became a plaintiff.

plane/plain An unending source of sidesplittingly comic headline fun – or so sub-editors would have us believe. However, when they put "plane sailing" and think they have made a clever pun on "plain" they have inadvertently got it right. In navigation *plane* sailing means "the art of determining a ship's place on the theory that she is moving on a plane, or that the surface of the earth is on a plane instead of spherical; navigation by a plane chart" (definition from the *OED*).

playing away / playing (fooling) around *Playing away* is now a standard tabloid way of describing what unfaithful partners do when allegedly "cheating on" their spouses or live-ins. It is borrowed from football and other sports – adultery committed elsewhere than at home. *Playing* or *fooling around* means unspecified dalliance and comes from America. A news report of an occasion when the British Prime Minister Harold Macmillan took his wife to a golf course famously caused a BBC news-reader to say: "Mr Macmillan then played around with his wife... I think that should have read 'a round – er – of golf'."

pocket/small *Pocket* used to be a common prefix word for a smaller-than-normal version of a familiar object – at first by implication small enough to be carried in the pocket, like a pocket-knife, but also used with derision or sarcasm. The *OED* quotes a Bishop Montagu complaining in 1621 about "pocket-learning", meaning little learning. The word came into its own, via MEDIA use, during the 1930s, when

Germans, preparing for World War II, began to produce "pocket-battleships" (an English coinage: there is no German equivalent). Although "pocket" is now largely superseded by "compact" or "mini", I spotted a small, portable and disposable BARBECUE which was marketed as a "pocket grill".

poignant/sad/plangent/pungent/piquant/pointed *Poignant* does not mean *sad* but *pointed*, from the French for a sharp point or prick, and ultimately from Latin *pungere*, to pierce, puncture or prick. Therefore "a *poignant* reminder of World War II" is not a sad reminder but a sharply affecting one; and such sadness may even make one *plangent*, from Latin *plangere*, to strike noisily, beat the breast or lament aloud. A *pointed* remark is a sharp one, but is not necessarily to the point. Things *piquant* are what pleasantly stimulate or excite keen interest – the mind as well as the PALATE – and can be applied to remarks. Although its immediate provenance is French (especially when used in food language), it has "pointed" or "sharp" connotations in Latin as well as Welsh and Nordic languages, e.g. pick, peck, prickle, prick, pike, etc. If you order *piccata* from an Italian menu you will get a dish of veal in sour lemon sauce, but you have to go to Italy or Spain for a dish described as *piccante*, or sharp-to-the-palate. Incidentally, when Italians speak of sharpness, rage or anger, as well as sharp-tasting dishes, they use *arrabiato*, which comes from Latin *rabere* to rage, as do rabid dogs. See also ACRID.

policeman/officer/constable *Policeman* is going out of use, pushed aside by the presence of numerous female police, so the song must now be: "If you want to know the time, ask a police *officer*." This at any rate is a safe form of address: a SERGEANT may prefer to be addressed as "officer". *Constable* has become almost archaic or even patronizing – a near-insult. Or else misunderstood: as the *Daily Mail* said, "Detectives found a Constable drawing in attic."

politically correct/ideologically sound/inclusive Although the term *politically correct* was at first one of approbation, invented by sociologists towards the end of the 20th century, it blew back badly in the faces of its inventors and soon became a term of opprobrium and ridicule. *Inclusivity*, too, acquired a political meaning, in that any suggestion of bias against any section of the human race or even the animal kingdom was deemed reprehensible. The bible of the politically correct is probably Rosalie Maggio's *Bias-free Word Finder* (Beacon Press, Boston, 1991) which gives "alternatives, explanations and definitions for more than 5,000 biased words and phrases". For example, right-hand man is wrong – twice over, as it discriminates against the left-handed as well as women. (The Isle of Man, however, is KOSHER, "as it has nothing to do with human beings".) Reader, it is a hoot – although good sense occasionally surfaces, e.g. "Do not refer to a person by a surgical procedure or missing body parts…", like amputee.

pore/pour/paw The three are almost homophones and therefore much confused. To *pore* is to look or gaze intently, usually *over* something, like a book. It has nothing to do with *pour* or *pouring*, causing a liquid to flow. Every paper at one time or another has people "pouring" over books or documents and barmen "poring" out drinks. And a hotel brochure: "Join us in the drawing room for a pre-dinner drink. Pour over the menu and place your order [but first mop it up?]." An added confusion is presented when *pawing* is pronounced with an intrusive *r*, "paw-ring".

portend/portent Latin *portendere* means to foretell, and the English verb that comes from it is (*to*) *portend*. Latin *portentum*, an omen or sign, produced the noun, which is (*a*) *portent*.

potable/portable *The Times* printed a 16th century quotation which, the paper claimed, described tobacco as "portable gold". The sub-editor probably thought it was the stuff the Three Kings had to carry to Bethlehem. The word was *potable*, from Latin *potare*, to drink, *potabilis*, drinkable. Potable or drinkable gold was a 16th century medicine made with real gold, as is the German liqueur *Goldwasser*. Tobacco was likened to gold when everyone except James I thought it would be a good thing to "drink" it (the verb "to smoke" was not yet used in this context): "The most divine tobacco that I ever drunk" – Ben Jonson in *Every Man in his Humour* (1598). The *Times* writer probably had written "potable" but found himself "corrected" by a sub-editor who suspected a typing-error.

pouffe/poof/cushioned footstool The French *pouf* means puff, and *pouffe* was until recently the legitimate English word for a round, tightly stuffed cushion, usually of leather – a word used in English since at least 1583: "Hee lay harde vppon a pouffe of straw…" It has no acute accent on the *e* and never had one, but is sometimes pronounced "poof-ay", either to make it sound desirably foreign or to avoid ambiguity. A reader of the *Independent* reported having asked for a *pouffe* in a big London furniture store: "Please madam", [he] was implored in hushed tones, "we are no longer allowed to call them that. I would be pleased to show you our range of *cushioned footstools*." *Poof* (Australian *poofter*), is an offensive name for an effeminate man, usually but not necessarily homosexual (plural either poofs or pooves), words that are generally seen in print only in the tabloids. The Australian *poofter* is applied more indiscriminately (say, to any man not holding a can of lager in his hand, or drinking its contents from a glass); but it seems to have been an English word first, if the *OED* reference dated "ca 1850–60" is to be believed: "These monsters in the shape of men, commonly designated Margeries, Pooffs, &c".

practice/practise/rehearse Classical musicians *rehearse* together but *practise* alone – and the noun for that activity is *practice* (though Americans have abandoned the *practise* spelling and write both with a *c*). Bands and choirs either rehearse or practise, and their meetings may be called band practice or choir practice. An opera singer running through her scales is practising, but as soon as her accompanist joins her they are rehearsing. By the same token orchestral or chamber-music players practise their individual parts but then rehearse together.

prat/twat *Prat* is a a mild term of abuse for a contemptible man (never a woman): "He made a prat of himself." It was defined in 1567 in Thomas Harman's *A caueat or warening for commen cursetors*: "Prat, a buttocke". By comparison with EXPLETIVES by present-day "cursetors" prat is weaker than ARSE: even polite Victorians cheerfully spoke of the music-hall comedian's *pratfall*. *Twat*, on the other hand is up (or down) among the worst four-letter obscenities. It dates from the Middle Ages and was considered so vile that it had to be defined in Latin, *pudendum mulieris* – "the shameful bit of woman" (more snappily euphemized as the "c-word"). Although now spurned by the foul-mouthed, twat figured in a literary *cause célèbre* that made the gentlemen's clubs of 1840s London buzz with SCHADENFREUDE. It was a howler by Robert Browning comparable with the later – anonymous – interpolation of "f*cking" in a *Times* parliamentary report. That was a malicious act, whereas Browning's use of twat was made in blissful innocence. He must have read, in *Vanity of Vanities* (1660) the lines, "They talk't of his having a Cardinalls Hat/They'd send him as soon an Old Nuns Twat." Always fascinated by the habits and rituals of the Roman Church, he assumed that a nun's twat was a nun's article of attire, something like a wimple (as in *The Barretts of Wimple Street* ?) – but no. So in his dramatic poem "Pippa Passes" (1841) Browning wrote:

> *Then, owls and bats,*
> *Cowls and twats,*
>
> *Monks and nuns, in a cloister's moods*
> *Adjourn to the oak-stump pantry!*

Spellings vary from *tweate* to *twaite*, *twayte* and (bad news for some families) *thwaite*; also the charming *twancle* (shades of the pantomime Widow?) and *twachylle*, an old word for a passage. It must have been widely used: a physician (especially a women's doctor) was a *twat-scourer* and a *twat-rug* a woman's pubic hair. "Pippa Passes", incidentally, is the mostly unsuspected source of the line, "God's in his heaven – All's right with the world!"

pray/prey *Praying* comes from Latin *precare*, to entreat – though not necessarily for good things: *imprecare* is to invoke evil or call up a curse or *imprecation*. *Preying* (usually *on* somebody or something) comes from Latin *praeda*, booty or spoil, *praedare*, to rob or plunder (hence *predatory*). The *Richmond Informer* published a story about "Workers who pray on Old Age Pensioners" – presumably while kneeling on them – and the *Independent*, conversely, captioned a group of praying Japanese, "Priests prey in the rain".

predate/pre-date/ante-date The hyphen makes a difference. To *predate* (pronounced to rhyme with sedate) comes from Latin *praedator*, a robber, and means to plunder, to be a thief or *predator*; to *pre-date* (pronounced with a long first *e*) means the same as *ante-date*, to date before the actual time, to occur earlier than.

predilection/"predeliction" *Predilection* comes from the Latin *praediligere* (participle *praedilectus*), to favour, choose or love one thing or person before others. *Predeliction* is a common misreading of it. There is no such word – though with a little effort it could be given a useful meaning – say, a predisposition to wrong-doing or law-breaking. For while *dilectus* means delight, a transposition of letters would relate it to

189

delictus, which is Latin for a crime, an offence (infinitive *delinquere*, to commit one, hence all our delinquents). There can be no better illustration (apart from the almost universal mispronunciation "ecksettera") of the deleterious (Latin *deleterius*, hurtful) effect of the loss of school Latin than "predeliction". A similar confusion-by-transposition affects SACRILEGIOUS/ "SACRELIGIOUS".

premier/premiere A *premiere* is a first performance – feminine because it is short for French *la première représentation*. A *premier* is a prime minister, imported and shortened from the French *premier ministre* – masculine because at one time only men held that office. (When Margaret Thatcher became the first British woman prime minister she could have called herself a *premiere*; but it would only have confused matters).

prestigious/prestigeful Pedants say that *prestigious* has nothing to do with prestige and everything with "deceits, impostures, delusions, iugling or cusening tricks", as a 16th century lexicographer wrote. It means juggling, Latin *praestigator*, a juggler, *prestigiosus*, full of tricks, a kind of portmanteau combination of *praestus*, quick + *digitus*, finger; hence also *prestidigitation*, sleight of hand (literally light-fingeredness). A prestigious hostess, therefore, is not a famous, grand or noble one, but one who with a bit of smart finger-work may pass off powdered coffee as freshly roasted, or who serves tinned soup in a fine tureen. In 1974 the *Times Literary Supplement* wrote about "...the prestigious balancing act" of a dissembling prime minister (is there an *honest* one?), but even by then the real meaning of prestigious had been lost to most of us, and people meant by it "having, showing or conferring prestige". The *OED* very correctly suggests using in its place "prestigeful or some other adjective".

prevaricate/procrastinate/prognosticate *Prevarication* comes from the Latin *varus*, bent, crooked, deviating from a true course or shuffling evasively. *Procrastination* is from Latin *pro*, for + *cras*, tomorrow – to put off or postpone something to another day. To *prognosticate* is to predict or forecast, e.g. the likely outcome of something, from Greek *prognostikos*, (having) foreknowledge.

priced at/worth Oscar Wilde, through his character Lord Darlington, in *Lady Windemere's Fan* (1891), defined a CYNIC as "a man who knows the price of everything and the value of nothing". This was confirmed when an Arts correspondent claimed in *The Times* that a heap of floor sweepings "by" Damien Hirst (a self-styled sculptor) was "worth £5,000". It was nothing of the sort, but someone was foolish enough to pay that amount.

primate/primate/primus All are derived from Latin *primus*, first, and *primas, primatis*, of the first or highest rank – and confusingly include monkeys as well as archbishops. The Church of England has *two* "first" bishops: the Archbishop of Canterbury and the Archbishop of York, both known as Primates. Ireland, too, has two – one for the North and one for the South: Armagh and Dublin respectively. Zoologists speak of mammals like apes and monkeys as *primates*; and an anthropologist allegedly caused consternation when he published a book, *Sex among the Primates*. To add further confusion, a *primus* can be either the presiding bishop of the Scottish Episcopal Church or an oil-stove: the proprietary name of the latter has been current since it was patented at the beginning of the 20th century, and like many household names is carelessly used in a generic, non-patent way.

principal/principle/principality *Principal* means first and foremost, in rank, quality or importance; also the main, original sum of money on which interest accrues. *Principles* (like scruples) are more difficult to define and too elusive for some to possess: see a good dictionary for the various meanings. A principality is anywhere ruled over by a prince, while *the* Principality is a rather affected way of speaking of Wales, often heard from Welsh nationalists who cannot wait to replace the Prince of Wales, their nominal chief, with a placeman (see NEPOTISM).

prise/prize/pry *Prise*, which is the French word for taking hold of something, means to lever. *Prizing* is concerned only with prizes (or as in "prized above rubies"). *Pry*, says the *OED*, is "to look, especially to look closely or curiously; to peep or peer, to look narrowly; to peer inquisitively or impertinently, to spy". Amerians do not distinguish between *prising, prizing* and *prying*: "Pierce lid and pry off", is printed on one of their potted supermarket products; and its English counterpart has been spotted with the inscription "Pierce with pin and push off". See also APPRISE/APPRAISE.

prise

prodigy/protégé/progeny/wunderkind A *Guardian* picture caption described a young painter who had been taken under the wing of an older artist as "his prodigy". The writer meant *protégé*, from Latin *protegere*, via French *protéger*, one who enjoys another's protection. A *prodigy*, from Latin *prodigium*, was originally a monster, a "prodigy of nature", unnatural or abnormal. Thomas Middleton, in *Women beware Women* (1626) has "A villain as monstrous as a prodigy and as dreadful". But prodigies might also have been benign marvels, like today's examples, who are generally youthful performers, the artistic phenomena the Germans call *Wunderkind(er)* — "wonder child(ren)". But Dea Birkett meant neither a monster nor a precocious child when she wrote, also in the *Guardian*: "DNA tests have confirmed that Hurley's son is the prodigy of American billionaire, Steve Bing…" What *she* meant was *progeny*, from Latin *progignere*, to beget. It seems to be a *prodigious* MINEFIELD. But perhaps the Hurley–Bing progeny will become a prodigy as well as someone's protégé.

proem/poem A *proem* is not a *poem* with an *r* waiting to be edited out but comes from Latin (earlier a Greek word) *præmium*, a prelude, preamble or opening, hence an introductory discourse or foreword to a book.

promise/assure A recent confusion has spread to all walks of life – even to the eminent playwright John Osborne, who wrote in his *Spectator* Diary: "The closing hymn, I promise you, was sung to the tune of 'I'm a blue toothbrush'." He meant to *assure*.

prone/supine In its *Londoner's Diary* column the *Evening Standard* claimed that "Sir Simon Rattle…would rather lie prone in a dentist's chair…than talk with the City Fathers of Birmingham". Unless his dentist is a contortionist he would probably prefer the conductor *supine* – i.e. on his back. Supine, from Latin *supinus*, means to lie on one's back, with the face upwards – seeing the stars, if you want a mnemonic to distinguish it from PRONE, Latin *pronus*, which means inclined downwards, or perhaps flat on one's front, facing the ground.

propaganda/spin/spin doctor/liar *Propaganda* goes back to 1622 when Pope Gregory XV founded the *Congregatio de propaganda fide* – the Congregation (or College) for propagating the Faith, a group of Cardinals who became informally and collectively known as "the Propaganda" –

clerical propagandists who might today be called Spin Doctors of Divinity. *Propaganda* is a modified verb which is treated as a singular noun – it is not the plural of *propagandum* (unlike CRITERIA and MEDIA, plurals of criterion and medium). Spin doctors entered English via American political jargon in the closing decades of the 20th century and were officially installed in government offices on a precise date: 1 May 1997, though they do not use this name, preferring "political assistant", "spokesperson", "a source" or other euphemisms. *Spin* here means slant, for the spin doctor's full-time job is to put a favourable slant on unpalatable facts or even downright lies. The doctor suffix is neither medical nor scientific but facetious and derisive (he is no more a doctor than a piss artist is an artist – though he tries to doctor the truth). In *my* book* the spin doctor nestles appropriately somewhere between "sphincter" and "sputum".

prostrate/prostate To *prostrate* oneself, from Latin *prostrare*, is to *lie* PRONE, with the face to the ground, perhaps before someone "...in token of submission or humility, as in adoration, worship or supplication". Latin *prostare*, with only one *r*, means to *stand* before someone or something, perhaps like a sentry. Hence the *prostate*, the gland that guards, or stands before, the path from a man's bladder to his urethra – and later in his life may try to obstruct it. An interesting (if slightly tautological) use of *prostate* in its adjectival, non-glandular sense occurred in a letter to the *Independent* from J. S. O'Reilly, which ended "...sufficient to have him prostate before the nearest magistrate", meaning he was "standing before" the magistrate. He would have been *prostrate* only if he had lain on his face.

protest/protest against A person before a British court who "protests his innocence" would in the USA be doing exactly the opposite, *protesting against* his innocence and by implication admitting his guilt. It is an Americanism that should be kept at bay for as long as possible – after all, an American suitor cannot protest his love without risk of a misunderstanding. Yet Jon Snow, on Channel 4 News, felt able to say, "They (Muslims) were protesting Tony Blair's action in Iraq." The noun is stressed on the first syllable, the verb, to pro*test*, on the second.

protest

---

* *Sick Notes* – a light-hearted dictionary of medical terms: Parthenon Books, 1995

provincial/regional The secondary *OED* definition of provincial, "Having the manners or speech of the provinces, exhibiting the...narrowness of view or interest ... wanting [i.e. lacking] the culture or polish of the capital", is not designed to please *provincials*, who prefer to think of themselves as people from the *regions*. In about 1745 Jonathan Swift got it right when he wrote of "...a country squire having only the provincial accent upon his tongue, which is neither a fault, nor in his power to remedy". Swift himself spoke in an Irish brogue. Calling them the regions is a safe ALTERNATIVE.

psychological/spooky When journalists invoke psychology – defined as "the science of the mind" – they usually mean something else. In football a goal comes "at the psychological moment" if it is scored just before half-time. "Psychological thrillers" are those that have an unexplained – perhaps even KAFKAESQUE – plot, but they are not necessarily *spooky*. For that they need the inclusions of ghosts or spectres (see SCEPTRE/SPECTRE).

pundit/guru The anglicized *pundit* is an expert in some specialized subject, especially one whom the MEDIA wheel out on news and discussion programmes. Originally a Hindi word, *pundit*, it means a wise man. The *pundit* is different from the *guru*, a Hindi spiritual teacher or influential mentor. Whenever Prince Charles asks someone for expert advice, that person is immediately trivialized in press reports as his "guru".

purse/handbag The Americans are great verbal innovators but this is one of their less successful efforts. A *handbag* is, well, a bag carried in the hand (though it may also be a shoulder-bag carried by a strap), mostly by women, to hold the many necessaries they must have to hand. Americans call this a *purse*, which in English use is usually smaller, made to hold only money or tickets. It comes from Latin *bursa*, hide, leather, giving us the ship's *purser*, the officer in charge of finances. Before that, the purser was a bag-carrier for the royals, who traditionally have no money on their person.

purulent/prurient/"prurulent" *Purulent*, from Latin *purulentus*, refers, or is related, to the nature of PUS – *pus, puris* being Latin for corrupt or putrid matter. *Prurient* is the adjective for something or someone "given to the indulgence of lewd ideas...lasciviousness of thought and mind" (*OED*). It comes from Latin *prurire*, to itch, *pruritus*, an itch (a common medical spelling *pruritis* is wrong, as the -*itis* suffix would suggest an inflammation). *Prurient* is now chiefly used with reference to sexual curiosity; with a hint of masturbation, to relieve a certain kind of itching. *Prurulent* is an erroneous spelling born of a misunderstanding and combining the two origins, which are as loosely related as itching is to scratching.

PUS/PUSS *Pus* is Latin for the PURULENT matter that exudes from a festering wound (see above); but has nothing to do with cats, as a *Times* obituarist assumed when he wrote of a deceased singer: "He was taken seriously ill with double pneumonia [and] two of his ribs were cut to drain off the puss."

Q

quantum leap/leap When physicists speak of a *quantum leap* (also *quantum jump*) they know what they are talking about, which is specifically "...an abrupt transition between one stationary state of a quantized system and another, with the absorption or emission of a quantum..." etc. What it does *not* mean is any old big advance or great metaphorical jump or *leap*. Indeed, a quantum can be of any size, even very small indeed – clearly not big enough for purveyors of clichés. Other specialist terms, like the done-to-death PARAMETERS and the musical CRESCENDO, also have their precise specialized meanings.

quondam/former/erstwhile *Quondam* is Latin for formerly and used to be seen on shop signs and business STATIONERY, where it stood for "formerly known as". Thus a well-known supermarket chain could have styled itself "Tesco – quondam Jack Cohen & Company". The word has been effectively used for incongruous or absurd effect, e.g. "the quondam pop singer", where both "singer" and "quondam" could be taken with a dash of sarcasm (see SARDONIC). *Erstwhile* also means former or formerly, but in speech sounds rather self-conscious (see YE OLDE/THE OLD).

quoth/said A self-conscious MEDIA archaism, like "methinks". "Quoth he" and "quoth I", and sometimes the ultimate facetiousness, "Quotha!" are, with other quothings, usually found in newspaper gossip columns or in "half-timbered" or "heritage" English, for which see YE OLDE/THE OLD.

—R—

racist/racialist Everyone knows what *racism* is, in the modern interpretation of the word, and some may detect it where it does not exist. Before its social transformation, however, it meant simply that different races had different characteristics, for example that Afro-Caribbeans are likely to have darker skins and curlier hair than Indian-Asians or those of Sino-Japanese origin. *Racist* diseases are those which afflict certain peoples. Thus the statement "Sickle-cell anaemia occurs mostly in black people" would be *racist* but not *racialist*. *Racialism* is a belief in the superiority of a particular race and the inferiority of others, leading to prejudice and antagonism towards some people. Unfortunately these dictionary differences tend to be lost under an onslaught of popular misuse, so that racism has both supplanted and included racialism.

racked/wracked/wrecked Both *racked* and *wracked* are seen in the papers but usually only when coupled with "guilt". Wracked is an alternative form of *wrecked*, e.g. as a result of a shipwreck; while racked is more like tortured, perhaps on the rack. So either will do: the *Guardian's* apology (in response to a reader's misinformed niggle) for having printed "wracked with guilt" instead of "racked", was unnecessary. As shipwrecks are now as rare as torturers' racks we might forget about the cliché altogether. See also FLOUNDER/FOUNDER and RECKLESS/"WRECKLESS".

railway/railroad Haters of things American dismiss *railroad* as an American invention and claim that the real English word is *railway*. Not true: the first passenger railway in the world, the line between Liverpool and Manchester, was initially called both railway and railroad, often with a preference for railroad. Maria Edgeworth, writing on 18th October 1830, only days after the inaugural train left Liverpool for Manchester, says "We were invited to go on the Liverpool railway…", but later in the same letter, "A regular communication goes on now by trains of cars on this railroad, backwards and forwards to Liverpool and Manchester." See also TRAIN STATION.

rain/reign/rein A king, queen or other ruler *reigns* (from Latin *regnum*, related to *rex*, a king); a horseman *reins* or *reins-in* his mount by grasping or pulling at the *reins*, from Latin *retinere*, to retain or restrain; and Shakespeare's *Love's Labour's Lost* (1588) has "Sweet Lord Longavill, reine thy tongue". And, as Shakespeare also observed, "the rain it raineth every day". The trouble is that the three words sound the same but are otherwise unrelated. Nevertheless, a leading political expert of the *Guardian* wrote: "The German finance minister has little respect for the opinions of other countries and could do a lot of reckless damage unless [the chancellor] reigns him in"; and the Education Correspondent (sic) of *The Liverpool Daily Post*: "[She] stepped in and handed over the reigns of power." See also CURB/KERB.

raise/raze Almost every newspaper claims – paradoxically – at one time or another, that a building had been "raised to the ground…" *Razed* means erased, obliterated, whereas *raised* suggests that the building in question started off below ground and was somehow given extra height.

rate/berate To *rate* is to count or estimate: "When we see the figure of the house, then must we rate the cost of the erection", Shakespeare says in *Henry IV Part 2* (1597). To *berate* is to scold or chide. Therefore "Liverpool are berated the best team in the north…" is nonsense. The same goes for LABOUR/BELABOUR and KNIGHTED/BENIGHTED.

rebel/rebel The *re*bel gets his stress on the first syllable, but the action described by the verb to re*bel*, on the second.

> Poor soul, the centre of my sinful earth,
> Fool'd by these *reb*el powers that thee array,
> Why dost thou pine within and suffer dearth
> Painting thy outward walls so costly gay?
> Shakespeare: *Sonnet 146*

> Aspiring to be gods if angels fell,
> Aspiring to be angels men re*bel*.
> Alexander Pope: *An Essay on Man* (1732–4)

reckless/ "wreckless" *Reckless* has been an English word since the early middle ages (adapted from an even older Germanic one – the Germans still say *ruchlos*). It means careless, or heedless of the consequences of one's actions. *Wreckless*, a favourite among headline writers, is nonsensical. One who is *reckless* lacks judgement, not a wreck.

record books/records *Record books* play a big ROLE in English journalism although they are just imaginary pegs on which to hang tediously facetious, allusive news prose. Thus diners "eat their way...", athletes "run their way...", pop entertainers "sing their way...", in *The Times* a javelin-thrower "threw his way..." and balloonists "fly into..." these strange tomes. The *Daily Telegraph* wrote its way into what must be a record of record-book silliness by heading a small article about global warming, "WORLD WARMS INTO THE RECORD BOOKS".

recover/discover The newsreader said, "Officers raided a flat and recovered weapons." Oh no they didn't. They *discovered* them, or uncovered them, as they had been hidden. To be *recovered*, the recoverer must have put them there in the first place. Pedantic, or what?

recuperate/recover Although *recover* is the simpler word of the two, no-one would now object to *recuperate*. But in 1864 it annoyed *Punch*:

"Another Yankeeism nearly as illiterate as 'reliable' [!] has just been imported by the *Etna* [a famous transatlantic steamship] in one of Reuter's telegrams. This communication, one of those evil ones which corrupt good language, informs us that General Grant is very ill, and that, 'as the army is about to settle into winter quarters, it is urged by General Grant's physicians that he should go home to recuperate'. Some years ago Mr Buckstone, in a farce, acted a Yankee's part, in which he had to say, 'If I live from July till eternity, I shall never obliviate this ...' The formation of 'recuperate' from *recupero* may be more defensible than that of 'obliviate' from *obliviscor*, but still 'recuperate' is a needless corruption of Latin. Why not stick to 'recover'? Besides, the French word *récupérer* has a distinct meaning and signifies to retrieve. An American might, without any impropriety beyond that of affectation, talk about action to recuperate his dollars, but how can people who call themselves members of the Anglo-Saxon family use such language? As for you who owe allegiance to Her Majesty, and are in duty bound to maintain the purity of the Queen's English, consider 'recuperate' Presidents's English, spurious, base, villainous; pray you, avoid it."

This little broadside must be taken with a pinch of salt; for "reliable" was never a Yankeeism: the *OED* has an instance of 1569 ("raliabill"); and gives a 1792 use of "a very reliable medicine". Mr Punch was being typically British and conservatively prescriptive. But the paragraph is interesting for its reflection on language-changes and our eventual acceptance of them. The same goes for "obliviate" – for which see OBLIVION.

red mist/anger According to a much-used cliché of sports-writers, a *red mist* descends on their pages whenever there have been sendings-off, fighting, bad temper and general MAYHEM in (usually) football. Players themselves have taken to using it as an excuse for bad behaviour: "A red mist came down, like…"

referendum/referenda Opinions vary as to the plural – *referenda* or *referendums* – but the *OED* prefers the second: "In terms of its Latin origin, *referendums* is logically preferable as a modern plural form meaning ballots on one issue (as a Latin gerund *referendum* has no plural); the Latin plural gerundive *referenda*, meaning things to be referred, necessarily connotes a plurality of issues. Those who prefer the form *referenda* are presumably using words like *agenda* and *memoranda* as models. Usage varies at the present time (1981), but *The Oxford Dictionary for Writers and Editors* (1981) recommends *referendums*, and this form seems likely to prevail." Put more simply, as soon as a Latin word becomes a much-used English one it tends to forfeit its "correct" ending, however much PEDANTS try to preserve it. But see PROPAGANDA/SPIN.

refuse/refuse/re-fuse "*Reff*-yooss" is put into sacks, after which the collectors may "reff-*ooze*" to collect it. Electricians putting a new fuse into an appliance "ree-*fyooz*" it.

refute/rebut/deny A *denial* is the opposing by, say, a defendant, of a claim, charge or accusation made against him. Such a denial may be false, and is therefore not the same as a *refutation* for which conclusive proof can be offered. Latin *refutare* means to repel or reject something, so it is safer to *rebut* (or reject) an allegation, as a rebuttal is neutral. See also JUSTIFY/DEFEND, REPEL/REPULSE.

reliant/reliable The two are not interchangeable: a *reliant* person relies on someone or something; but if he is *reliable* he can be relied upon. None of this worries writers in search of a feeble joke, who like to play, for example, on the name of a popular three-wheeled car, the Reliant Robin, by describing anyone called Robin, Robbie or Robert, as reliant when they really mean reliable.

remembrance/memory "This has not occurred within living remembrance..." (The *Observer*). Correct, if stilted: since the aftermath of World War I and again after 1945, *remembrance* has become so closely associated with the commemoration of the dead that it might be better avoided for the living. Besides, "within living memory" is simpler and has a comfortingly familiar ring.

renaissance/renascence *Renaissance* is French for a rebirth, the state of being born again, from *naissance*, birth. Since the middle of the 19th century *Renaissance* has been the appropriate word for the great revival of Classical art and letters which began in 15th-16th century Italy – and is pronounced in approximately the French manner, each of its three syllables equally stressed. For any other kind of renewal, revival or rebirth the English word *renascence* is superior (its stress on the middle syllable) and has been in use in that context since the early 18th century. However, it is nonsensical to speak of "the great Renascence composers", as some BBC Radio 3 speakers do.

repel/repulse Both come from Latin *repellere*, to drive back. *Repulse*, from *repulsus*, from the same Latin stem, is usually more suited to describing a physical driving-back in a fight or battle. *Repulsive* ("what a repulsive fellow") is colloquially more common than the milder *repellent*, but both can be used in an insulting manner. (So can *repugnant*, which comes from Latin *pugnare*, to fight.) In the Parish Church of Romney, Kent, there is (or was) a tablet, "In 1066, near this Church, the Normans attempted a landing. They were repelled by the men of Romney." Underneath, in a feminine hand, the annotation, "So am I."

repellent/repellant An advertisement for Boots the Chemists recommends that travellers "...use insect repellent" to avoid catching malaria. *Repellent* is an adjective, used to describe someone or something that repels one; but the substance, e.g. a spray or powder, that repels something or somebody, is a *repellant*.

201

replete/complete A BBC Radio 3 record reviewer informed readers that a certain concerto recording came "replete with Beethoven's own cadenza". He might just have meant it, as the cadenza in question *is* rather long; but the movement is by no means crammed full with it. He meant *complete with*, but felt that a little elegant verbal variation might impress his listeners. To be *replete* is to be physically full, filled to satisfaction with – usually – food or drink, satisfied, gorged. Latin *repletus* is from *replere*, to fill. It is not the same as *complete*, which hardly needs to be defined but is also concerned with filling, Latin *complere*, to fill.

restaurant/restaurateur Just to catch the unwary, a *restaurant*-keeper or -owner is by convention – and against modern usage – not a "restauranteur" but a *restaurateur*. Both restaurant and restaurateur come from the Latin restaurator, one who restores; but since restaurant is from a French word (the present participle of *restaurer*, to restore or refresh) and *does* have an *n*, one can in a strict sense find no fault with the anglicized "restaura*n*teur". But then some people seem to think food tastes better when served in French. As in a menu item, *Kipper sur Toast*.

restive/restful The two have almost opposite meanings. *Restful* means free from disturbance, quiet, full of repose; but *restive*, unwilling, obstinate, stubborn – now often said of troublesome or disobedient children but formerly commonly applied to horses, for example an animal that obstinately moves backwards or sideways and resists control. And see COSTIVE/COSTLY.

review/revue A *review* is a (re)consideration or critical examination; a *revue* a theatrical performance ("more or less topical and musical", as the often whimsical *Chambers' Dictionary* defines it) which originated in the 19th century on the French stage, where revue entertainments examined recent events and commented upon them in SATIRE. However, the British fleet, or what is left of it, is reviewed – the Review of the Fleet being a large-scale seaborne inspection. In former times it was a show of military might.

rhyme/rime Earlier editions of the *OED* (including the second-edition CD-Rom version used for this book) quaintly prefer *rime* to *rhyme*, but few other authorities do. Rime may be the correct and original form but it also means hoar-frost or frozen mist, so perhaps rhyme is to be preferred.

right/rite/wright/write Four homophones that set up a kneejerk reaction among newspaper headline-writers, who inevitably caption a picture of the Wright brothers' historic 1903 flight with the oh-so-witty quip "The Wright stuff". These "jokes" have become so common that in the end they cannot tell *rite* from wrong. So one man has Ancient Greeks "performing their rights and rituals", and another accidentally describes Harold Pinter as a "playwrite". As mother used to say, "If you keep making silly faces, dear, one day one of them will stick!"

rings/rinks/circles/cycles/bees Five words with mixed good and bad connotations: *rings* are for lovers, boxers, shady antiques-dealers at auctions, spies and PAEDOPHILES; whereas families, knitters and socialites, etc., move in *circles*. Wagner's *Ring Cycle* has connotations of both good and evil and refers to an actual metal ring, that of the Nibelung. Homosexual rings had a brief vogue, but were dropped and replaced by the inevitable COMMUNITY. In the 1930s there was a vogue for *bees*, like knitting-bees and quilting-bees for housewives, and spelling-bees – an idea worth reviving for MEDIA social gatherings. *Rinks* are areas covered with ice on which skaters go round in circles and have nothing to do with rings but date back to the 14th century, adapted from an old French word, *ranc*. This was a course on which sports like jousting, running or racing took place – not necessarily in circles. See also ROUND ROBIN.

riposte/reply The National Portrait Gallery, the *Daily Telegraph* claimed, was "the visual riposte to *Who's Who*". What the writer meant was that the Gallery was the pictorial equivalent of, or the answer to, that British directory of famous people. A *riposte* is more than a mere *reply*: in the sport of fencing it is "a quick thrust given after parrying a lunge", but for the rest of us "an effective – and usually speedy – reply by word or act". That is why adjectives like "barbed" or "witty" often precede it. See also REFUTE/REBUT/DENY.

rise/raise British employees ask for a WAGE/SALARY *rise*, Americans put in for a *raise*. The Americans are wrong here, for *rise* is a noun, (as well as an intransitive verb), *raise* a transitive verb.

rocks/stones In a report in the *Independent* about hooligans in Bristol a photograph showed a child about to throw a *stone*. The caption read, "A girl carrying a rock…" The child was about six and the "rock" she was carrying was the size of a small apple. Journalists keep repeating AD NAUSEAM the stale cliché that "size doesn't matter". Well, here it does. A *rock* is a stone too big to be picked up and HURLED. Will future Bibles be inviting him that is without sin to cast the first *rock*? And leave no *rock* unturned? The confusion is in one direction only: no-one has yet changed the famous hymn to "Stone of Ages". See FLOOR/GROUND.

role/roll The same remarks apply as for RIGHT/RITE/WRIGHT/WRITE. Thus the *Malvern Gazette* published an advertisement for an Executive Head Chef able "to fill this important roll" (a sausage roll?). A *roll*-call is the act of calling out a list, which would formerly have been inscribed on a roll, of persons' names, to check their presence or absence. Whatever *roles* these persons might play it is not a role-call, but the role played by actors (originally written *rôle*, being a French word) harks back several centuries, to a time when theatre CAST-lists were written on real rolls of paper or parchment.

romance/"roe-mance" Americans – and growing numbers of Britons – who watch American TV and cinema *roemances* mis-stress *romance* with a strong and elongated first syllable. English poetry proves them wrong. The very lines that produced the over-used cliché "high romance", from Keats's *In a Drear-nighted December*, illustrate this:

> When I behold upon the night's starr'd face
> Huge cloudy symbols of a high ro*mance*.

Romance was also a favourite word in Kipling's poetry, and in every instance he stresses the second syllable.

rood/rude A *rood* is a cross: not any old cross but one used as an instrument of execution, like the cross upon which Christ died. Rood screens are found, separating the nave from the choir, in most cathedrals and many churches, of richly carved wood or stone and properly surmounted by a rood. They are not "rude screens", as the *Liverpool Daily Post* has claimed.

root/route The writer who alleged that "Britain was now taking the root pioneered in the USA..." had probably read too many HOMOPHONE headline quips of the RIGHT/RITE/WRIGHT/WRITE kind and became confused.

rotund/orotund Something that is *rotund* (from Latin *rotundus*, related to *rota*, a wheel) is round or circular; a podgy person may also be euphemistically described as *rotund*. But not *orotund*, which is now almost always applied to a pompous and inflated style of speech and comes from the Latin *ore rotundo*, "spoken with a round mouth": you can just see it on a speaker fond of his own eloquence.

round robin/circular letter/petition *Round robin* is now almost always interpreted as a *circular letter* – circular not in shape but because it is sent round to various persons to read or sign its contents. The real round robin was nautical in origin, or at any rate several nautical definitions survive, including this from 1730: "A Round Robin is a Name given by Seamen, to an Instrument on which they sign their names round a Circle, to prevent the Ring-leader being discover'd by it, if found"…a wise precaution, when even the mildest complaint might have been interpreted as mutiny. (The old military saying, "No names, no pack-drill" confirms the need for some kind of anonymity.) The earliest appearances of the round robin hinge on religion and blasphemy, and perhaps on priests' attempts to prevent the Gospels from being translated into the vernacular. Miles Coverdale (1546): "Certayne fonde talkers applye to this mooste hooly sacramente names of despytte and reproche, as to call it Jake in the boxe and round roben…" Round robins are discussed every Christmas as growing numbers of people send (now also e-mail) them to their friends.*

rowing/rowing A story in the *Daily Telegraph* reported how a couple tried to take a rowing-boat from England to the USA but failed in the attempt because they were constantly quarrelling. The writer, who must have been both word-deaf and word-blind, kept alluding to the fact that "they rowed across the Atlantic", without telling readers which meaning (and pronunciation) of "rowing" he had in mind.

rubensesque/"rubenesque" Used to describe a woman with a full, rounded figure, as was often painted by Sir Peter Paul Rubens (1577–1640) – not "Ruben", so the almost customary spelling *Rubenesque* is wrong.

* In the early days of the English postal system the postmen were nicknamed *Robins*, because of their red uniform jackets.

— S —

sacrilegious/"sacreligious" The noun is *sacrilege* – hence *sacrilegious*, pronounced "sacri-leegious", not "sac-religious", which is either based on a mis-spelling or may cause one. *Sacrilege* is the profanation or theft of anything held sacred by others, especially holy relics, and comes from Latin *sacra legere*, to steal sacred objects. There is no noun "sacrelige", and *sacreligious* means nothing except that the writer has transposed the *i* and the *e*. Much the same applies to PREDILECTION/"PREDELICTION".

salmon/salmonella In spite of sounding like a plural word, *salmonella* is a singular formation – plural *salmonellae* – and there is no such thing as a "salmonellum". Nor is there a connection with *salmon* except as a tribute to the American veterinarian pathologist Daniel Elmer Salmon (1850–1914), who discovered the BACTERIUM. He himself died of pneumonia.

salvia/saliva *Salvia* is the Latin and botanical name for sage and other plants of the genus. It is one of the danger words which may be "corrected" to *saliva*.

sanitary/sanatory/sanitor/sanitarium/sanatorium etc. All come from Latin *sanare*, to heal, but the English and the Americans cannot agree about the spellings, developing various competing forms. In English usage *sanitary* and *sanatorium* seem to be the settled spelling.

sardonic/ironic/sarcastic/laconic The first three of these four words serve related purposes: *sardony* a sharp, bitter or cutting expression or remark, a gibe or taunt, with *sarcasm* the more "biting", coming from the Greek *sarx*, flesh. *Irony*, says the *OED*, is "a figure of speech in which the intended meaning is the opposite of that expressed by the words used, usually taking the form of sarcasm or ridicule in which laudatory expressions are used to imply condemnation…" Sardony maligns the

Sardinians, whom the Greeks cuttingly called Sardonios, after the Sardinian plant *Herba sardonia*, which was said to produce "facial convulsions resembling horrible laughter, usually followed by death". Neither irony nor sardony nor sarcasm are generally effective in journalism, and irony fares worst, as writers of letters to newspapers discover when readers take their remarks seriously. *Laconic* is not to be confused with the others, though a speaker could be all four. To be laconic is to be brief, concise or sententious, named after the Laconians, who were regarded as men of few words. Perhaps they didn't know many, or preferred to keep those they knew to themselves. King James VI asked a correspondent (1589) to "excuis me for this my laconike writting I ame in suche haist". See also IRONICALLY/(CO)INCIDENTALLY.

sargent/sergeant/serjeant As is stated elsewhere in this book, English spelling evolved in a haphazard manner, with few rules and many inconsistencies. There is no public body to issue rules, as there is in some continental countries, and no government interference in either usage or spelling (but see FLAMMABLE). The only determining factors are custom and habit. The spelling of family names is governed by ancient traditions that preserve ancient spellings. Thus – to take only one example – the conductor Sir Malcom Sargent and the painter John Singer Sargent were written thus; whereas the three-striped non-commissioned army or police officer is a *sergeant*; and a certain official in the English royal household a *serjeant* – one of the Serjeants-at-Arms. There were formerly also Serjeants-at-Law, the now obsolete name for high-ranking barristers. All forms are derived from the Old French, written either *sergent* or *serjant*, a servant of official. See also POLICEMAN/OFFICER/CONSTABLE.

satire/satyr In ancient Rome a *satire* was a poem in which prevalent follies or vices were held up to ridicule – and much the same goes for modern satire. This had only an incidental connection with the *satyr*, a mythical woodland god or demon "with a body that was partly human and partly bestial". His behaviour, too, was rather beastly, for he was given to lustfulness and sexual excess, enough to cause many a FRISSON of temptation and excitement. In Caxton's *Fables* "The woodwose [wild man of the woods] or Satyre ledd the pylgrym to his pytte"; and even the Bible, in *Isaiah* 13.21, says, "Satyrs or hegoats shall daunce there." The respective adjectives are *satirical* for the writings and *satyric* for the beasts.

scab/blackleg/fink "I'll tell you what a scab is," said a trades union leader cryptically when interviewed on television, "a scab is an Ealing wound." In the *OED* a scab is indeed an unpleasant and unsightly skin condition (whether healing or not), but also someone who "takes the place of a worker who is on strike, thereby helping the employer to carry on his business and defeat the ends of the strike". Another name for this kind of *scab* is *blackleg*, which is also a skin condition, but one that attacks sheep – the four-footed kind, not the unquestioning follower of policies. In the USA a blackleg or scab is called a *fink*, arising from the famously broken "Homestead" strike of 1892, after which the fink, also *rat fink*, became a word for a person held in contempt by his peers. *Fink* is the German word for the finch and also a family name. In about 1970 the German Embassy in London had a Herr Fink with the rank of Counsellor – *Rat* in German – who startled callers by barking, "Rat Fink here!" down the phone. See also BLACK/NEGRO and FRANKENSTEIN.

scarify/scare The confusion is common, almost logical and quite old: The *Newfoundland Journal* as long ago as 1794 wrote, "If a Clergyman was [!] to make his appearance in his Canonical Robes...I have little doubt but the Weomen and Children would be scarified out of part of their senses" – perhaps a facetious portmanteau combination of *scared* and *terrified*. Scared is derived from an old Scandinavian word brought by Viking invaders, who would have scared the natives by frightening, terrifying and probably also *scarifying* them, if not worse. To scarify is to cover with scratches, to make sore or wound, from Latin (via Greek) *scarificare*, to sketch an outline or scratch lightly. It has remained a medical and horticultural term for shallow incisions or scarring.

sceptic/septic A *sceptic* is one who tends to doubt the validity of claims or assertions, from Latin *scepticus* and Greek *skepsis*, the critical philosophical examination of a proposition. *Septic* is a medical word (Latin *septicus*, Greek *sepein*, to putrefy) though better known among patients in its negative form *antiseptic* and among country-dwellers from the septic tank in places that lack public drains. If sceptics used the more common and classically correct spelling "skeptic", which hints at the pronunciation, fewer people would say "septic" for both, or use the now common misspelling "(euro)septic". See also CYNIC/STOIC.

sceptre/spectre *Sceptre* is from Latin *sceptrum*, a rod or staff; and the sceptre is a symbol of state and authority, usually coupled with the equally symbolic crown, both carried by the Monarch on special ceremonial occasions. A *spectre* (Latin *specere*, to look) is an apparition, a vision or ghost, usually of a threatening nature. John Prescott, Her Majesty's Deputy Prime Minister, was not alone when he assumed (in Prime Minister's Questions, 1999) that the two words meant the same; and condemned "the sceptre of unemployment stalking the North East".

schadenfreude/gloating English has no word for the German *Schadenfreude*, which literally means "damage-pleasure", and must therefore paraphrase it as "a feeling of pleasure at another's or others' misfortune". The Germans, conversely, possess no word for "sense of humour", and use the English term. It would be quite wrong to draw any conclusions from this exchange of ideas. For a famous instance of literary *Schadenfreude* see under TWAT, via PRAT.

schizophrenic/undecided *Schizophrenia* is a defined mental disorder, and although the word is made up of two Greek elements denoting "split" and "mind" respectively, it is too strong a term for general journalistic use when speaking of a divided opinion, of being "in two minds". Most newspapers list it as a forbidden term in frivolous or inappropriate applications. See also JEKYLL AND HYDE.

schoolchildren/school students What used to be *schoolchildren* – schoolboys and schoolgirls – are now grandly and politically correctly called *school students* – part of the movement that has turned office-boys into "junior executives" and refuse-collectors into "public waste disposal operatives".

scottish/scots/scotch The *Scots* like to be described as *Scottish*, *Scotsmen* or *Scotswomen*, or else just *Scots*. *Scotch* is what they drink (though they call it whisky). Apart from the drink, Scotch is considered suitable only for expressions like scotch mist, or a scotch that is a mark or line scored on the ground (hence the game of hopscotch); or a different form of scotch that is a block or wedge placed against a wheel, barrel or suchlike, to stop it moving; to scotch something, like a plan or intended action, is to prevent or frustrate it. Many derogatory or facetious slang terms, like Scotch fiddle for the itch, Scotch bum for a bustle, etc., helped to discredit its legitimate use, though Dr Samuel Johnson and numerous other luminaries used it naturally and without intended insult. See WELSH/WELCH/RENEGE and the WHISKY/WHISKEY difference.

scottish

scull/skull A *scull* is a kind of oar used for propelling a boat; a *skull* the bony container that encloses the brain of man or other animals. Both words are said to be of obscure origin, and may be related to a hollow vessel – perhaps because a scull or half or part of a hollow vessel may have been used for pushing water backwards and a boat forwards.

sea captain/sailor Britannia once ruled the waves, and England had many, many ships. But not so many that *everyone* can claim as they now seem to do, in television and radio interviews, "My great-grandfather was a sea captain." This has become an almost stock reply when antiques or heirlooms are under discussion or their alleged provenance explained. The claim should be taken with a dose of old salt. For every "sea" captain there were dozens of bosuns, midshipmen and first lieutenants. Among real naval officers, traditional British understatement still obtains. Ask any admiral, "What do you do for a living?" and he will reply, "I'm a sailor".

set/expected/about to The sun *sets*, jellies set, but events are *expected* or *about to* happen. The brevity of set has made it into a regular element of snappy newspaper headlines, but from there it moved into news text and, more absurdly, spoken news. "The Chancellor is set to up his spending...", a newsreader solemnly intoned.

sew/sow To *sew*, meaning to fasten or join something with needle (or awl) and thread, is written thus and pronounced "sow" (rhyming with "flow", not with "few" or "how"). *Sow*, as in the placing or scattering of seed, is written differently but pronounced the same, though even Elizabeth Barrett Browning seemed unsure about her sewing:

> The clock stands at the noon;
> I am weary, I have sewn,
> Sweet, for thee, a wedding-gown.

But not as unsure as the writer of a *Guardian* article about pupils "who were sewing the seeds of dissent" in classrooms; the context made it clear that they were not doing needlework.

sexton/sextant The *sexton* is a church officer who performs (in bigger churches oversees) the duties of grave-digger and bell-ringer, and is also charged with the care of the church fabric – without pay. As that inveterate punster and patron saint of tabloid headline-writers Thomas Hood (1799–1845) wrote:

> His death, which happen'd in his birth
> At forty-eight befell:
> They went and told the sexton, and
> The sexton tolled the bell.

Sexton comes from mediaeval Latin *sacristan* – which, if you say it quickly with a rustic burr, comes out as *sexton*. Or it might be misheard for *sextant* (Latin for "the sixth part"), an instrument enabling sailors to ascertain latitude at sea by observing celestial objects. However, this statement from the *Guardian* was more than either pun or mishearing: "David, John and Jay [made a 2,000-mile ocean voyage with only] woefully inaccurate 18th century charts and a sexton."

sheepish/sheeplike "All we like sheep have gone astray," sang Handel in his *Messiah* (by courtesy of the Bible) but the *sheeplike* human sheep who face the reckoning may look *sheepish* – embarrassed or out of countenance – for having allowed themselves to be misled.

shofar/chauffeur The *shofar* is a ram's horn which is played in Jewish religious services, a *chauffeur* the paid driver of a motor vehicle; so a *Guardian* writer's assertion that "A chauffeur was heard in the synagogue" was presumably a homophone confusion (though one can never be sure about the often wicked *Guardian* humour). The chauffeur is an example of an Anglo-French mix-up. In French it literally means a heater, and a chauffeur was initially the fireman or stoker on a steam-engine. The subsequent introduction of the motorcar (of which the French were pioneers) changed the job without changing the job-description. The shofar's musical history is interesting in that it is the only surviving instrument from biblical times. It must be made from the horn of a ram or wild goat and has a range as limited (and a sound as coarse) as the foxhunters' horn. Sir Edward Elgar called for a shofar in his oratorio *The Apostles*, which has occasionally provided work for a real rabbi but is now usually played on a non-KOSHER Flügelhorn.

siamese/conjoined twins A concern for people's sensibilities tells us that it is wrong – and often inaccurate – to name medical conditions after foreign peoples. Siamese twins entered the language in 1811, when Chang and Eng, natives of Siam, were born joined at the waist, and factually described in the *Times* of 25 November 1829 as "the Siamese United Twins" (which now makes them sound like a pair of footballers).

siamese

Chang and Eng were much exhibited and lived until 1874. Doctors now call such babies *conjoined twins*, though the *con-* (indicating togetherness) seems unnecessary. To what are they joined except each other? Why not just "joined twins", in the same way as identical twins are not "co-identical"?

silicon/silicone A cartoon in *Punch* showed a tanker-load of *silicon* being delivered to the *Baywatch* studios. The supposed joke was intended to be a reference to the implanted breast enlargements which featured prominently on near-naked actresses in that TV show (and were usually more startling than the story-line). The material from which false bosoms may be made is *silicone*. Silicon is sand, which was not in short supply on the *Baywatch* beaches.

singer/crooner/vocalist/entertainer If Pavarotti, Sir Thomas Allen, Sir Peter Pears and the rest are (or were) *singers* then clearly Sir Paul McCartney, Sir Mick Jagger, Sir Elton John, "Eminem" and Gareth Gates are *something else*, however excellent of their kind. But so far no satisfactory word has been coined. *Vocalist* would theoretically be appropriate but covers anyone who uses his or her voice, successfully or not, in song or speech. Since the presentation of pop music involves not merely the voice but also, simultaneously, dancing, prancing, strutting, pointing at the audience (why?) and, in the case of girl entertainers, pouting, the most suitable word might be *entertainer*. *Crooner* is now outmoded, as it describes a specific 20th-century style, characterized by the musicologist Eric Blom in about the 1950s as a form of singing "…that established itself in light entertainment music about the 1930s. The principle of crooning is to use as little voice as possible and instead to make a prolonged moaning somewhere near the written notes, but preferably never actually on those notes. The smallest vocal equipment is sufficient for the purpose of crooning, one of its admirers' delusions being that it does not become wholly satisfactory until it is amplified by a microphone." The presence of the microphone absolves crooners from using their full voice: they can be heard even if they whisper. Pop and rock entertainers, on the other hand, try to outshout their amplification which (together with a feigned American accent) often makes their words indiscernible. The verb to *croon*, curiously, is apt for both activities, as it meant (from ca 1500) "to bellow as a bull, to roar" and also (from ca 1460), "to sing in a low murmuring tone, to hum softly".

sitting/sat/standing/stood/falling/fell etc. The slide into "yoof" English that began in the1990s has gathered unstoppable momentum and is sweeping in its wake teachers, police officers, TV and radio reporters – and of course print journalists. Where any journalist with an inkling of grammar would a generation ago have said, "I am standing/sitting in Parliament Square..." today's parliamentary reporters will tell us they "are (or were) stood/sat", or that they are (were) "headed/pointed/faced" in a certain direction. A senior BBC commentator who covers State occasions told us: "King Hussain will be sat next to the Queen." We know that the late King of Jordan was not exactly king-sized, but surely no-one would have disrespectfully lifted him up and plonked him down on his chair? By way of inelegant variation a BBC reporter declared he "would have went" – and no doubt "would have drove", given the chance. Another said that someone "had ate a meal" and that an aircraft "had took off from Woodvale airfield". One journalist reported "...a freak storm in which two inches of rain had fell". In spite of all the films about World War I and World War II, the young seem to be puzzled by a reference to those who "fell in the War", thinking they had just fallen over (or "had fell over", as they would say); borne out by a *Sunday Telegraph* sub-editor who produced a particularly choice headline about a naval officer who "was felled in 1940" (so Laurence Binyon's famous poem of 1914 will just have to be retitled "For the Felled"). But the wackiest examples noted so far come, respectively, from the *Liverpool Daily Post* and Granada TV News, claiming that someone had been "found knelt in prayer" and that "the court will not be sat until February". Verily, the Yoof Bible will have the Lord asking Adam, in Genesis 3.11, "Hast thou ate of the tree whereof I have commanded thee that thou shouldst not of ate?" Lord, which way are we faced? We are faced with an apparently unstoppable MEDIA force dumbing-down the language at an unprecedented pace. See also HAVE/OF.

snooty/snotty *Snooty* means supercilious, superior, haughty, conceited. Its first *OED* attribution is to Aldous Huxley (1894–1963), in a letter of 1919. *Snot* is older:"the fylthe of the nose", as a writer of 1440 described it. When Anne Robinson in *The Times* accused the Government of having "become incredibly snotty and superior" she was slightly wide of the mark. See also BOGIE/BOGEY.

snort/snifter *Snort* is "a sound made in driving breath through the nostrils with some force", but in fashionable slang of the early years of the 20th century it took on the same meaning as a *snifter*, the taking of a quick and short alcoholic drink. That was what P. G. Wodehouse meant in *Carry on, Jeeves* (1925) by "...taking a quiet snort in a corner". By the middle of the 20th century Wodehouse would have risked being dangerously misunderstood: "A dose or measure of cocaine or heroin which is taken by inhalation" (*OED*). Anyone who is now said, without further explanation, to be "snorting", is taking cocaine, not "audibly expressing contempt or disdain" or indeed imitating a horse. The language sometimes changes dangerously fast.

sod/sot To call someone a *sod* is an insult, as it is short for sodomite, which will be found under CATAMITE/SODOMITE. *Sot* is not much better, as this implies that he is a drunkard, one who dulls or stupefies himself with drinking alcohol.

softly softly/gradually/salami tactics *Softly Softly* was the title of a BBC TV police-and-crime drama series in the early 1970s. The show helped to keep alive an almost proverbial saying, "Softly softly catchee monkey", which originated with British forces serving abroad, meaning that it is sometimes necessary to move slowly and with stealth (see STEALING) to gain one's objective. Another term for the gradual introduction of measures is *salami tactics*, often to accomplish political or social changes. This comes not, as might be supposed, from America, the fount of many imaginative clichés, but from Hungary, the home of the world's finest salami. In May 1952 *The Times* reported that the Hungarian politician Matyás Rákosi described it as "...salami tactics, by which slices of the Smallholders' Party were cut away and its strength worn down". Like salami itself, the term found wide acceptance in the USA. See also the more homely MARMITE POLICY.

sophomore/semaphore "Mr Clinton was then a semaphore at Oxford University...", claimed the *Liverpool Daily Post*. The writer meant *sophomore*, the standard name in the USA for a second-year university student, although it was originally an English varsity term. From the 17th century onwards, first-year university students were known as freshmen ("freshers" when women joined them); and second-year students "Sophy Moores", a jocularly wilful corruption, by those senior to them, of sophomores – itself a jest at their expense, from Greek *sophos*, wise and *moros*, fool (see also OXYMORON). In other words, students who by their second year foolishly thought they knew all there was to know. This nickname fell into disuse in England but survived in the USA, where it is extensively used, though without pejorative associations. Most British people are more familiar with the signalling-device, the *semaphore*, from the Greek *sema*, a sign or signal, plus *phorein*, to bear or carry. For related terms see ALMA MATER, ALUMNUS/OLD BOY and GRADUATE/ (POST)GRADUATE.

spacious/specious *Specious* is an endangered word which some sub-editors and computer checks "correct" because they think it should be *spacious* – from Latin *spatius*, relating to space. *Specious* comes from *speciosus*, fair, beautiful, though in modern use it is mostly arguments that are specious, that is to say, fair and plausible but wanting in genuineness, truth or sincerity. When John Aubrey, in his *Brief Lives* in 1697, referred to "the specious town of Richelieu" he meant it as a compliment.

spinster/unmarried woman *Spinster*, a useful and evocative old word, has been all but driven out by political correctness. Originally it described a person – not necessarily but by tradition always a woman – whose occupation or pursuit was spinning. Not until the early 18th century did *spinster* come to mean an unmarried woman (presumably one who, having no husband to look after, would spin all the family's wool and flax, etc). "Spinster of this Parish" is often seen on old gravestone inscriptions and in parish records, and was until well into the second half of the 20th century used in official documents, such as marriage certificates, to indicate a woman's unmarried state. During the 1930s and 40s there was a monthly magazine for unmarried women called the *Spinster*, intended particularly for those looking after elderly parents. See also CELIBATE and ELDERLY/OLD. Also MRS/MISS/MS.

staggering/surprising *Staggering* is a MEDIA cliché to describe the surprising or astonishing, as STUNNING is for things desirable or beautiful. The *Independent* said, "Britons will buy a staggering nine million roses for their valentines"; and the *Liverpool Echo* lamented "a staggering rise in drunkenness on Merseyside".

standard/regular As descriptions of sizes, as perhaps in reference to packaged goods like soap or cereal products, *standard* is the British form, *regular* the American. To English people something that is regular occurs

standard

at measured intervals of time or space, whereas to Americans it means usual, customary, ordinary. To them "regular sex" means not that it happens regularly but that it is neither kinky nor perverted.

stately homes/grand houses The expression *stately homes* is often misapplied, for the building under discussion may be merely a grand or big house that is far from stately. It is widely credited to Noël Coward's eponymous song from his show *Operetta*, produced in 1938:

> The Stately Homes of England
> How beautiful they stand,
> To prove the Upper Classes
> Have still the Upper Hand.   etc.

though he was in fact parodying a once popular ballad published in 1827 by Felicia Hemans (1793–1835):

> The Stately Homes of England
> How beautiful they stand!
> Amidst their tall, ancestral trees
> O'er all the pleasant land   etc.

Nor was Coward the first to see its comic possibilities. *Punch* in 1874 had:

> The Cottage-homes of England—
> Alas, how strong they smell!
> There's fever in the cesspool,
> And sewage in the well.   etc.

Mrs Hemans bequeathed another much-(mis)used or parodied quotation to headline-writers and political cartoonists, "The boy stood on the burning deck" (or, as is doubtless now said by some, "WAS stood on the burning deck"); but Coward unwittingly coined many other MEDIA clichés for journalists: Poor Little Rich Girl; A Room with a View; Chase me, Charlie; Mad Dogs and Englishmen; and the two much-quoted "Don'ts" alluded to and punned upon *ad nauseam*, in both stories and headlines: Don't Let's Be Beastly to the Germans and Don't Put your Daughter on the Stage, Mrs Worthington.

stationery/stationary In the 17th century and for some time afterwards a *stationer* was a bookseller who traded from a bookshop, and was therefore *in stationem*, not on the road, like the itinerant hawker of books, ballads and pamphlets who CATERED FOR the majority of the reading population. This is doubtless how the *-ery/-ary* distinction arose, though being in a fixed abode the seller of *stationery* was also *stationary*. The distinction was probably preserved by the founding in the 18th century of Her Majesty's Stationery Office (in the late 20th baldly renamed "The Stationery Office"). Another *a-e* confusion that concerns stationers will be found under FAINT/FEINT.

statue/sculpture "Bronze statues of three ducks…have been stolen from a Moscow park" (*Sunday Telegraph*). They may have been standing rather than sitting ducks, but even then *sculptures* would have been a better description. *Statues*, from Latin *stare*, to stand, should strictly be *standing* representations, and usually only of humans: that of a seated US President Franklin D. Roosevelt is a *sculpture*. When the subject is seated on a horse it becomes an *equestrian statue*, even though only the horse is standing.

stealing/stealing/stealth Shakespeare had his characters *stealing* in both senses of the word: in *Othello*, "…the handkerchief …which so oft you did bid me steal", and in *Cymbeline* "We may steal from hence…" but the meaning "to proceed by stealth", which is the older one, has been almost forgotten – or at any rate submerged under a growing crime wave. Abraham Cowley, who lived later than Shakespeare, confessed that "[As a boy] I used to steal from my playmates" – by which he meant he quietly left their company, not that he picked their pockets. The noun *stealth* formerly referred to both forms of stealing but has in the thieving sense been supplanted by *theft*. "Stealing a march" is first-dated by the *OED* as 1716, and comes from military use: "to succeed in moving troops without the knowledge of the enemy, hence, to get a secret advantage over a rival…" This once alarmed my late Austrian aunt, who read in the "Peterborough" column of the *Daily Telegraph* a favourable review of a piece of music I had published: "Fritz Spiegl has stolen a march on today's aleatoric composers." My aunt cried, "But you are a *good* boy – you wouldn't *steal* anyone's composition, would you?"

stilted/elevated/pompous The literal meaning of *stilted* is of something raised above the general level. When applied to language or writing style it means affectedly lofty, excessively formal or *pompous*. The EGREGIOUS also "stand out".

stomach/belly/abdomen The *stomach* and *belly* are not the same part of one's anatomy, although some people use stomach because they think belly, an early mediaeval word meaning a bag or sack, is crude or vulgar. *Abdomen* is even more polite, but is best left to doctors, who usually know what they are talking about. This, too, is a euphemism, probably from Latin *abdere*, to conceal or cover. Tell it to NAVEL-ringed teenagers...

story/storey "I live three stories above a shop..." claimed a writer in the *Independent*. By current English (though not US) custom a *story* is something that is written or told (plural *stories*) and a *storey* (plural *storeys*) a stage or portion of a building, placed one above the other. Americans accept stories for both sorts.

strained/(con)strained When we "did" Shakespeare's *Merchant of Venice* (1596) at school, I did not understand the meaning of "The quality of mercy is not strained". Was this mercy, I asked, strained like a *rope*, or strained as through a *sieve*? There was a long silence. Obviously the teacher himself had not a clue. In desperation he brushed my question aside with a peremptory "Well, boy, as you can see, it says, 'The quality of mercy is *not* strained'. So it doesn't matter *either* way, does it! Get on!" In fact it means neither stretched taut nor sieved: an implied apostrophe indicates the contraction *'strained*, i.e. constrained. Shakespeare uses this word in all three possible stressings, as one syllable, strained, as above; with two, constrained; or three, as in *Macbeth* (1605): "None serve with him, but *constrainéd* things/Whose hearts are absent too."

straighten/straiten To *straighten* is to make straight. As it says in the Book of Isaiah (and in Handel's *Messiah*) : "Make straight in the desert a highway for our God" – thus ordering the first freeway long before the Romans had the idea. To *straiten* something is to contract or constrict it, which in a road would create a bottleneck. The word straiten(ed) is rarely used unless linked to "circumstances", implying some degree of poverty. Many writers doubt its existence when they first encounter it and try to correct it – like the author of an article in *History Today*, who had Britons of the 1950s "living in straightened circumstances". Only the Hunchback of Notre Dame would have hoped for such treatment. The same confusion afflicts straitlaced and straightlaced, with its suggestion of a SURGICAL corset and orthopaedic purpose of *straightening* posture.

strategy/tactics/plans *Strategy* is now an essential ingredient in the jargon of corporate business, politics and other areas. Captains of industry, ministers, educationists and especially government spin doctors (see PROPAGANDA), broadcasters' focus groups and policy advisers, all spend an inordinate amount of time and money determining "strategies", when they could just as meaningfully call them *plans*. Strategy was originally concerned only with warfare: a *strategos* in ancient Greece was a commanding general, who would draw up battle plans. In modern war, strategic weapons are big long-range ones (modern cliché: "of mass destruction"), whereas the tactical ones would be deployed on the battle-field. In the quaint language of the MEDIA, *strategic* places are those parts of the human body that are normally kept from public view: "She was wearing only three small triangles of silk, strategically placed". In the MEDIA Bible Genesis 3.7 would read, "They [Adam and Eve] sewed fig leaves together and made themselves aprons, strategically placed"; and in personal relationships, "Come to my place for coffee" is *strategy*, but the hand on a woman's knee, *tactics*.

stunning/good/beautiful/desirable etc. If participial adjectives were gender-specific, *stunning* would be feminine, for it is the single most favourite word in fashion, interior decoration, food and glamour magazines, glossy catalogues, colour supplements – in short, in all women's pages. Everything that is allegedly *desirable* – hats, clothes, handbags, books, music (also good-looking men and women) – all are thought to possess the power of knocking one senseless, though Erik Levi in the *BBC Music Magazine* has "stunningly fluid playing" by a Dutch orchestra; and the *Independent* deplored "the stunning rise in the proportion of lone parents". If a strong word were called for, such a rise might have been alarming or calamitous, even deplorable or devastating. But stunning? See also STAGGERING/SURPRISING.

subject/citizen Americans are sensitive to the difference. A *subject*, says the *OED*, is "one who is under the dominion of a monarch or reigning prince", but adds to that definition "one who owes allegiance to a government or ruling power, is subject to its laws and enjoys its protection" – which should accommodate even the most ardent left-breast-clutching singer of the *"Star-spangled Banner"*. A *citizen*, strictly, is an inhabitant of a city; and in a secondary but now more common sense, a member or inhabitant of a state, especially if he is enfranchised and not a foreigner or ALIEN.

subordinate/suborn President Robert Mugabe of Zimbabwe, at an international summit soliciting help for African countries, complained that Europe was "subordinating African sovereignty". To *subordinate* is to render someone (or a country) DEPENDENT on the authority, power and resources of another. That was indeed the point of the summit meeting (i.e. Africa demanding yet more financial support from Europe) but not what Mugabe meant. The word he was searching for was *suborn*, to bribe or corrupt – and he and most other African leaders have no need of Europe to bribe and corrupt them.

substantial/substantive Orotund (see ROTUND) politicians and others who love the sound of their own words like to say *substantive* when they mean *substantial*. *Substantive* means independent and self-sufficient; *substantial*, having substance that is absolute or, more often, considerable, as in *substantial size*.

suburb/suburbs Latin *urbs*, a city, from which comes the expression *sub urbe*, i.e. "below" the city – in rank, not geographical position. In modern usage the *suburbs* is outside, or on the edge, of a city. Its use varies between the derogatory, i.e. something or someone not cosmopolitan, and therefore allegedly inferior, to that which is found *in* the outer parts of a city. *Suburbs* is both singular and plural, so "suburb" is a false singular back-formation.

suffrage/suffering/sufferance *Suffrage*, from Latin *suffragium*, a prayer or petition, was used by Wyclif in about 1380, to denote an opinion. Only since the 17th century has it meant the right to vote. In this sense it appears in the US Constitution of 1789: "No state shall be deprived of its equal suffrage in the Senate", which was how it became increasingly associated with the voting-rights of minorities, especially women. Latin *sufferre* or *sufferire* means to undergo or endure, and is unrelated to both voting and praying, which the extra *e* should make clear. In about 2001 a practical joker set up a table in a London street bearing a placard with the message "Abolish Women's Suffrage NOW!" and invited passers-by to sign a "petition" to that end. They signed in droves and went happily on their way, believing they had struck a blow for oppressed womanhood. In modern English *sufferance* has little to do with *suffering*, and means endurance or acquiescence.

suppositious/supposititious A *suppositious* work, such as a book or piece of music, is one whose authorship is hypothetical and based on supposition, so that its genuineness may be in doubt. A work that is *supposititious* is fraudulently substituted in the place of another, or spurious. This word, with its all-important extra syllable, comes from Latin *suppositorium*, that which is "placed underneath", as is a suppository, or a cuckoo's egg in another bird's nest.

surgical/orthopaedic *Surgical* strictly should pertain to a *surgeon*, from the medieval Latin *surgicus*, a medical person who attempts to cure by cutting, as opposed to the *physician*, who uses medicine or *physic*. In news jargon a precise military attack, an air-raid etc., is often described as a "surgical strike", from the notion that surgeons always work with CLINICAL precision. But the adjective surgical also has an amusing history as a sexually charged English euphemism. For example, early 20th-century English men needing contraceptives would go to "surgical stores" to buy them, though the chief purpose of such shops was to fit and sell artificial limbs, "surgical" corsets and other garments designed to cure, correct or alleviate an illness or deformity. See also STRAIGHTEN/STRAITEN and CLINICAL/PRECISE.

surprise/astonish *Surprise* in the modern sense is a chiefly abstract emotion, and to be *surprised* is now almost always understood as being overcome by some unexpected fact or feeling, pleasurable or otherwise. It was formerly the action of taking, or being taken, unawares, especially in combat. The difference is illustrated in a probably apocryphal story about the American lexicographer Noah Webster (1758–1843). He was at work – or supposed to be at work – on the great dictionary that bears his name, when his wife unexpectedly entered his study and found him in the arms of their housemaid. She cried, "Oh Mr Webster, I am surprised!" He replied, with as much dignity as he could muster in the circumstances, "No, my dear. *We* are surprised. *You* are astonished." Older writers almost invariably use it in this earlier sense, e.g. Shakespeare's *Titus Andronicus* (1588): "Treason, my lord, Lavinia is surpriz'd", which does not mean someone made a startling statement to her or crept up on her from behind. Webster, incidentally, laid the foundations of some of the American spelling simplifications that tend to irritate the English. He would have objected to archaic spellings like "surpriz'd", but this has itself been modernized.

surprise

221

surplus/surplice A charming picture in *The Times* of three choirboys accompanied a story by Anthea Lawson, who stated that the choristers "were presented with bibles and surpluses to wear over their jade cassocks". At around the same time an article in the *BBC Music Magazine* about choral music was headed "Surplice to Requirements". The *surplice* comes not from an Army *Surplus* shop but from the Latin *super*, above + *pellis*, skin or fur, in other words an over-garment. Also, in nominally Christian countries, the Bible takes a capital B, as the Koran takes a K. The same remarks apply as under RIGHT/RITE/WRIGHT/ WRITE. See also CASSOCKS/HASSOCKS.

sweet bread/sweetbread(s)/sweetmeat(s) *Sweetbreads* are not sweet but savoury, and come from the pancreas or thymus gland of an animal (usually a lamb or calf). They are a great delicacy when deep-fried in breadcrumbs or stewed in a piquant, creamy sauce. *Sweetmeats* is a charming old English word going back to the 1400s, for sugary or honeyed confections or candied fruit. Shakespeare's *Romeo and Juliet* (1592) has the line, "Their breath with Sweet meats tainted are"- and as early as 1626 Roger Bacon warned, "Teeth are much hurt by Sweet-meats." *Meat* in this early sense does not necessarily mean the flesh of an animal but food in general (see MEAT/MEET/METE). In archaic usage sweetbreads also meant a small bribe (like the originally French word *douceur*, in English still "a sweetener"; though in France the edible, savoury sweetbreads are called *ris*). When a contemporary of Samuel Pepys wrote, in about 1670: "I obtain'd that of the fellow...with a few Sweetbreads that I gave him out of my Purse" he did not mean meat but a bribe. But in English public-school slang the "sweetbreads" are (were) a boy's testicles, especially when hurt ("The full-back kicked me in the sweetbreads!"). This gave rise to a common misconception that the sweetbreads sold by the butcher (now alas rarely) come from those parts of an animal, also euphemized as FRIES.

swingeing/swinging Both the curious word *swinge* and the more common and familiar *swing* go back to Middle English *swengen* (like modern German *schwingen*), to swing something, such as a golf-club or cudgel, but from the 1500s *swingeing* and *swinging* parted company and swingeing came to mean to flog, whip or thrash, chastise and castigate: like "Saint George that swindg'd the Dragon..." in Shakespeare's *King John* (1595). Swingeing seems today to be used only for "swingeing cuts" and "swingeing tax increases", etc: apart from these clichés no-one seems to swinge any more and it appears to be a one-application word: nobody says things like "I swinged him in the gob!" See also WHINGEING/WINGING.

sybarite/voluptuary A *sybarite* is one devoted to self-indulgent and LUXURIOUS living, formerly "a native or citizen of Sybaris, an ancient Greek city of southern Italy, traditionally noted for its effeminacy and luxury" – perhaps a sort of Brighton of its time, or male counterpart of Lesbos. As the *OED* defines a *sybarite* as (among other things) "an effeminate voluptuary" and a *voluptuary* as (among other things) just a plain "sybarite", we may INFER that the implied difference in the pleasures lies in sexual preferences. A voluptuary is non-geographical, coming from Latin *voluptas*, one of many words that language offers for pleasurable delights.

sympathy/empathy/fellow-feeling. *Empathy* is an English, Greek-based, translation of the German *Einfühlung*, psychologists' jargon for the ability to project one's personality into (so as to comprehend fully) the object of contemplation. It is stronger, in a sense more internal, than the EVERYDAY *sympathy*, which literally means "with-feeling" (German *Mitgefühl*), or a *fellow-feeling*. Here a hyphen is essential: a fellow-feeling in the bosom is not the same as a fellow feeling in the bosom.

(the) system/government/authority/employer/apparat *The system* is something intangible and undefinable that seems to exist only for the purpose of being fought against, complained about and, wherever possible, exploited. It can be the prevailing political order, the *government*, the local council, social conditions, the class structure, the bosses and foremen – all may be reviled for being "part of the system". Whatever it is, he who expresses his hatred for it is never part of it. Beating the system is as important for the millionaire as for the pauper: the one beats it by striving to AVOID/EVADE taxes, the other by joining the black economy. The French and Germans also have their systems, and the Russians an *apparat* and its *apparatchiks* (from the German), in their case meaning the party machine (superseded, at least nominally, since the fall of Communism, by the government). See also INDIGENT.

system

T

tamarind/tamarisk The *tamarind* is a tropical tree, *Tamarindus indica*, whose sweet-sour fruit has long been familiar (though not by name) to Britons as an ingredient of the bottled "brown sauce" condiment that graces so many dining-tables, but tamarind first came to England as a laxative in the 16th century. It has nothing in common with the *tamarisk* (except as an early medicinal decoction), for this grows in the south of England – and is mentioned in Genesis 22.33: "Abraham planted a tamarisk tree in Beer-sheba."

taoiseach/irish prime minister *Taoiseach* is a fine and ancient Irish word, meaning leader – just as *Duce* does in Italian, *Caudillo* in Spanish and *Führer* in German – though it is now generally translated as "prime minister". The word holds a bizarre fascination for English journalists – although it is difficult to spell and harder to pronounce – something like "tea-shack". They always follow it with the explanation "the Irish prime minister" anyway, so why not say so in the first place? Why stop at Taoiseach? Why not find out what Finns, Hungarians or Turks call *their* prime ministers? Taoiseach was reclaimed early in the 20th century from the then all-but-defunct Irish Gaelic, specifically for Eamonn de Valera, the first leader of Sinn Fein and first President of the Irish Republic. It was an explicit anti-English gesture. Although he was a fine Irish patriot, the British government regarded him as a terrorist and potential dictator. His personal choice of the title Taoiseach was made in direct imitation of his close friends, the fascist leaders Mussolini, Franco and Hitler, whose regimes he supported on the principle that "my enemy's enemy is my friend" (he also cheered for the Kaiser in World War I and sent condolences on Hitler's death). A famous press photograph shows him marching side-by-side with the three dictators (perhaps more tagging along than marching): they in their resplendent uniforms, he ludicrously out of style in a flapping flasher's mac and battered trilby.

target/shot man In police-speak, ELEMENTS may sometimes end up as *targets*. This was confirmed by an officer who described how a known criminal was shot dead while stark naked and in bed with his partner: "We had reason to believe the target may have been armed." See also ELEMENTS/PEOPLE/MALES/FEMALES.

teacher/treacher *Teacher*, one who teaches, is pronounced in the customary manner, whereas *treacher* rhymes with lecher and means a deceiver, cheat, or sometimes a traitor. It comes from Old French *tricher*, to trick or cheat: thus treachery and trickery spring from the same root. See also ASTRONOMY/ASTROLOGY.

tempera/tempora/tempura A *Guardian* writer described a typist correcting errors "...with a blob of tempura". This would be greasy as well as wasteful, for *tempura* is a Japanese kind of battered and deep-fried fish, chicken, etc. *Tempora* usually occurs today only in the Latin tag from Horace, in which he complained about the manners of his day, *O tempora, o mores!* – "O what times – o what habits!" *Tempera* is artists' paint mixed with water and gum (in the past also egg yolk, as egg tempera), and is short for Latin *pingere in tempera*, to paint in DISTEMPER. And anyway, the typist would probably have used Tipp-Ex. See also YOKE/YOLK.

testament/testimony Robert Fisk wrote in the *Independent* about "...a shoal of testaments [for a terrorist] including one from Lord Gilmour". Not unless Lord Gilmour left them some money. A *testament*, from Latin *testamentum*, is a will, or the formal declaration of a person's wishes as to the disposal of his property after his death. A *testimony* is the same as a *testimonial*, something that gives evidence or furnishes proof.

there's/theirs/"their's" *There's* is a contraction of "there is", formerly used in formal English only when informal spoken English or dialogue was reported (like "isn't" for "is not"), and purists hold that it should otherwise be written out in full. *Theirs* is a form of the possessive pronoun *their*, indicating possession – a double possessive, says the *OED* – and takes no possessive apostrophe. *Their's* is a non-word which exists only in the imagination of those who use it in place of *theirs*. This confusion is so widespread that it reaches the highest ranks of writers. For example, the most often quoted lines of Tennyson's famous poem

225

The Charge of the Light Brigade appear in the *Oxford Dictionary of Quotations* (and in Tennyson's manuscript) as:

> Their's not to make reply,
> Their's not to reason why,
> Their's but to do and die:
> Into the valley of Death
> Rode the six hundred...

As Tennyson himself said: "someone had blundered". See also IT'S/ITS.

thrill/thriller Thrills have not been the same since certain kinds of books, films or videos became known as *thrillers*, possibly PSYCHOLOGICAL ones. The meaning of thrills, thrilling and being thrilled changed during the course of the 20th century. In 1912, for example, the *Musical Times* was able to report that "The foundering of the Titanic...thrilled civilized humanity". Today this would suggest that humanity *enjoyed* hearing the news.

throes/throws The *Guardian* reported that someone had been "...in the throws of booze-fuelled indiscretion". Curiously enough the *throes* (now usually in plural use only) which are a sign of pain, violent spasms or even death, were indeed at first related to the other kind of *throws*.

titivate/titillate *Titivate* has nothing to do with tits or titties but is really "tidyvate", which describes perfectly what women do in front of a looking-glass before they go out: tidy themselves up and make running repairs to their appearance. *Titillate* is also unconnected with female breasts, although it is exactly what the *Sun* sets out to do. Titillate comes from Latin *titillare*, to tickle – or, as the *OED* puts it: "To excite or stimulate as by tickling, to excite agreeably, gratify (the sense of taste, smell or touch, the imagination)". A reporter on BBC 1 News thought he could have it both ways: "Rapid titillation is under way in preparation for the visit of the Queen and the Duke of Edinburgh," he said. See also BEAUTIFY/BEATIFY.

torso/body There is a growing tendency for newspaper writers to use *torso* when they mean the (dead) *body* of a person. From Latin *thyrsus*, a stem or stalk, e.g. of a plant and without side-growths, torso was later used by sculptors for the trunk of a statue, without head or limbs. Thus to qualify as a "human torso" it must lack these features, now uncomfortably called "body parts". (Among the many delights and surprises offered by the second edition of the *OED* is the magisterial entry, "torso-tosser, *slang* [for] a hootchy-kootchy dancer", with a cross-reference to "hootchy-kootchy, *origin unascertained*, a kind of erotic dance".)

tortuous/torturous *Tortuous*, from Latin *tortuosus*, means full of twists and turns, perhaps like a winding road or path – hence figuratively also a complicated or longwinded argument or other process. *Torturous* is from Latin *tortura* and relates to torture. It had become obsolete by the end of the 19th century and today is almost certain to be a misspelling of tortuous. The *OED* cites a quotation from the *Standard* of 23 August 1890, which makes punning use of both: "Tortuous, as well as torturous, renderings of Psalms, Te Deums, Canticles and responses".

toupee/wig/rug/merkin "He wears a toupee" is the usually euphemistic way of saying that the man under discussion is trying to hide his baldness with a *wig* (women wear wigs or hairpieces, never *toupees*, but usually as fashion accessories, and are therefore less secretive about it). However, the proper distinction, now often ignored, is that a wig covers the full head, a toupee only a bald patch. Toupee is actually an old English word adapted from the French *toupet*, which referred not only to artificial hair worn by men but also to the real head-hair of horses ("That part of the mane which lies between the ears" – *Sporting Magazine*, 1797). Calling someone's wig a *rug* is now usually meant as an insult, implying that it is a bad one. But a rug may also be a pad of the wearer's own hair, TORTUOUSLY trained and teased to attempt the same hopeless deception. The *merkin*, sometimes used in the papers on the assumption that it is an ordinary wig, is detachable hair to cover the pubic region; or, as Grose's *Dictionary of the Vulgar Tongue* (1796) explains, "*Merkin* – counterfeit hair for women's privy parts". Why such wigs would have been used in the 17th and 18th centuries is anyone's guess (except for one instance when a Cardinal was given one on pretence that it was "St Peter's Beard"); but merkins came into their own again in the 20th, used by very blonde actresses required to appear naked on stage, in films or television. In military slang a merkin was "a mop to clean cannon".

touting/toting *Touting* means to look out importunately for customers or employment; originally a common word for peeping, peering or keeping a look-out. From this came the touting that is associated with the tout who looks for possible customers, especially those to whom he can sell overpriced tickets to plays or sporting events, or introduce to the services of a prostitute (and by the curious conventions of that trade, while men tout and importune – e.g. for those undefined "indecent purposes" – women solicit). The *Daily Telegraph* confusingly reported that "PLO men were touting guns" but did not make it clear whether they were waving them about as a threat, i.e. *toting* them, or hoping to sell them.

towing/toeing *Towing a line* is something nautical people do – a line being a rope, which usually has another vessel or floating object attached to its other end. *Toeing a line* is derived from sports in which all competitors are expected to use the same starting-point, hence also to submit to rules or discipline by coming into line with others. "Towing the state line", as a correspondent to *The Times* wrote, is a confusion of two expressions.

town/township *Township* is an ancient name for an urban division of land, often purposely laid out by planners, like the early 19th-century Township of Toxteth and Township of Harrington in Liverpool. In modern use it has become associated more with areas set aside (as in South Africa) for non-white occupation, townships which in the Middle East would be called refugee camps rather than *towns*. See also EMIGRANTS and CAMP.

train station/railway station/station *Station* has served travellers well for nearly two centuries, and there was never any risk of confusion with a comfort station, a bus station or one of the Stations of the Cross. Thus Victoria Station in London was always understood to be the *railway station*, situated next to the newer Victoria Coach Station, which had to be specified. *Train station* is an American fad, replacing railway station – and indeed ignores the US RAILROAD difference.

transport/transport Both in the happiness sense and in what Americans prefer to call, needlessly, *transportation*, the stress in the noun is on the first syllable but shifts to the second for the verb. Goods are (and slaves were) trans*ported*.

> Oh *trans*port! how can this
> Be true to heaven's bliss?
> Anon.

> Trans*port*ed with celestial desire
> Of those fair forms, may lift themselves up higher.
> Edmund Spenser (1552?–1599): *The Faerie Queen*

tribute/imitation/plagiarism In normal use, a *tribute* is a testimony or form of praise such as might be accorded to a famous or recently dead person; or to an idea; or it might be an act of homage. The standard form is to *pay* tribute, which was originally a fiscal term for the payment of tax. But tribute can also indicate *imitation* – even *plagiarism* – as in "tribute band", when a pop-music group closely models itself on an earlier and more successful one. One suspects that the warm word "tribute" is chiefly intended to ward off accusations of plagiarism or copying, or lawsuits for breach of copyright. Plagiarism has an interesting history, for in ancient Rome a *plagiarius* was an abductor or kidnapper of children. This almost PAEDOPHILE meaning was widened by Martial (ca 40–104 AD) to include the theft of intellectual property. See also DOPPELGÄNGER/DOUBLE.

trooper/trouper When the Daily Telegraph described an elderly and much loved ACTRESS as an "old *trooper*" it suggested that she had been in the Army, not a member of an acting *troupe*. To balance one wrong with another the *Guardian* had someone "swearing like a trouper".

tumultuous/momentous "The Queen Mother's coffin was driven past Buckingham Palace, where she reigned for fifteen tumultuous years" (BBC Radio News). *Tumultuous*: "full of tumult or commotion; marked by confusion and uproar; disorderly and noisy; violent and clamorous; turbulent"- none of them reminiscent of Queen Elizabeth. What was meant was *momentous*, an appropriate word to describe times that included her brother-in-law's abdication, World War II and its aftermath, and the loss of the British Empire – to name only three momentous events.

twofer/bogof *Twofer* is American, dating from ca 1911, and is or was commercial slang for a cigar sold at half-price: in other words *two for* the price of one. Later it referred to any object sold at a 50% discount if the customer bought two. The twofer has been joined (and in the UK almost ousted) by the *bogof*, a word seen in supermarket advertisements and on shop shelves, acronym of "Buy One Get One Free". But the twofer also has a later meaning – referring to a black or otherwise ETHNIC woman, or one from some other minority group, who is given a desirable job that would normally be done by a white male. Or, as the *OED* delicately says, "*twofer*: a Black woman appointed to a post, the appointment being seen as evidence of both racial and

twofer

sexual equality of opportunity". The supporting quotation, from *Time* (1977), explains: "By appointing her, Carter got a kind of 'twofer': as a black and as a woman, she is proof that the President-elect is trying to open his Cabinet to both groups." No connection with GOPHER.

— U —

unexceptional/unexceptionable The *unexceptional* is nothing out of the ordinary; the *unexceptionable*, that to which no exception is taken, or objection made.

union jack/union flag Letters Editors of newspapers could paper their walls with complaints every time a writer mentions the *Union Jack*. "Should be Union *flag*!", the PEDANTS cry. Not so. It depends on its size – for, as papers keep reiterating *ad nauseam*, "size matters". In Royal Navy speech a *jack* is a *small* flag, smaller than the ensign, and usually flown from the jack-staff at the bow of a vessel. As the English Court decreed via the *London Gazette* as long ago as 1674, "...from henceforth they [the ships' masters] do not presume to wear His Majesties jack (commonly called The Union Jack) in any of their Ships or Vessels without particular Warrant". Whatever the precedent, Union Jack is so deeply ingrained in the popular consciousness that we should ignore the pedants and continue to have "children waving Union Jacks".

unknown/unnamed "The solo was sung by an unknown choirboy," wrote a music critic in the *Liverpool Daily Post*. The writer, probably thinking of the Unknown Soldier, revealed that the choirboy was *unknown* to *him* and the rest of the congregation. The boy's mother and his classmates would have known him. An *unnamed* choirboy?

unloaded/unladen A ship is *unloaded*, but once empty is *unladen*. But a gun without ammunition is always unloaded, never unladen.

until/till/to/through The American use of *through* (or *thru*) to indicate a point or position to be reached has been slow to gain acceptance in British English, although it MIGHT provide a useful distinction. "Monday through Thursday" means from Monday until the *end* of Thursday, in other words "through" the day, whereas an English speaker has to say,

231

"Monday till (or to) Thursday inclusive". But a book title like *Chamber Music Brahms through Stravinsky* still rings disagreeably foreign to English ears. See also WHILE/WHILST/AS WELL/UNTIL.

upbeat/downbeat *Upbeat* and *downbeat* are musical terms with precise musical meanings. In conducting, for example, the *downbeat* is the *first* beat of every bar and therefore the strongest, whereas the *upbeat* (say, the third, upward, beat in waltz-time or the fourth in common-time) is the one that precedes it, and therefore the weakest. Popular usage has got hold of the wrong end of the stick and calls that which is strong or positive *upbeat*, while a *downbeat* mood is subdued, depressed, etc. The confusion probably arose from *uptempo*, which is a light-music term for a quick and cheerful beat.

uxorious/conjugal Only a man can be *uxorious* in its strict sense, that is "dotingly or submissively fond of a wife, devotedly attached to a wife", though only PEDANTS will point this out. In the foregoing definition the *OED* omits to specify *whose* wife, but the implication is of home-loving fidelity on the man's part. There appears to be no converse equivalent of a wife's devotion to her husband – perhaps because this was taken for granted – but *conjugal*, from Latin *con*, with + *jungere*, to join would fit the sense, in an admirably mutual kind of way.

— V —

valet/varlet Both words originally denoted manservants. A *valet* is a gentleman's male personal servant, perhaps popularly perceived as resembling P. G. Wodehouse's Jeeves, a servant employed only by the rich. The French origin of the word is betrayed by the pronunciation "vallay". The same Old French word produced *varlets*, originally attendants to a knight or other mediaeval personage. These are now even harder to find than valets, except in jocular or facetious writings. Families called Varlet, Varley, Vassal and Valley, etc., are descended from one or the other kind of manservant.

valuable/invaluable At first sight *invaluable* seems to negate what is *valuable*, as *invalid* invalidates the valid. But the *in-* in invaluable is an intensifier, making that which is invaluable beyond price, something which *can not* be valued. See also FLAMMABLE/INFLAMMABLE/ INFLAMMATORY.

venal/veinal/venereal/veneral/venery Things *venal* are those that are offered for sale, including political honours that should be conferred on merit alone. This sense comes from Latin *venum*, that which is sold or for sale. Another sense of venal (also *veinal*) is that used by doctors, from Latin *vena*, a vein. *Venereal* diseases and other things to do with sex are related to neither, but are so named after Venus, the Roman goddess of love. The adjectives *veneral* and *venereal* are ambiguous, coming from both Venus and *venery*, the sport of hunting. But perhaps it is all about the excitement of the chase.

vibrant/vibrato/wobble/bleat *Vibrant* comes from Latin *vibrare*, to vibrate, and the dictionary says it means "agitated with anger or emotion; moving and quivering rapidly", etc. But by the end of the 20th century vibrant had established itself as an over-used "blue skies" word. When critics describe a stage production, or politicians their policies, as

233

"vibrant" they should be invited to qualify: vibrant with *what*? *Vibrato* is a musical term for intentional undulations in the human singing-voice or in the sound produced by an instrument. More than about eight per second make it a *bleat*; fewer, and it becomes a *wobble*. Wind instrumentalists produce their vibrato invisibly, like singers, by diaphragm-supported fluctuations in air pressure; string players with a visible movement of the note-finger on the string. Like most professional terms it is best left to professionals; and the music-critic who complained of a famous DIVA's "excessive use of her powerful vibrator" was either puzzled by a musical term or the victim of an over-zealous sub-editor. Another kind of vibrato worth noting is that of a famous, sweet-voiced, self-taught girl-soprano, whose vibrato is/was achieved simply by wobbling her chin, like a cat longing for an unattainable bird.

vicious/viscous/viscose *Vicious*, from Latin *vitium*, a fault, took some time to develop its modern meaning of fierceness or bad temper: it was formerly connected with wickedness. *Viscous* was derived from Latin *viscum*, birdlime, which was made from mistletoe berries and therefore means sticky, so the *Guardian* was wrong to claim that "Railtrack was able to embark on a viscous circle of underinvestment". *Viscose* is related to the sticky substance, and is the name given to a form of cellulose from which film and synthetic fabrics like rayon are made.

visit/visitation Some feel that by adding an *-ation* suffix to a word they make it sound grander: "The last time the Queen made a visitation to the university…" *Visit* and *visitation* mean much the same, but usage has it that humans make *visits*, while *visitations* are best left to the Virgin Mary or ghosts, both holy and secular; also to supposedly divine punishment, like visitations of sicknesses or the plague.

W

wage/salary A social division exists: "blue-collar" and manual workers get *wages* – and are *waged* (if unemployed "unwaged"- a new verb-creation), whereas "white-collar" employees draw a *salary*. These are *salaried* (as William Caxton wrote as long ago as 1477: "How...shall I be salaryed of suche payement in the recompensacion of the saluacion of your lyf?"). Wages come from an old Teutonic word, but salary from Latin *salarium*, a reference to the fact that Roman soldiers drew a salt allowance – in much the same way as British sailors received an issue of rum. In the UK wages are traditionally paid weekly and in cash, salaries monthly and by cheque. According to a famous plural confusion in the Bible (Romans 6. 23), "The wages of sin is death." Is they really?

wax/wane *Wax* means to grow or increase, a useful word sadly neglected. It comes from the old Teutonic and modern German *wachsen* and in modern English is used chiefly of the moon and in semi-facetious applications like "He waxed enthusiastic (or eloquent)." It has no connection with the stuff from which candles are made. Its opposite, *waning*, or *on the wane*, to lessen or decrease, is derived from Old English *wana*, and while more common, is also chiefly used in relation to the moon.

weather/wether *Weather-eye* (hyphenated in the *OED*) is a nautical term reflecting the need for sailors to keep an eye on the weather; also generally to be watchful and alert, keeping one's wits about one. It dates from the early 19th century but may be related to an old Norse word for "keen-eyed". A *wether*, as in wether ram, is early mediaeval Teutonic, possibly Frisian, and means a male sheep, usually a castrated one. A *bell-wether* is the leading sheep (not necessarily male) of a flock whom the rest follow blindly (SHEEPISHLY?), and from this comes a convenient expression for a (political) leader. Bell-wether has also become an opprobrious term for a loudmouth, though (the always free-spelling)

Shakespeare himself used the "wrong" form in *The Merry Wives of Windsor* (1598): "To be detected with a jealious rotten bell-weather". He wasn't too meticulous about jealous, either.

welsh/welch/renege The obsolete *Welch* for *Welsh* is appropriate only for the Royal Welch Fusiliers, a regiment of the British Army which retained the archaic spelling it has used since its founding in 1702, when spelling was loose and free. *Welshing* (sometimes *welching*) means to fail to carry out an agreement or promise, or *renege* on a debt, usually one incurred in betting. The expression is undoubtedly offensive to the Welsh, and should be forgotten, along with the ancient nursery-rhyme, "Taffy was a Welshman, Taffy was a thief". See also SCOTTISH/SCOTS/SCOTCH.

were/was Shakespeare has Macbeth (1605) saying, "If it were done when 'tis done, then 'twere well it were done quickly." Today few bother with this form of expressing contingency, doubt or future time. They prefer, "If it *was* done...'twas well if it *was* done quickly." This leads to such time-shifting absurdities as, "If he *was* there by three he would be too late." Was he there or wasn't he? Another waswolf, presenting a music programme on Radio 4, said, "Here's John McCormack singing a version of the 'Londonderry Air' with words beginning 'Would God I was a tender apple blossom'." John McCormack then started to sing and, with his wonderfully clear diction, sang, "Would God I *were* a tender apple blossom". Even the famous song from *Fiddler on the Roof* is sometimes dumbed down to "If I *was* a rich man".

were/where When Dame Vera Lynn recorded that very English song *"We'll meet again"* she did *not* sing "...don't know *were*, don't know *wen*": she sang "*where*" and "*when*" – as clearly as any well-brought-up person of her generation would have said it. Alas, no amount of nostalgia for the good old days will persuade don't-care speakers to emulate her (and the Scots) by distinguishing between *wh* and *w*. The Scots actually know the difference between Wales and whales, even if the Welsh themselves tend not to. WET/WHET have the same problem.

wet/whet Appetites, knives, scissors, scythes and other sharp implements are *whetted*: though at least two TV-celebrated chefs write about "wetting" their readers' appetites. Whet, meaning to sharpen, comes from an Old Teutonic and modern German word *wetzen*.

while/whilst/as well/until *While* has connotations of time or duration, something that happens at the same time as something else. It can also mean "as well as" or "in addition"; also "although"; and as a variation of "and". It is all very confusing. For example, "Mrs Jones sang a Handel aria while her husband played a solo on the trombone" suggests they did so simultaneously. Even more confusingly, in parts of northern England *while* is still used for "until", as it was in Shakespeare's time: "While then, God be with you" – *Macbeth* (1605). The old warning notice at level-crossings, "DO NOT CROSS WHILE BELL IS SOUNDING", would have caused some Lancashire farmers to wait dutifully *until* the bell sounded and a train *was* approaching. See also UNTIL/TILL/THROUGH.

while/wile See previous entry. *Wile* is deceit, so "wiling away the time" (which the advertising-agents of Iberia Airways invite passengers to do) is a misspelling as well as a blunder.

w(h)ingeing/winging Although now a vogue slang-word, *whinge* (or *winge*) goes back to about 1100, as *hwinsunge*, meaning to whine like a dog or complain peevishly. *Winging* is a misspelling when this sense is intended and is pronounced differently. Compare *whingeing* with the modern German *winseln*, which is the noise a complaining dog makes. The *whingeing/winging* pronunciation-difference also occurs in SWINGEING/SWINGING.

whisky/whiskey The Scots – or their ancestors – called the spirit they distilled *uisgebeatha* (or *usquebaugh* – authorities differ); and have traditionally called it *whisky*, while the Irish spell their own near-equivalent *whiskey*. For a time there was available on the Isle of Man a Manx spirit, distilled in the same manner as whisky/whiskey which, though colourless, was sold under the name "Manx Whiskey" – until the large whisky/whiskey industry came down on the small distiller with a heavy hand. The Gaelic words above mean "water of life", which relates it to the French *eau de vie* and the Norwegian *Aquavit*, but the latter is more like the German *Kümmel*, only much stronger. See also SCOTS/SCOTTISH/SCOTCH.

who/whom The trend in informal speech is towards using *who* where *whom* should be used, e.g. "Who d'you mean?" (just as the "incorrect" *me* often sounds more natural than *I*, as in "It's me"). Thus "Whom do you mean?" sounds affected or STILTED; and "Whom are you kidding" puts a pedantic horse before a colloquial cart. Unfortunately many speakers, in trying to be correct at all costs, commit the greater sin of pretentiousness, using *whom* because they think it is posher. Almost daily one hears on radio and TV, and reads in newspapers, statements like, "Police want to interview a man whom they believe is armed…" The best way of avoiding these solecisms is to isolate the elements with appropriate punctuation, and then mentally replace *whom* with *him* and *who* with *he*. Thus "Police want to interview a man whom, they believe, is armed…" sounds and looks absurd. Was *him* really armed? Was it *him* they believed? Conversely, ask yourself when you read, "An armed man who police want to interview…" – do they want to interview *he*? (The same applies to the I/ME, HE/HIM and LAY/LIE confusions). According to the pseudo-posh the Psalmist (and Handel in his *Messiah*) would have sung, "He trusted in God that He would deliver He, let He deliver He if He delights in He". On the other hand – let *him* who is without sin cast the first stone…

— Y —

ye olde/the old *Ye olde* is the most familiar example of what might be called "Bogus Heritage", or "Half-timbered" English, (or, to be consistently phoney, Englysshe). It is the linguistic equivalent of "distressing" (i.e. damaging) mock-antique furniture to make it look older and more saleable. "Half-timbered" English seems to have begun as a Victorian fad, as the earliest uses of "ye olde" as a sales tool are thought to have been spotted in 1896 on a then new pub in London, "Ye Olde Bagnigge Wells", and "An Olde Almanack in forme of a Booke of Reference for this Preſent Yeare of Grace 1883", from the Leadenhall Press, London – though the intention here was to amuse, not to deceive. Charles Dickens called his novel *The Old Curiosity Shop*, without the phoney spelling, but it inspired numerous Ye Olde Curiositie Shoppes, Ye Olde Willow Patterne Tea-rooms; and, in many a pub, Ye Olde Snugge. An interesting variation has been seen in Ye Ploughman's Lunche: a piece of cheese, a hunk of French bread and a pat of pasteurized butter, also available with brie as an upgraded "Executive Ploughman's Lunch" – and this time without silly spellings. Once the MEDIA discovered Ye Olde Englysshe they never looked back – or rather, forward. There has already been spotted an example of Ye Olde Shoppynge Malle with, perversely, "Old-Tyme Dancing" and, OXYMORONically, "Ye Modern Dresse Shoppe). *Ye olde* is usually pronounced "yee oldie…", which is absurd on two counts. The *y* of *ye* is pronounced like *th*, being an approximate representation of the runic thorn, an Old English character which stood for the *th* sound, for which the modern alphabet makes no provision (there were also words like *yis* for "this", and *yat* and *yt* for "that", *yeir* for "their", etc); and the *e* at the end of "olde" would have been soundless, at any rate during the period that is usually mimicked. When Ye Olde Bagnigge Wells was named, people were more familiar than we are with the language of the King James Bible and its use of *thee*, *thou* and *thine*, but since the spate of modernized, colloquially matey updates of the Bible, prayer, service and hymn books, much of it has been forgotten.

Thus Lloyds Bank paid good money for an advertisement which exhorted the reader to "Taketh a Leaflet!" Another example occurs in George and Ira Gershwin's *Porgy and Bess*, which has the remarkable line, "He foughteth Goliath, who laid [sic] down and dieth" – but then the Gershwin brothers were being facetious, whereas Lloyds' copywriter was just plain ignorant. Let him write out a hundred times: "I take, thou takest, he taketh, we take, ye take, they take…" – and just to confuse him, this "ye" is a real ye, not a "the" as in Ye Olde. The Technology Editor of the *Independent* was also being facetious when he wrote, "The gasman will no longer cometh, at least not to read the meter…." Another "ye olde" confusion is caused by the pre-1800 typographical "long" s, which is often mistakenly represented as an f: "the afsembled company then fang a fong" (the double-s being printed in the 18th century as ß) – which caused the *Guardian* DIARY to write about "a fop to the masses".

yoke/yolk The *Guardian* cited "…dried yokes [as] evidence that things [had] recently been hurled". The things hurled were presumably eggs not the wooden couplings, or *yokes*, that join draught animals. Eggs figure also in TEMPERA/TEMPORA.

— Z —

zip code/post-code In the UK *zip* is now associated mostly with the zip fastener, registered in 1925 as the "Zipper", whereas zip is a 19th-century onomatopœic word suggesting speed. From the early 1960s ZIP has been the contrived acronym for the US zoning *i*mprovement *p*lan which issues numbers to postal delivery areas. *Zip code* is appropriate only for the US, not the UK, where the earlier and badly thought-out *post-codes* prevail (Norwich post office was a pioneer). These mix digits with letters – easier to remember but harder to write legibly – for while most people take care writing figures, as money may be at stake, many are careless with the letters of the alphabet, which in the context of words may be guessed but standing alone can cause confusion between 2 and Z, 5 and S, 9 and G, etc.

Index

247

index

index

Praise for Contradictionary

*'An amusing and comprehensive dictionary of
frequently-confused homonyms.'*
INDEPENDENT

'Splendid'
SUNDAY TELEGRAPH

'His final blast against the maltreatment of the English language.'
THE TIMES

*'Reliable, fascinating [...] great for dipping into
at random or as a reliable reference tool.'*
GOOD BOOK GUIDE

*'The English language owes a debt of gratitude to Fritz Spiegl.
This latest book adds to the debt.'*
John Humphreys

'Bringing clarity to your writing and a pleasure to dip into.'
WRITING MAGAZINE

*'The ideal gift for anyone delighted by language, crossword addicts,
over-zealous conversationalists and the terminally pedantic!'*
PRIZE QUEST

Rudyard Kipling
The Complete Verse

With a foreword by M.M. Kaye

978 1 85626 952 0 / £14.99 PB

A fully revised and meticulously researched edition of Kipling's Complete Verse with an authoritative introduction from M. M. Kaye.

With the possible exception of Shakespeare, no other poet has so enriched the English language with his vivid prose and verse as Rudyard Kipling. His poetry has been perpetually popular – from his Nobel Prize for Literature in 1907 to the 1995 BBC opinion poll that voted his poem 'If—' The Nation's Favourite Poem.

Though at times controversial, especially after the decline of the Empire, Kipling has always entertained and spoken to people. He has been described as 'the greatest democratic English poet' and 'a man of genius.' With over 700 pages, this edition of his complete verse bears weighty testimony to that claim.

W. B. Yeats
The Love Poems

Edited and annotated by A. Norman Jeffares

978 1 85626 953 7 / £9.99 PB

This collection of Yeats's love poetry follows the changing tides of his life – beginning with his youthful, romantic idealism and following his rejection by Maude Gonne and disillusionment into middle age.

Yeat's comments on his loves in later life are particularly evocative and provide deeply moving portraits of people and places. They combine much of the beauty he created and imparted to the Celtic Revival with his later outspoken, sardonic treatment of sexuality. Right up to his death his love poems reflect the developing mind of a genius, still capable of remaking himself and his ideas with compelling immediacy.

Professor A. Norman Jeffares was widely recognised as the world's foremost authority on Yeats.